TEACHING VOCABULARY IN ALL CLASSROOMS

SECOND EDITION

CAMILLE BLACHOWICZ
National-Louis University

PETER FISHER
National-Louis University

Merrill
Prentice Hall

Upper Saddle River, New Jersey
Columbus, Ohio

Library of Congress Cataloging in Publication Data

Blachowicz, Camille L. Z.
  Teaching vocabulary in all classrooms / Camille Blachowicz, Peter Fisher.—2nd ed.
    p. cm.
  Includes bibliographical references and index.
  ISBN 0-13-041839-0
  1. Vocabulary—Study and teaching. I. Fisher, Peter, II. Title.

LB1574.5 .B53 2002
  372.44—dc21

                                                                        2001032968

Vice President and Publisher: Jeffery W. Johnston
Editor: Linda Ashe Montgomery
Editorial Assistant: Lori Jones
Production Editor: Mary Harlan
Design Coordinator: Diane C. Lorenzo
Cover Design: Thomas Borah
Cover Photo: The Stock Illustration Source, Inc.
Photo Coordinator: Valerie Schultz
Production Manager: Pamela D. Bennett
Production Coordination: Lea Baranowski, Carlisle Publishers Services
Director of Marketing: Kevin Flanagan
Marketing Manager: Krista Groshong
Marketing Coordinator: Barbara Koontz

This book was set in Sabon by Carlisle Communications, Ltd. It was printed and bound by R. R. Donnelley & Sons Company. The cover was printed by The Lehigh Press, Inc.

Photo Credits: Camille Blachowicz, p. 22; KS Studios/Merrill, p. 65; Barbara Schwartz/Merrill, p. 122.

Pearson Education Ltd., *London*
Pearson Education Australia Pty. Limited, *Sydney*
Pearson Education Singapore Pte. Ltd.
Pearson Education North Asia Ltd., *Hong Kong*
Pearson Education Canada, Ltd., *Toronto*
Pearson Educación de Mexico, S.A. de C.V., *Mexico*
Pearson Education—Japan, *Tokyo*
Pearson Education Malaysia Pte. Ltd.

Merrill
Prentice Hall

10 9 8 7 6
ISBN 0-13-041839-0

To the three J's (who also love words)—
Jim (wwnotwmad), Jake, and Jesse

To Sheila

And to our colleagues who have so
generously shared their ideas

PREFACE

Vocabulary instruction is like the weather: Everyone talks about it, but no one is quite sure what to do about it. This text is therefore written for preservice and in-service teachers of *all* grade levels and in *all* content areas who recognize the importance of vocabulary development but aren't sure what to do with it in the classroom. This text is also written, however, for teachers who have a sense of direction but who want some new, classroom-tested strategies to renew their curriculum.

Focus of the Text

Research and practice emphasize that attention to learning vocabulary is an important part of all content learning as well as a significant part of any literacy program. Therefore, many of the techniques for teaching vocabulary that are explored in this book have the broader goal of enhancing the acquisition of content knowledge. Also explored are independent means of learning vocabulary, such as using metacognitive and contextual cues. New features of this edition include greater attention to the ESL student and an added chapter on spelling and word structure. Also, websites for vocabulary exploration are included for each chapter.

Special Features

This book has the following special features to help guide the reader.

- *Prepare Yourself*   A knowledge rating activity that introduces the major content issues by asking you to evaluate your own prior knowledge.
- *Strategy Overview Guide*   A guide to the instructional strategies highlighted in the chapter. It can also be used as a quick reference tool.
- *Teaching Idea File Cards*   Shorthand references to a number of strategies and resources most practical to duplicate into a teacher resource file or curriculum resource guide.

- *For Further Learning*   Selected, teacher-friendly references that encourage greater investigation.

If you are a reading and language teacher or a content area teacher, if you teach in kindergarten or in high school, if your students are gifted or at risk, this text has ideas for your classroom. If you are a student or a teacher of methods classes in reading and language, in social studies, in science, or in special needs instruction, this book will supplement your other texts by giving you ideas for handling the important vocabulary unique to your classes. We hope that you will use the ideas in the text as springboards for experimentation in your own classrooms.

Acknowledgments

Most of the ideas we share in this text have been developed over the years by teachers in many different classroom situations. We thank you. We have tried to give credit to our contributors wherever possible but know that ideas get adapted, modified, or changed as they meet individual classroom needs. If you, the readers, have any new adaptations or suggestions that we could credit to you in future editions, we would love to hear from you.

Our thanks do also go to our colleagues and students at National College of Education of National-Louis University and to the many teachers with whom we work closely. Special thanks to Amy McCann, Becky McTague, Elsie McAvoy, Lily Rodriguez, and Joan Stahl for their ideas and assistance. We are also grateful to our reviewers whose thoughtful ideas helped refine this text: Irene Mosedale, Plymouth State College, New Hampshire; Roger Passman, Ed.D., Texas Tech University; and I. LaVerne Raine, Texas A&M University–Commerce.

Lastly, we would like to thank Linda Montgomery and Mary Harlan for helping us bring our work into print.

Camille Blachowicz
Peter Fisher

DISCOVER THE COMPANION WEBSITE ACCOMPANYING THIS BOOK

THE PRENTICE HALL COMPANION WEBSITE: A VIRTUAL LEARNING ENVIRONMENT

Technology is a constantly growing and changing aspect of our field that is creating a need for content and resources. To address this emerging need, Prentice Hall has developed an online learning environment for students and professors alike—Companion Websites—to support our textbooks.

In creating a Companion Website, our goal is to build on and enhance what the textbook already offers. For this reason, the content for each user-friendly website is organized by topic and provides the professor and student with a variety of meaningful resources. Common features of a Companion Website include:

FOR THE PROFESSOR—

Every Companion Website integrates **Syllabus Manager™,** an online syllabus creation and management utility.

- **Syllabus Manager™** provides you, the instructor, with an easy, step-by-step process to create and revise syllabi, with direct links into Companion Website and other online content without having to learn HTML.

- Students may log on to your syllabus during any study session. All they need to know is the web address for the Companion Website and the password you've assigned to your syllabus.

- After you have created a syllabus using **Syllabus Manager™,** students may enter the syllabus for their course section from any point in the Companion Website.

- Clicking on a date, the student is shown the list of activities for the assignment. The activities for each assignment are linked directly to actual content, saving time for students.

- Adding assignments consists of clicking on the desired due date, then filling in the details of the assignment—name of the assignment, instructions, and whether it is a one-time or repeating assignment.

- In addition, links to other activities can be created easily. If the activity is on-line, a URL can be entered in the space provided, and it will be linked automatically in the final syllabus.

- Your completed syllabus is hosted on our servers, allowing convenient updates from any computer on the Internet. Changes you make to your syllabus are immediately available to your students at their next logon.

FOR THE STUDENT-

- **Topic Overviews**—outline key concepts in topic areas
- **Strategies**—these websites provide suggestions and information on how to implement instructional strategies and activities for each topic
- **Web Links**—a wide range of websites that allow the students to access current information on everything from rationales for specific types of instruction, to research on related topics, to compilations of useful articles and more
- **Electronic Bluebook**—send homework or essays directly to your instructor's email with this paperless form
- **Message Board**—serves as a virtual bulletin board to post—or respond to—questions or comments to/from a national audience
- **Chat**—real-time chat with anyone who is using the text anywhere in the country—ideal for discussion and study groups, class projects, etc.

To take advantage of these and other resources, please visit the *Teaching Vocabulary in All Classrooms*, Second Edition, Companion Website at

www.prenhall.com/blachowicz

CONTENTS

CHAPTER 3

INTEGRATING VOCABULARY AND READING STRATEGY INSTRUCTION   39

CHAPTER 4

LEARNING VOCABULARY IN LITERATURE-BASED READING INSTRUCTION   61

CHAPTER 5 — LEARNING VOCABULARY IN THE CONTENT AREAS 83

CHAPTER 6 — USING DICTIONARIES AND OTHER REFERENCES 109

CHAPTER 9	**VOCABULARY AND SPELLING INSTRUCTION USING STRUCTURAL ANALYSIS 189**

CHAPTER 10	**WORDPLAY IN THE CLASSROOM 203**

APPENDICES

NOTE: Every effort has been made to provide accurate and current Internet information in this book. However, the Internet and information posted on it are constantly changing, so it is inevitable that some of the Internet addresses listed in this textbook will change.

CHAPTER 1

VOCABULARY IN THE CLASSROOM

A Theoretical and Practical Perspective

✓ Prepare Yourself

Prepare yourself by evaluating your own knowledge. Rate your ability to answer some of the key questions for this chapter. Check the boxes that best describe your prereading knowledge.

Key concept questions	Well informed	Aware	Need ideas
1. *What is some of the basic instructional research on vocabulary learning?*	❏	❏	❏
2. *What goals emerge from the research on vocabulary instruction?*	❏	❏	❏
3. *What guidelines for vocabulary instruction can be drawn from research?*	❏	❏	❏

☑ Strategy Overview Guide

This chapter presents background, ideas, and strategies to help you understand the research foundations for vocabulary instruction. In subsequent chapters, this Strategy Overview Guide will describe the instructional strategies introduced in the chapter, their goals, and useful comments for selecting and using them in the classroom. Vocabulary instruction is like the weather—everyone talks about it but nobody knows what to do about it! In this chapter, we set the stage for the instructional ideas that constitute the main part of this book by introducing you to some of the research that underpins good vocabulary instruction. Because the history of research on vocabulary is so rich and varied, we have organized our discussion around three research questions that are critical to the choices you'll have to make for your own classroom: What does the research tell us about vocabulary, what does it mean to "know" a word, and what is effective vocabulary instruction? Each of these questions will be introduced, discussed, and used to generate some guidelines for classroom instruction.

WHAT DOES THE RESEARCH TELL US ABOUT VOCABULARY?

One of the longest, most clearly articulated lines of research in literacy education describes the strong connection between the vocabulary knowledge of readers and their ability to understand what they read (Davis, 1944, 1968). This relationship makes good, intuitive sense not only to a noneducator, who might suggest, "You certainly will understand what you read better if you know the words!," but also to teachers and researchers who observe and study the ways in which complex, unfamiliar, or technical vocabulary makes reading difficult. An interesting side of this connection, however, is the fact that, despite this strong and persistent relationship, programs designed to teach vocabulary have often had surprisingly little effect on reading performance (Dale, Razik, & Petty, 1973; Mezyinski, 1983; Stahl & Fairbanks, 1986).

One issue that contributes to this difficulty is the lack of clarity across research as to what is being referred to as "vocabulary learning." This learning can involve the growth of either receptive or expressive vocabulary in general language development, can mean the learning of new concepts or new labels for already known concepts, and also can refer to the learning of words through many modalities, such as in speech and conversation, through listening, and from reading and writing. The use of a single term to describe all these types of learning seems to be a paradox; using an overly simplified interpretation of the connection between vocabulary knowledge and comprehension might lead to inappropriate classroom decisions. As in all areas of education, teachers must consider many factors in constructing their own framework for vocabulary development in the classroom. While vocabulary development is a product of learning, that learning can take place in many ways, not always as a result of teacher-directed instruction. Learning and instruction are the focus of the next part of this chapter. Let's look first at what it means to know a word.

WHAT DOES IT MEAN TO "KNOW" A WORD?

There are several ways to use your knowledge of what learners know or don't know to make instructional decisions in your classroom. First, we must look critically at what it means to "know" a word. Most researchers agree that word learning is not an all-or-nothing proposition, like a light switch that turns a light on or off. A better metaphor is that of a light dimmer switch that gradually produces an increasingly richer supply of light. Most researchers agree that learners move from not knowing a word, to being somewhat acquainted with it, to attaining a deeper, richer, more flexible word knowledge that allows them to use new words in many modalities of expression (Carey, 1978; Dale, 1965; Graves, 1984; McKeown & Beck, 1989; Stahl, 1985). Repeated encounters with a word in rich oral and written contexts provide experiences and clues to the word's meaning that build over time and help develop and change our mental structures for a word's meaning (Eller, Pappas, & Brown, 1988; Nagy, 1988; Vosniadou & Ortony, 1983).

Reading Builds Vocabulary.   Rich exposure to words, such as that provided by wide reading, helps students construct and retain meaningful personal contexts for words (Whittlesea, 1987). For example, the word *wardrobe* in *The Lion, the Witch and the Wardrobe* (Lewis, 1950) becomes meaningful in a way it never could in its dictionary definition or in an isolated sentence. Specific events in the novel help the learner note that a wardrobe is a piece of furniture that can be located in a bedroom, that it has a front door, and that it is big enough to walk through. Readers who have read that wonderful book have no trouble conceptualizing or remembering the term *wardrobe*.

Connecting New to Known.   As learners read or meet words in other meaningful contexts, they begin to build frameworks of relationships that we refer to as "the word's meaning." Each time a word is encountered, another bit of information is added to the framework, enlarging or changing it. For example, the student reading the sentence

I saw two frimps.

may start to build a framework for frimps that looks like this:

> **Class** = visible objects
>   *frimps* can be seen
>   can be counted (there are two)

Reading on and seeing the sentence

They looked tasty to me.

adds further information to the reader's framework:

```
Class = food
        frimps   can be seen
                 can be counted (there are two)
                 look edible
                 look attractive
```

Reading further to the sentence

I picked them off the bush, and peeled and ate them. Yummy!

modifies the framework somewhat to include this information:

```
Class = fruit or vegetable
        frimps   can be seen
                 can be counted (there are two)
                 look edible
                 look attractive
                 grow on a bush
                 have peels
```

Reading the last sentence

My stomach turned cold; I died.

results in a framework that looks like this:

```
Class = poisonous fruit
        frimps   can be seen
                 can be counted (there are two)
                 look edible/but are poisonous
                 look attractive
                 grow on a bush
                 have peels
```

Any reader who already has a knowledge of food, fruits, fruit peels, and poisonous fruit can add *frimp* to an already existing network of meaning connecting those categories. However, for a student who is not familiar with the anchor concepts of "food," "fruit," "peels," and "edible or poisonous food," picking up the information from the context might be more difficult. If frimps are important to the curriculum, a teacher might wish to handle instruction differently based on what the students already knew.

Using a more realistic example, imagine a group of fourth-grade students who are familiar with the term *crown*. Teaching the meaning of the word *diadem* won't be too difficult. Students already have the concept of a "crown" and are learning only a new label for a related term. Little, if any, instruction might be needed. Alternatively, an associational, mnemonic, or imaging method might be used, with the teacher encouraging students to create their own relationship for the word by connecting it to the reading selection in some general or personal way, such as with a drawing of one of the characters with clothing labeled. For the same students, in the same selection, the word *nostalgia*, however, would probably be harder to teach because it is an abstract concept that might not be too familiar to most 9-year-olds. To teach the word, the teacher would have to help students establish a rich network of related concepts, such as "longing" and "the past." So it makes sense to look on "knowing" a word as a continuous process that can be affected by meaningful encounters with words and by instruction aimed at helping learners develop a network of understanding. The instructional situation that the teacher selects will vary depending on both the framework of knowledge the learners already have and the importance of the term to the task at hand.

Learning from Context. Researchers have also examined the questions of learner knowledge by analyzing what young students typically learn during their school years. The question here is, How many words do most students learn during their school careers? Researchers have made many attempts to answer this question, attesting to the interest it holds. From 1891 to the present, researchers have struggled with issues about vocabulary size, with widely varying estimates resulting. Estimates of vocabulary size for first graders have ranged from 2,500 to 25,000 words (Graves, 1986). Concerns about students who may be underprepared for school stimulated a renewed interest in this question in the last 20 years (Becker, 1977). Most recent estimates suggest that school-age students learn, on average, 3,000 to 4,000 words per year (Nagy & Anderson, 1984; Nagy & Herman, 1987), with some researchers still suggesting that this average varies widely based on the background of home and school experiences (Becker, 1977; White, Graves, & Slater, 1989). *Learning* in most of these studies refers to growth in familiarity of recognition for certain frequent words as measured on wide-scale tests or through research studies such as those carried out for *The Living Word Vocabulary* (Dale & O'Rourke, 1976). This rapid and large growth again suggests that a significant amount of vocabulary learning takes place through incidental or environmental learning, from wide reading, discussion, listening, and media, for example, rather than from direct instruction. We learn from interacting with and using words in meaningful contexts.

Vocabulary Learning Is Problem Solving. Examining the two strands of research on how words are learned and how many are learned during the school years can also shed some light on the paradox noted earlier in the chapter: Why does the preteaching of vocabulary not always affect comprehension? We know from our own reading experiences and from research (Freebody & Anderson, 1983b) that we can comprehend stories fairly well without knowing every word. Reading materials are redundant; they give us lots of information to help us get the gist of the story without knowing every word. For example, consider the following paragraph with the keyword *glunch*:

> The *glunches* were walking toward the house. Their antennae bobbed in anger. Each paw held a different weapon: swords, guns, bludgeons, and truncheons.

Several clues tell us that whatever a *glunch* is, more than one are coming toward the house: The word has a standard plural ending *(-es)*, the verb *were* indicates plurality, and the word *their* in the following sentence refers to more than one. *Glunches* are capable of locomotion (walking) and have paws. Because of what we know about *anger* and *weapons* and their use, and from past reading and experience, we can infer that the glunches may be about to attack. Further, our knowledge of stories suggests that if this paragraph occurs in a longer selection, there will be some sort of battle or other resolution of their anger in later paragraphs. We could also read passages prior to this paragraph to try to find out what motivated the glunches to anger. It's clear that we could understand quite a bit about this paragraph without knowing the keyword *glunch*. Learners' knowledge of the syntax, grammar, stories, concepts, and the world in general can help them overcome their lack of word knowledge. This explains why wide reading and a wide range of exposure to both oral and written language are critical factors in incidental word learning. We learn about grammar, syntax, and stories—all information that allows context to help us understand even when we don't know every word. For many narratives, prior knowledge and context can help students understand without the need for preteaching of specific vocabulary. There are, of course, limits to the support that rich context and our own prior knowledge can provide. If there are many unknown words, comprehension will be too difficult. There are also situations in which the context is not rich enough to support readers without help (Jenkins, Stein, & Wysocki, 1984). For highly technical reading, or reading with many new concepts, building a conceptual base, with new terminology, may be necessary before adequate understanding can take place.

Good Instruction Builds Vocabulary.   Further, some learners come to school knowing fewer school-type words (Becker, 1977) or have limited networks of meaning for the words that are familiar to them (Graves & Slater, 1987). This lack of knowledge makes it harder for these students to make new connections of meaning that support contextual learning. Some learners also lag behind others in their ability to use strategies that allow them to gain new word meanings from context (McKeown, 1985). Research suggests that judicious attention to concept development and vocabulary can have a positive effect on the growth of usable vocabulary and can also positively affect comprehension (Beck, Perfetti, McKeown, 1982; Mezynski, 1983; Stahl & Fairbanks, 1986). With the understanding that all instruction must deal with the variable of what the learner already knows, we can move on to the next issue—what do we know about vocabulary instruction?

WHAT IS EFFECTIVE VOCABULARY INSTRUCTION?

There are many ways to organize the vast quantity of research that exists on effective vocabulary instruction (see Blachowicz & Fisher, 2000, for a research review).

With the understanding that instruction will vary based on what the learner already knows and the level of knowledge that is needed for understanding, we can tease out a few aspects of good classroom instruction. Let's look at four guidelines that characterize what effective vocabulary teachers do:

- Guideline 1: The effective vocabulary teacher builds a word-rich environment in which students are immersed in words for both incidental and intentional learning.
- Guideline 2: The effective vocabulary teacher helps students develop as independent word learners.
- Guideline 3: The effective vocabulary teacher uses instructional strategies that not only teach vocabulary effectively but model good word-learning behaviors.
- Guideline 4: The effective vocabulary teacher uses assessment that matches the goal of instruction.

Although we will consider these guidelines separately, it is important to note at the outset that they are interdependent. For example, the fact that vocabulary learning should be active is necessarily connected to the fact that vocabulary learning takes place in a word-rich environment. The purpose of this section is to introduce you to research-based practice.

Guideline 1: The effective vocabulary teacher builds a word–rich environment in which students are immersed in words for both incidental and intentional learning.

Just as teachers use the phrase "flood of books" to talk about situations in which students have many and varied opportunities to read (Anderson, Wilson, & Fielding, 1988), so "flood of words" is an important concept for general vocabulary development. Reading to children has been shown to have an effect not only on their recognition knowledge of new words but also on their ability to use these words in their own retellings (Eller, Pappas, & Brown, 1988; Elley, 1988). Wide reading is another hallmark of word learning, with many studies suggesting that word learning occurs normally and incidentally during normal reading (Herman et al., 1987; Nagy, Herman, & Anderson, 1985). Furthermore, discussion, both in the classroom (Stahl & Vancil, 1986) and around the dinner table (Snow, 1991), is another correlate of incidental word learning. While this type of learning through exposure cannot guarantee the learning of specific vocabulary words, it does develop a wide, flexible, and usable general vocabulary.

So our students need "word-aware" classrooms, where time is taken to stop and discuss new words, where words, dictionaries, puzzles and word games, word calendars, books on riddles, and rhymes form the environment for enthusiastic word learning. Besides doing the things that result in greater incidental learning, teachers also need to *intentionally* focus on vocabulary and make word learning a part of every day, not just during those times called "vocabulary instruction." In a detailed study of word learning in the middle elementary grades, Beck, Perfetti, and

McKeown (1982) found one classroom where the students outperformed others in word learning. Looking around the classroom, they saw a 79-cent piece of poster board on the wall with words entered on it by different students. When the researchers asked about this, they were told by the teacher, "Oh, that's just a little something we do each day. If the kids encounter a new and interesting word, they can tell the rest of the class about it, put it on the chart, and earn points for their team." The students became attuned to listening for new and interesting words and had this interest validated in the classroom on a regular basis. Techniques like "word of the day," "mystery word," and so forth are easy, low-maintenance, inexpensive, and time-effective ways of making sure that kids are intentionally exposed to words each day and are motivated to do their own word learning.

One necessary requirement is that teachers are models of word learning. We can probably remember the year we learned lots of new words in school, when we had a teacher who was an avid punster, or was a crossword puzzle aficionado, or was otherwise involved in word play. By being a good model of enthusiastic and pleasurable word learning, teachers can be sure that they and their classrooms are models of best practices.

Guideline 2: The effective vocabulary teacher helps students develop as independent word learners.

Good learners take control of their own learning (Nagy & Scott, 2000). Studies that focus on student self-selection of vocabulary suggest that having students themselves identify words they need to learn results in powerful vocabulary learning. Haggard (1982) interviewed adults and secondary school learners about their memories of learning new words and found that these learners most easily retained words that were usable in their peer groups—popular among peers, occurring frequently in their readings, buzzwords in the media. Her subsequent teaching studies, involving self-selection of words to be learned (1982, 1985), suggested that the control offered by self-selection was an important factor in building a generalized vocabulary. Moreover, for ESL students, some self-selection is critical to getting a true picture of words that confound learning (Jiminez, 1997).

In light of the popularity of wide reading approaches and cooperative group models of classroom instruction, Fisher, Blachowicz, and Smith (1991) examined the effects of self-selection in cooperative reading groups on word learning. The fourth-grade groups analyzed in this study were highly successful in learning a majority of the words chosen for study. In a later study with older fifth- and seventh-grade readers (Blachowicz, Fisher, Costa, & Pozzi, 1993), the results were repeated and new information was added. The students' teachers who were co-researchers in the study, were interested not only in whether or not the words were learned, but in whether or not the students chose challenging words for study. In all groups studied, the students consistently chose words at or above grade level for study. These and other studies indicate that self-selection and self-study processes can be viable choices for some of the word study in the classroom. Collaborative word choice, with the students selecting some words to be learned and the teacher also contributing words for study, may be called for in content area learning and with difficult new conceptual topics (Beyersdorfer, 1991). Combined with teacher selection and support, helping students learn to select words for self-study is a powerful tool for independent learning.

Besides knowing which words to choose for study, students have to be able to use the tools they need to gain new word meaning. Research on learning from context emphasizes that it is a major avenue to word learning but points out that it is unreasonable to expect single contextual exposures to new words to do the job (Baldwin & Schatz, 1985; Schatz & Baldwin, 1986). Students need to understand context and how to use it.

While several studies have provided intensive instruction in contextual analysis (Jenkins, Matlock, & Slocum, 1989; Patberg, Graves, & Stibbe, 1984; Sternberg, 1987) with mixed results, recent instructional studies (Blachowicz & Zabroske, 1990; Buikema & Graves, 1993; Nicol & Graves, 1990; White, Sowell, & Yanagihara, 1989) suggest that context-use instruction that involves explicit instruction (with good planning, practice, and feedback), scaffolding that leads to more student responsibility, and a metacognitive focus can help students become conscious learners from context. Similarly, instruction focusing on structural analysis or morphology, the learning of word parts, suggests that such instruction can be generative in learning new words when the instructional support emphasizes problem solving.

Students also need supportive instruction to learn how to use the dictionary, an important word-learning tool. Every teacher who has watched a student struggle in looking up a word knows that using a dictionary can be a complex and difficult task. Stories of dictionary use often take on a "kids say the darndest things" aura: The student whose only meaning of *sharp* has to do with good looks feels vindicated by finding *acute* as one meaning for sharp in the dictionary (as in "That sure is acute boy in my class"). Another, noting that *erode* is defined as "eats out," produces a sentence, "Since my mom went back to work, my family erodes a lot" (Miller & Gildea, 1987). Aside from providing humorous anecdotes for the teacher's room, dictionaries and dictionary use are coming under closer scrutiny by those involved in instruction. Students don't automatically understand how dictionaries work or how they can most effectively take information from them.

For contextual analysis, morphology instruction, and work with dictionaries, it is wise to remember to work from the known to the unknown. As students engage in learning any one of these processes, it is important for them to understand the underlying rationale. This is best achieved through exploration of the "how to" with familiar words and phrases. Once they have mastered the process with easy words, they can practice with more and more difficult words until the process becomes automatic.

Guideline 3: The effective vocabulary teacher uses instructional strategies that not only teach vocabulary effectively but model good word-learning behaviors.

Along with helping students develop control of their own word learning through self-selection, supported selection, and the use of context, word structure, and reference tools, the effective vocabulary teacher presents new vocabulary in ways that model good learning. This type of instruction involves developing learners who are active, who personalize their learning, who look for multiple sources of information to build meaning, and who are playful with words. Good learners are active. As in all learning situations, having the learners actively attempting to construct their own meanings is a hallmark of good instruction. Many comparisons of instructional methodologies suggest that having the learners take an active role in constructing a network of meaning for a word is critical. Learning new words as we have new experiences is one of the most durable and long-lasting ways to develop a rich vocabulary. Words like *thread, needle, selvage, pattern,* and *dart* are naturally learned in the context of learning to sew, just as *hit, run, base,* and *fly* take on special meanings for the baseball player. This is particularly important with learners whose primary language is not English. They may need the additional contextual help of physical objects and movement to internalize English vocabulary. Another way for students to become actively involved in discovering meaning is by answering questions that ask them to evaluate different features of word meaning (Beck & McKeown, 1983). For example, answering and then explaining one's answer to the question, "Would a recluse enjoy parties?" helps students focus on the important features of the word *recluse,* a person who chooses to be alone rather than with others. As noted above, discussion is another way to involve learners in examining facets of word meaning.

Making word meanings and relationships visible is another way to involve students actively in constructing word meaning. Semantic webs, maps, organizers, or other relational charts, such as the one shown in Figure 1.1, not only graphically display attributes of meanings, but provide a memory organizer for later word use. Many studies have shown the efficacy of putting word meaning into graphic form such as a map or web (Heimlich & Pittelman, 1986), semantic feature chart (Johnson, Toms-Bronowski, & Pittelman, 1982) (Anders, Bos, & Filip, 1984), or advanced organizer (Herber, 1978). It is critical to note, however, that mere construction of such maps, without discussion, is not effective (Stahl & Vancil, 1986).

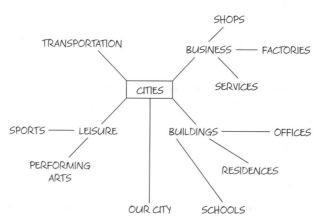

Figure 1.1 Web Example

Other approaches that stress actively relating words to one another are clustering strategies that call for students to group words into related sets, brainstorming, grouping and labeling (Marzano & Marzano, 1988), designing concept hierarchies (Wixon, 1986) or constructing definition maps related to concept hierarchies (Bannon, Fisher, Pozzi, & Wesse, 1990, Schwwartz & Raphael, 1985), and mapping words according to their relation to story structure categories (Blachowicz, 1986). All these approaches involve student construction of maps, graphs, charts, webs, or clusters that represent the semantic relatedness of words to other words and concepts. Again, discussion, sharing, and use of the words are necessary components of active involvement, as is feedback and scaffolding on the part of the teacher.

Making learning personal is another strategy of effective learners. We have already commented on the way in which learning words in the context of learning some important skill or concept is one of the most durable ways to learn words. These meanings are personalized by our experiences. Words not learned in firsthand experiences can also be personalized; relating new words to one's own past experiences has been a component of many successful studies. Eeds and Cockrum (1985) had students provide prior-knowledge cues for new words, a method related to that used by Carr (Carr & Mazur-Stewart, 1988); who asked students to construct personal cues to meaning along with graphic and other methods. Acting out word meaning (Duffelmeyer, 1980) has also led to increased word learning.

Creating one's own mnemonic or image is another way to personalize meaning. While active, semantically rich instruction and learning seems best for learning new concepts, tagging a new label onto a well-established concept can be done through the creation of associations. Mnemonic strategies, those strategies aimed at helping us remember, such as ROY G. BIV for the colors of the spectrum (red, orange, yellow, green, blue, indigo, violet), are time-honored ways to assist memory. Keyword methods are the best known of these word-learning strategies. They involve the creation of a verbal connection, an image, or a picture to help cement the meaning in memory. For example, to remember the word *phototropism*, the bending of plants toward light, a student created the picture shown in Figure 1.2 as a visual mnemonic. The verbal labels _*photographer*_ and *tropical _plant_* aided memory for the word, and the drawing of the tropical flower bending to the light (the sun) supplied a visual image to support it.

For the same word, another student created a keyword sentence, "A photo was taken of the plant bending toward light." So for the two students we have two variations upon a mnemonic theme. When trying to remember, one student would call up the picture of the plant and the light in her mind; the other would think of the sentence, with *photo* providing an acoustic cue and *the bending toward light* a meaning clue. A significant amount of research has been done on the use of the keyword method as a remembering technique (Pressley, Levin, & Delaney, 1983), for special education students (Scruggs, Mastropieri, & Levin, 1985), for second-language learners, and for adult learners (McCarville, 1993). While reviews of the research suggest that the keyword method may be limited in its application, it remains a useful approach for remembering specific word labels, especially combined with imagery, drawing, and other tools for personalization.

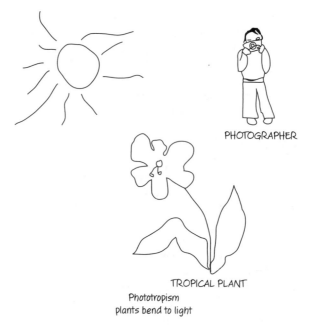

PHOTOGRAPHER

TROPICAL PLANT

Phototropism
plants bend to light

Figure 1.2   Keyword Image—Phototropism

Helping students gather information across text and sources is another way teachers can model mature word-learning strategies. It's important for students to keep looking for different types of information that will flesh out the meaning they need to understand. For learning specific words, rather than for building a generalized, nonspecific vocabulary, research suggests that providing students with multiple sources of information, along with opportunities to use the words in meaningful communication situations, results in superior word learning. Numerous studies comparing definitional instruction with incidental learning from context or with no-instruction control conditions support the notion that teaching definitions results in learning (Kameenui, Carmine, & Freschi, 1982; Pany & Jenkins, 1978; Stahl, 1983).

However, the performance of students who received instruction that combined definitional information with other active processing, such as adding contextual information (Stahl, 1983), writing (Duin & Graves, 1987), contextual discovery (Gipe, 1979–80), or rich manipulation of words (Beck & McKeown, 1983), exceeded the performance of students who only received definitional instruction. A meta-analysis of studies that compared different types of instruction (Stahl & Fairbanks, 1986) concludes that methods with multiple sources of information for students provide superior word learning. In effective classrooms, students encounter words in context as well as work to create or understand appropriate definitions, synonyms, and other word relations.

On

(On top of the world)

Figure 1.3 A wuzzle is a word puzzle that uses strategically placed words (or letters or numbers) and pictures. The wuzzle shown here illustrates "on top of the world."

Along with instruction, students need to experiment with and use new words. Different types of instruction can result in different types and depths of learning. When the goal is to have students gain control of vocabulary to use for their own expression, students need many experiences that allow them to use words in meaningful ways. Use in writing and conversation, where feedback is available, is essential to durable and deep learning. Creating personal word books and dictionaries is a good first step to word ownership; use in many situations is a second step. Using new words in discussion, in writing, in independent projects, and in word play develops real ownership and moves those words into students' personal vocabularies.

Play is also an important part of word use and word learning. Part of creating a "positive environment for word learning" involves having activities, games, materials, and other resources that allow students to play with words. Who wouldn't enjoy a few minutes each day spent figuring out a "wuzzle" or word riddle (see Figure 1.3).

Guideline 4: The effective vocabulary teacher uses assessment that matches the goal of instruction.

The final guideline relates to the complexity of vocabulary instruction that was suggested in our introduction. We teach words for many different purposes, and require varying levels and types of understanding according to the task, the word, and the subject area. In general it is helpful to think of two main dimensions for vocabulary knowledge—depth and breadth.

Depth refers to how much is known about a particular word. Can you recognize the meaning in text or conversation? Can you use it appropriately? Can you define it? We all have the experience of being asked, "What does *energetic* mean?" and replying, "Well, Bonny, my dog, is energetic when she runs all over the house and barks at everything." That is, we tend to supply examples to illustrate meaning rather than to give a definition. This is appropriate in many situations, and relies on the questioner's ability to use the context we provide to elaborate on the basic meaning of the word. We often do this even when we could give a definition. However, there are many occasions when we do it because we know how to use a word—say, the word *calligraphy*—but are unsure of the precise meaning. Other times we can understand some of the meaning of a word when we hear or see someone use it, but not feel comfortable about using it ourselves. We learn more about words each time we see or hear them—that is, we increase our depth of understanding. In relation to classrooms it is helpful to consider what level of understanding is needed for successful completion of the task. Perhaps, when reading a particular selection, it is enough to know that a *pallet* is a form of bed, or maybe it is necessary to know what distinguishes it from other beds (it is made of straw) because it is part of a social studies unit that connects living styles to the environment.

Breadth of knowledge of a word is related to depth insofar as it can add layers of understanding, but it is concerned primarily with how a word is connected to others in a domain of learning. For example, do students understand the relations among the words *plains, rivers, mountains, foothills,* and *erosion?* Students in fourth grade may need to see how each relates to the other when studying a unit on the plains. And their depth of understanding of *erosion* may be small when compared with that of a high school geography student or a geomorphologist. Baker et al. (1995) have argued that an important principle of vocabulary instruction is that it should be aligned with the depth of word knowledge required in any setting. We would add that the assessment should match the instruction in relation to both depth and breadth of word knowledge. This may sound complicated, but it is not. Many instructional techniques can also be used as assessment techniques, so that a teacher can evaluate a student's understanding in authentic learning situations. We will look at this in more detail in Chapter 8.

Some Last Thoughts

The learning of new words is not a simple issue, and neither is instruction for word learning. Though there is still much to be learned about vocabulary learning and instruction, teachers need to use the best practices they know and the best available research to help students build their vocabularies. This checklist might help you think about your classroom using the guidelines we proposed above.

Looking Back and Looking Ahead

In this chapter, we have presented a theoretical and practical overview of some of the research on vocabulary instruction. We looked at what learners know (and don't know) about words and what the research suggests about instruction. Included were descriptions of situations that foster word learning and guidelines for structuring instruction. The rest of the chapters in this book contain practical teaching ideas for different instructional situations. One common situation is the teaching of reading strategy lessons. Chapter 2 describes how vocabulary can be learned from context and how strategies of independent word learning can be developed.

HOW WILL I KNOW A GOOD VOCABULARY PROGRAM WHEN I SEE ONE?

(A classroom checklist)

Word-Rich Environment

Teacher shows enthusiasm for words and word learning.

_____ Daily read-aloud
_____ Word of day or word activity of day
_____ Students indicate teacher *loves* words and word play
_____ Understands differences *and* connections between spelling, phonics and vocabulary

Classroom shows physical signs of word awareness.

_____ Word charts or word walls (showing student input)
_____ Books on words, word play, specialized dictionaries (where students can easily access them)
_____ Labels in classroom
_____ Word games
_____ Puzzle books and software
_____ Student-made word books, alphabet books, dictionaries, hypercard stacks

Builds the Base for Independence

_____ Students show enthusiasm for words and word learning and are responsible for their own learning
_____ Spend part of each day reading on appropriate level
_____ Can name a favorite word book, puzzle activity, and/or word game
_____ Have personal dictionaries or word logs
_____ Can use dictionary on appropriate level
_____ Have a strategy for dealing with unknown words
_____ Have strategies for self-selection and self-study
_____ Develop a knowledge base for independent strategies (word parts, context, word references, etc.)
_____ Develop strategies for using knowledge base

Models. Supports, and Develops Good Strategies

_____ Rich instruction on content area vocabulary words where definitional and contextual information provided
_____ Use of mapping, webbing, and other graphics to show word relationships
_____ Multiple exposures and chances to see, hear, write, and use new words
_____ Wide reading with follow-up discussion of new words
_____ Emphasis on students using strategies
_____ Word play and motivation activities

Uses Varied Assessment

_____ Differ depending on goal
_____ Differ depending on entry knowledge level of learners
_____ Assess both depth and breadth

Resources for Further Learning

Blachowicz, C. L. Z., & Fisher, P. (2000). Vocabulary instruction. In M. Kamil, P. Mosenthal, P. S Pearson, & R. Barr, (Eds.), *Handbook of Reading Research, Volume III.* White Plains, NY: Longman.

Graves, M. F. (1986). Vocabulary learning and instruction. In E. Z. Rothkopf (Ed.), *Review of Research in Education,* Vol. 13, (pp. 49–89). Washington, D.C.: American Educational Research Association. (A readable and comprehensive summary of research)

Irvin, J. L. (1990). *Vocabulary knowledge: guidelines for instruction.* Washington, D.C.: National Education Association. (Part of "What Research Says to Teacher" series—clear and accessible)

Report of the National Reading Panel (2000), Chap. 4. Report on Vocabulary. http://www.nationalreadingpanel.org/.

CHAPTER 2

LEARNING VOCABULARY FROM CONTEXT

☑ **Prepare Yourself**

Prepare yourself by evaluating your own knowledge. Rate your ability to answer some of the key questions for this chapter. Check the boxes that best describe your prereading knowledge.

Key concept questions	Well informed	Aware	Need ideas
1. *What do we know about learning from context?*	❏	❏	❏
2. *How can we encourage informal word learning?*	❏	❏	❏
3. *How can we help students learn strategies for problem solving with context?*	❏	❏	❏
4. *How can teachers use context to present new vocabulary?*	❏	❏	❏

✓ Strategy Overview Guide

This chapter presents background, ideas, and strategies to help you understand learning from context, a term that is used in several different ways. We'll talk about how words are learned informally by students placed in a word-rich environment, how strategies for inferring specific meanings can be developed, and how teachers can use contextual methods for introducing new words. The following chart can help you choose suitable instructional strategies for your classroom.

Instructional strategy	Goal—use when you want to . . .	Comments
Read-alouds (p. 20)	*Provide meaningful listening experiences with new words.*	*Also good for motivation and language development.*
Dual-language charts (p. 21)	*Create synonym lists.*	*Helps show value of bilingualism.*
Classroom labeling (p. 21)	*Associate words with concrete objects; develop concept of word.*	*For ESL and foreign language; for science or technology classes.*
CD-ROM books (p. 24)	*Increase motivation; provide dual-language and multimodal input.*	*For independent learning; learning labs; motivation.*
Metacognitive context instruction (p. 26)	*Develop a framework for independent learning.*	*Useful as a structure for mini-lessons.*
Cloze procedure (zip, maze, synonym cloze) (p. 30)	*Build skill at inferring word meaning.*	*Useful in individual or small-group instruction.*
Vocabulary self-selection strategy (p. 32)	*Give students control of word selection.*	*Use for literature circles.*
C(2)QU (p. 33)	*Present words in a problem-solving format.*	*Effective prereading strategy.*
Sentence game (p. 35)		
Personal contexts (p. 36)	*Help students remember new words.*	*Discussion develops oral language and listening skills.*

LEARNING FROM CONTEXT

How many new words do school-age students learn, on average, in a school year? Chances are that you estimated well below 4,000 words, which many researchers estimate is the number of new words students learn, on average, each year of their school careers (Nagy & Anderson, 1984). Compare this number with the roughly 400 words formally introduced in a year of reading instruction. How do students learn all these words if they are not formally taught?

As teachers, parents, and word learners ourselves, we know the answer. From our own experience, as well as from studies of children's word learning, we know that the majority of words we learn are learned in situations where words are used in meaningful contexts. Take up a new hobby and the vocabulary of that hobby is learned as a by-product. For example, *knit* and *purl* become part of the knitter's vocabulary; *c-clamp* and *contact cement* are typical words in a woodworker's vocabulary. Firsthand learning supplies us with many of our word tools. In school, this learning often takes place in content area classes and in thematic study. In a science class, the teacher may say, "OK, now we light this *Bunsen burner* carefully before we can boil the water in the *beaker*." Students observing the lesson can easily attach labels or characteristics to the tools being used. A *Bunsen burner* is something you light to give heat, and the *beaker* is the thing with the water in it. Students might not know these words well enough after one exposure to use them or remember them, but over time they learn and remember the words as they use them in learning and in discussion.

We also learn through more vicarious experiences. The watcher of Olympic figure skating will not have the same knowledge of skating vocabulary as a figure skater but will soon come to recognize the terms *triple lutz, axel,* and *edge* as terms related to skating actions. Similarly, we learn words in listening to others speak and from having them read to us. Research with both preschoolers and older students has shown that students learn new words when they are read to (Eller, Pappas, & Brown, 1988; Elley, 1988). As students read and reread books, they develop increasingly sophisticated understandings of new word meanings and begin to use those words in story discussions, retellings, and responses. Lastly, we know that silent, personal reading is a rich source of incidental word learning. So a critical part of word learning happens when students have rich experiences, both firsthand and vicarious, that expose them to new words used in meaningful contexts.

Repeated meaningful encounters with words in direct experience, in read-alouds, in conversation, in personal reading, in discussion, and in drama or television watching can lead students to produce an immediate label for an object or concept or to build clues to these word meanings over time. This informal learning from context can be facilitated by instruction that will be described in the following section on developing oral vocabulary and is the first avenue to learning from context.

Although this incidental learning from context is a powerful means for building vocabulary, teachers also have other options for working with context. We can help students develop the ability to problem-solve using new words and their contexts.

This type of instruction involves modeling the thinking processes we use when trying to figure out word meaning and can also help students understand how contexts work. For example, writers commonly use apposition, a direct statement of a synonym or explanation as a context clue, as in science project directions that note, "The pipette, or eyedropper, should be used to measure the ingredients."

Developing strategies for problem solving with context will be the second focus of this chapter.

A third way teachers focus on context in instruction is to use contextual methods to present new vocabulary words directly. We'll examine each of the processes, enhancing incidental, informal day-to-day learning, developing the ability to use context, and using context to directly present vocabulary words in the remainder of this chapter.

ENCOURAGING INFORMAL WORD LEARNING

Developing Rich Language Environments

Wide exposure to words is a powerful force for word learning, particularly for the development of oral vocabularies. For students of all ages, but particularly for preschoolers or students who are not secure in English, having lots of time for classroom talk is an essential aspect of encouraging informal word learning. Using activities such as "show and tell" at the lower levels and current events and cooperative grouping for older students maximizes the opportunities your students have to hear and use language. Repeated story and poetry readings are excellent stimuli for word learning. Connecting new vocabulary to rich illustrations and engaging story lines helps to make new words comprehensible and memorable (Freeman & Freeman, 1993). As with all things happening in classrooms, some judicious attention and planning by the teacher can maximize student learning (Elley, 1988). For example, read-alouds can enhance word learning when the teachers:

1. Use illustrations to express and clarify meanings. For example, in Audrey and Don Wood's delightful *King Bidgood's in the Bathtub* (1985), words such as *battle, trout, masquerade, feast,* and *plug* are clarified by the superb illustrations.

2. Use new words in questions, "If you were going to be in a battle, what would you take?" Such questions involve students in meaningful thoughtful responses to new words, and the students tend to use these words in their responses. "Well, for the battle, I'd take. . . . " This technique also gives teachers a chance to clarify meanings when students have a misconception.

3. Involve students in creating images for new words to cement their meanings in a personal way. For example, ESL students working with *King Bidgood* were asked to draw and label the objects in scenes from the book. One student's feast looked like the one drawn in Figure 2.1.

4. Read and reread favorite books and recommend that students take them home to be read for and by parents. Research indicates that students learn more about a word's meaning each time the word is used in a meaningful way.

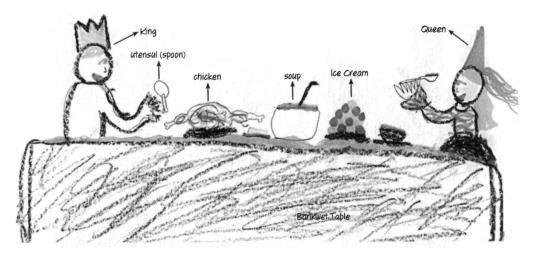

Figure 2.1 Student's Drawing and Labeling of a Scene from *King Bidgood's in the Bathtub* (Wood & Wood, 1985)

Table 2.1 English–Spanish Chart

English	Picture clue	Español
trout		la trucha
battle		la batalla
mask		la máscara
plug		el tapón

5. For ESL students, create word lists that use words in their native language as well as in English. For example, for *King Bidgood* the word list created by a bilingual English-Spanish teacher for her class looked like the one shown in Table 2.1, with spaces for students to provide their own picture clues.

Use of good literature, repeated exposure, use in discussion and image making, and relation to first languages are all ways vocabulary from a read-aloud book can find its way into students' oral vocabularies.

Classroom Labeling

In addition to read-aloud sharing, classroom labeling is a good way to teach new vocabulary. Objects and situations in the classroom provide natural contexts for learning. Using a label maker (a large one for young students and a smaller size for older students), students can label classroom objects to produce a vocabulary set that is contextualized by the classroom. This process can also assist the students in spelling when they want to describe the classroom aquarium or write about the mealworms in science class. Students in advanced classes can use a professional label maker to label new equipment in a science lab. Gym class students can label the bins for storing sports gear. Figure 2.2 shows some uses of labeling in a kindergarten.

This is Nora's work of art and she used blocks of colors and she didn't use black and brown. She even used white

This is a flower that Julia made.

Figure 2.2 Kindergarten Labels

These Richard Scarry books contain detailed and labeled drawings of objects and other concepts in both English and Spanish.

Learn to Count

Great Big Schoolhouse

Great Big Air Book

Busiest People Ever

Naughty Bunny

My House

What Do People Do All Day?

ABC Word Book

At Work

Nicky Goes to the Doctor

Best Word Book Ever

Story Book Dictionary

Figure 2.3   Dual-Language Books by Richard Scarry

Context clues in the form of labeled pictures also provide useful, contextualized information, particularly for older, second-language, or LEP students. Volumes illustrated by Richard Scarry can be useful in advanced classrooms when basic vocabulary is needed. Scarry also produced a series of books in many languages so that terms can be compared across languages and used by all students. Figure 2.3 contains a list of his books that are available in Spanish. Many are also available in other languages such as French, Italian, and German.

Wide Reading

Wide reading is also a powerful determiner of vocabulary growth. **Sustained Silent Reading,** the process of including independent reading in each day's instructional program, ensures that students regularly receive new words and see these words repeated. Experiments such as the "book flood," which involved students in a large volume of independent reading (Anderson, Wilson, & Fielding, 1988), have indicated that wide reading means wide vocabulary growth. Also, "low-workload" techniques such as keeping a word wall or bulletin board of interesting words that are discussed as they are added have proved to be productive tools for informal word learning. Teaching Idea File 2.1 summarizes some of the ways you might encourage informal word learning.

Using Technology

Capitalize on students' love of technology by using technology that can teach. For example, you could consider using captioned TV and videos for instruction. These

Teaching Idea File 2.1

Encouraging Informal Word Learning

1. Use illustrations, pantomime, and objects to clarify meaning and make new words comprehensible.
2. Use new words in questions and discussion.
3. Have students create personal images as mnemonics.
4. Reread favorite selections to "imprint" new words.
5. Create multilingual synonym lists.
6. Use labels whenever possible.
7. Keep English and non-English books in sets so that students can use one for reference.
8. Set aside time for personal reading and encourage wide reading at a comfortable level.

From Blachowicz & Fisher, *Teaching Vocabulary in All Classrooms*, p. 22.

are useful for making new vocabulary more comprehensible not only for students with hearing impairments, but also for students who are nonnative speakers of English. Videos can also be rented in captioned form. Newscasts, presidential addresses, and other topical events are often captioned. Taping them for use in current events class can help students hear and see new words at the same time.

Computerized and CD-ROM books and computer word processing programs can also be useful for providing multiple types of context clues to word meaning. (Figure 2.4 contains some CD-ROM sources.) Many of these computer-based books allow students to hear the story at the same time they see the words. Several versions, such as those by Discis Books, also allow readers to highlight words to hear them pronounced again and defined. There are also word processing programs, such as *Kids Works 2,* that print in primary or regular type, have a file of vocabulary rebuses, and use synthesized speech to read back to students what they have written. Music can also be a means of acquiring new vocabulary. CD-ROM music videos often provide words to match the music, and students also enjoy karaoke singing, which involves reading lyrics to match the music. Technology has a motivational factor that will frequently interest students who would be reluctant to learn in other ways. Put a computer mouse in a kid's hand and you have instant motivation.

LEARNING TO PROBLEM-SOLVE WITH CONTEXT

Besides ensuring that students are surrounded by words in contextual settings, teachers also want to help students hone their abilities to figure out new words from context. This process involves several stages of active problem solving (McKeown, 1985) and ongoing reflection. The strategic process of context use can be envisioned as having three components:

Bravo! Books
Publisher: Computer Curriculum Corp.
1287 Lawrence Station Rd.
Sunnyvale, CA 94089
(800)-227-8324
For Macintosh LC or better

Stories and More
Publisher: Eduquest/IBM
One Culver Rd.
Dayton, NJ 08810-9988
(800)-426-3327
MS-DOS computers

Integrated Language Arts-Primary
Publisher: Josten's Learning Corp.
7878 N. 16th St. Suite 100
Phoenix, AZ 85020-4402
(800)-221-7927
Macintosh, Tandy, or Josten's Computers

Living Books: Just Grandma and Me
Publisher: Broderbund Software
P.O. Box 6125
Novato, CA 94948-6125
(800)-521-6263
Macintosh and Microsoft windows

Discis Books (various titles)
Publisher: Discis Knowledge Research
P.O. Box 66
Buffalo, NY 14223-0066
(800)-567-4321
Macintosh

Figure 2.4 CD-ROM Storybooks and Publishers

1. Students must know why and when to use context. Studies of at-risk readers frequently reveal great cognitive confusion about the potential uses of strategies (Downing & Leong, 1982). Controlling the why and the when involves awareness of both the limitations and contributions of context to word learning. Sometimes the context is quite explicit about word meanings; at other times the clues given by the author merely suggest an attribute or relationship. Students need to see and discuss various levels of context explicitness to develop sensitivity to the different levels of help context can provide.

2.   Students must have a general idea of what kinds of clues may be provided by the context. The following section on teaching about context will describe these characteristics.

3.   Most importantly, students must know how to look for and use these clues. Several strategy sequences have been suggested that involve looking at the word and around the word (Herman & Dole, 1988), and proposing and verifying meanings (Blachowicz & Zabroske, 1990; Buikema & Graves, 1993).

Teaching About Context

To sensitize students to the types of information that context can supply, try to have them examine and collect different types of context clues that authors provide. This type of instruction is typically included in school curricula and commercial instructional materials in the middle grades. Instead of worksheets focused on single paragraphs, consider mini-lessons built around entire selections in anthologies or periodicals. Introduce examples of context use in mini-lessons and have students examine and discuss them. Then make wall charts with examples they discover in their own reading. For instance, one class discovered that context helps provide readers with the following types of information:

1.   *Synonyms.* The farrier, the man who makes shoes for the horses, had to carry his heavy tools in a wheelbarrow.

2.   *What a word is or is not like.* Unlike the peacock, the *mudhen* is not colorful.

3.   *Something about location or settings.* The *shaman* entered the Hopi roundhouse and sat facing the mountains.

4.   *Something about what a word is used for.* He used the *spade* to dig up the garden.

5.   *What kind of thing or action it is.* Swiveling his hips, waggling the club, and aiming for the pin, he *drove* his first four golf balls into the water.

6.   *How something is done.* He *expectorated* the gob of tobacco juice neatly into the spittoon.

7.   *A general topic or ideas related to the words.* The dancing bears, the musicians, the cooks carrying huge plates of food all came to the church for the *fiesta.*

From their own reading, students can collect, explain, and display new words so that they will have concrete examples of the ways in which context explains word meaning. These examples will provide models for writing, and their own creations can also be displayed.

Metacognitive Context Instruction

Once students have a basic sensitivity to some of the ways context reveals meanings, structure some group lessons that help them build and test hypotheses about word meaning. Direct students to:

- *Look.* Before, at, and after the word.
- *Reason.* Connect what they know with what the author has written.
- *Predict a possible meaning.*
- *Resolve or redo.* Decide if they know enough, should try again, or consult an expert or reference.

Introduce this strategy through teacher modeling, group work, and discussion. To prepare, select a passage and target a word or words for discussion. For example, before reading *Fog Magic* (Sauer, 1943), a story of a young girl's time travel into the past, the teacher chose to take out the term *cellar holes.* She prepared a transparency by photocopying the passage and putting masking tape over the word *cellar holes.* Then she presented it to the class (see Figure 2.5). The class discussion that resulted was rich and thoughtful.

> T(EACHER): Remember that for the last few weeks we have been talking about using context clues. Can anyone tell me why we do this?
>
> S(TUDENT)1: When there's a word you don't know, sometimes you can get an idea by looking at the rest of the story for clues.
>
> S2: You can think about what you already know and then see if you can figure out what the new word means or something about it from what the author says.
>
> T: How do we do that?

Greta knew what this part of the mountain was like in clear weather. To the south of the road there was still unbroken forest—scarred here and there with burned patches, but otherwise dark, mysterious, treacherous, with unexpected chasms. Along the edge of the road to the north a high protective hedge of spruce and alder had been left, cut here and there with entrances. Beyond the hedge lay a clearing that sloped gently toward the sea. And dotting this clearing were _____. Smooth little depressions they were, covered with the quick-springing growth of the pasture. It looked almost as if the homes of the departed inhabitants had sunk quietly into the earth.

Greta had often played in these _____. It was fun to imagine where each house had stood, where the doorways had been, where the single street had led. Sometimes the shape of the depressions gave a clue; often a flat stone marked the doorstep. Once she had dug up a tiny spoon in a _____. A salt spoon it was, with a strange name engraved on the handle.

The missing term is *cellar hole.*

Figure 2.5 Text with a Keyword Blanked Out for Contextual Discussion

S3: We look before the word, we look after the word, and we look *at* the word, too, for prefixes and roots and stuff, but we can't do that here because you took that all out (laughter).

T: That's right. I'm making it a real challenge for you. Can you tell me anything about the missing term?

S2: Well, she's outside, so it's something outside.

S5: It's something on the ground 'cause she's digging later on.

S1: It says, "Smooth little depressions they were . . . " but I don't understand that because I know depressed and this doesn't make sense.

T: Anyone have anything to say about that? (Students make no response.)

T: Remember to look further on. Is there anything else about depressions?

S4: Later it says that "The shape of the depressions gave a clue," so it's not a feeling. It's something on the ground.

S5: She played in them, so they were holes or like where walls of old stones were left.

T: What made you think of walls?

S5: Well, they keep talking about the houses and said "houses had stood there . . . the doorways had been there," so I think she is somewhere where houses used to be. Like after an earthquake or tornado.

S1: "It looks as if the homes had sunk into the earth," so they must be holes.

T: Would (the word) *holes* make sense?

S4: Yea, they could be depressions. She could play in them, and you could dig a spoon out of the hole.

S5: If it's the hole where a house was, then it could be the basement hole, like the hole they dig when they start to build a house.

S1: Basement makes sense; it's a hole for a house.

T: Well, what do you think?

S1: I think we should stop. We know enough.

T: Should we stop or keep thinking? (Students agree to stop and uncover the term *cellar holes*.)

S2: Well, they are holes.

S5: My gram has a fruit cellar in her house, and it's like, it's the same as a basement.

S4: OK, we figured it out. Let's see what this story is about.

T: Good idea.

Where a word is unknown to all the students in a group, or in an individual tutorial situation, the word itself is a place to look, for roots and affixes and to make associations with what is already known. For example, in the same selection, a single student identified *depressions* as a hard word that he was not sure about.

T: Can you find some clues?

S: I've heard of being depressed.

T: Does that make sense here?

S: Not to me.

> T: Do you know any other meanings?
>
> S: It has "press" in it. When we rode the subway to the museum, we talked about not touching that handle where it said "To stop train, depress lever." We figured it meant press it down.
>
> T: So . . . ?
>
> S: So these could be pushed-in parts. Like later it says she dug in them. So they're like holes.

In this instance, looking at the word itself and asking what other associations he had about the word helped the student match what he knew with ideas from the context.

After students become familiar with using a contextual process, student teams can lead the lessons. Working with the teacher, they can choose two words a week they think would be unfamiliar to the group and model the process with the first word and lead the discussion on the second. Students also like to play "Mystery Word," in which photocopied pages, news articles, and magazine articles are posted on the chalkboard daily with one or two words designated as mystery words. Students note on index cards what clues they pick up about the word and where they were located and then make hypotheses about the word's meaning. The cards are placed in an envelope tacked below the selection. At the end of the day, the student team that posted the word would review the cards and discuss the word. If needed, students would consult a dictionary to see if their reasoning about the word clues and the word was consistent with established definitions.

When context wasn't helpful, students often rewrote sections of text to make the surrounding text more explanatory or provided a synonym version for later study. Many of these versions have been collected and kept for next year's students, who will use the same textbooks. A brief summary of a strategy for using context is shown in Teaching Idea File 2.2.

Teaching Idea File 2.2

Strategy for Context-Use Lesson

1. Make a transparency of a passage and omit a contextually explained word.
2. Direct students to:
   - *Look.* Before, at, and after the word.
   - *Reason.* Connect what they know with what the author has written.
   - *Predict a possible meaning.*
   - *Resolve or redo.* Decide if they know enough or should stop.
3. Discuss—discussion is critical.
4. Reveal the author's word choice.
5. Discuss further. Use references to elaborate.

From Blachowicz & Fisher, *Teaching Vocabulary in All Classrooms*, p. 27.

Using the Cloze Procedure

The **cloze procedure** can also help students learn to use context to infer word meanings. It is a particularly useful strategy in individualized instruction, such as in Chapter 1 programs. When done with an overhead, as with the zip cloze procedure, the cloze procedure can be effective with a small group as well. In a cloze passage, selected words are omitted from the text and replaced with a line or space. Reading a cloze passage requires readers to use their knowledge of context to supply appropriate words and concepts to create a meaningful passage. For example, a cloze passage might look like this:

More direct instruction and _____ with vocabulary may be given by using

the _____ procedure in its many modifications. A cloze passage _____ selected

words from the _____ and replaces them with a line or _____. Reading a cloze

passage requires _____ to use their knowledge of _____ to supply appropri-

ate words and concepts to _____ a meaningful passage.

In completing a cloze passage, the teacher should have the students supply sets of words that might be appropriate to create a meaningful passage. For the passage above, several words could fit many of the omissions. For example, you might have supplied:

experience/practice; cloze; deletes/omits/leaves out;
passage/paragraph/text; space; readers/students; meaning/context;
complete/create/finish/fillin.

While cloze passages used for assessment typically remove every fifth word, cloze for instruction can be structured more selectively and flexibly. Oral cloze, with rich discussion around the choices, can be used for emergent readers or any students who need practice with oral expression. Selected content words can be deleted from a high-interest, natural language, or predictable selection from any book or pupil-made story used in the classroom. For best results, choose interesting content, predictable structures or refrain, clear and captivating illustrations, and familiar experiences. In using a selection for oral cloze, the teacher first shares the illustrations that carry information and clues and then reads aloud, substituting a pause for each of the words omitted.

For example, a class who had read Judith Viorst's *Alexander and the Terrible, Horrible, No Good, Very Bad Day* (1972) made their own versions of a very bad day. The teacher used several of these for oral cloze, having the students hold up their illustrations for the class. One student's example is shown here:

I went to bed with candy in my <mouth> and now there's candy on my <face>. When I got up this morning I tripped on the <toys> that were all over my <floor>. While I ate, I dropped <food> all over my <shirt>. Then I went to school but I forgot my <homework> so the teacher was <mad>. I could tell it was going to be a terrible, horrible, no good, very <bad> day.

As the teacher reads the story, the students supply possibilities for the words omitted. Student enthusiasm for the original book and their adaptations makes the "contribution rate" high and provides many alternatives for discussion of possible vocabulary and contextual appropriateness. After the story or segment has been read and a number of suggestions offered, students often like to tape-record different versions to keep oral records of "Room 101's Different Terrible Days." The goal is not to limit choices to the author's vocabulary but to generate a range of words that would fit the context. This technique helps students to develop sets of synonyms and a sense of flexibility of vocabulary choice.

Zip Cloze.   One problem that readers sometime encounter when using context is a total loss of the sense of the selection some place in the passage. Where more sophisticated readers might push on and attempt to recapture the meaning, less flexible readers often become frustrated and give up. The **zip procedure** (so named by a second-grade class with an innate sense of onomatopoeia) supplies constant feedback to readers to "keep them going" in the context.

The story to be used can be an ordinary book, big book, or wall chart, but the most effective format involves putting the story or passage on an overhead transparency. Masking tape is used to block out the words that have been chosen for deletion. The children first skim for gist and then supply the masked words one at a time. As each possibility is predicted and discussed, the tape is pulled off (or "zipped") so that readers receive immediate feedback from the text as well as being given more of the context from which to make further predictions. The zip procedure can be used in individual books by rubber banding a sheet protector over the page and using a marking pen to blank out words. Children enjoy preparing zip selections for others and can work on individual goals to increase their own awareness of certain word classes (for instance, they could tape over the nouns) or sentence elements (they might tape over the words or phrases that describe something).

Maze Cloze.   For students who might need more support or practice in distinguishing between related words, the **maze procedure** can be used. Rather than deleting words from a passage, teachers provide students with several choices at each contextual point. The first exercises of this type should offer clear, unambiguous choices. The following example illustrates such choices:

	house
The boy on the hill lived in a yellow	cat.
	umbrella

	very
The house had seven	stars.
	rooms

After students become comfortable with the procedure, more sophisticated exercises can be structured to draw attention to specific word classes, pronominal references, connotation and denotation, and so on. For example, students might be asked to choose words with positive (or negative) connotations in the following maze cloze:

The young man wanted to make a good impression on his date. He described the restaurant they were heading for as being popular and (inexpensive/cheap). The decor was (simple/plain), and you could dress (casually/sloppily).

Maze gives students a chance to evaluate possibilities for contextual appropriateness without having to generate terms from their own memory. It is especially useful for students who might have word-finding problems or who might have limited-English-recall vocabularies.

Synonym Cloze.   **Synonym cloze passages** use context to provide students with a support system. As in a regular cloze passage, words are deleted, but further cues are provided by placing a synonym or synonym phrase under the space. For example,

The boy petted his <<u>puppy</u>> before going <<u>outside</u>>.
little dog   outdoors

In this type of exercise, students have access to additional cues, which is especially useful for students who need to broaden their vocabularies by building stores of synonyms.

Self-Selected Vocabulary from Context

In addition to using context as a formal device, many teachers have students create personal word lists or word files from the new words they meet in context. In Chapter 4, we will look at many different ways this process can be used with literature circles and other literature-based approaches. Students should be instructed to choose words that are important to understanding a selection or words that they find interesting. When recording the words, students should record the location and a bit of the context. Students can then proceed to use a reference book (see Chapter 6) or participate in an activity such as the vocabulary self-selection strategy (Haggard, 1982).

The **Vocabulary Self-Selection Strategy (VSS)** is a group activity in which each student, and the teacher as well, is responsible for bringing two words to the attention of the group (for larger groups, reduce to one word or have students alternate weeks). Students are encouraged to choose words they have seen, heard in conversation or on TV, or come across in pleasure reading or in textbooks. Students place their words on the board, with spelling assistance offered by the teacher.

Each pupil, in turn, talks about his or her word, where it was encountered, what it might mean, and why he or she thinks it is important for the class to know. After all the words have been presented, the class narrows the list to a predetermined number (five to eight per week is typical). Once the final list is picked, students again talk about their words, and the teacher leads discussions to clarify, refine, or extend the definitions. Discussion is a critical part of the process. Students then enter the words in their vocabulary logs and practice using the words in activities ranging from doing crosswords to researching word histories to creating a class assessment. The cycle starts again the next week.

The process can be modified in many ways to suit a particular class. The teacher can ask students to focus on words in particular areas or ones that are related to a specific content under study. Because of the emphasis on explanation from context (telling where the word was found, what it means, why it is important to know), VSS is especially useful for students learning English as a second language. In discussions, students can explore synonyms, word histories, and personal experiences. Because the teacher also brings words, teacher modeling takes place, which is helpful to students who need additional guidance. Students enjoy choosing their own words to learn, and they like the variety of words presented. Haggard's (1982) strategy for having students self-select vocabulary words is shown in Teaching Idea File 2.3.

USING CONTEXTUAL METHODS TO PRESENT NEW VOCABULARY

Besides helping students develop strategies for using context, teachers can also use contextual methods to present specific vocabulary or to help students create contexts to learn new words. The next two strategies can be used for prereading presentation of new vocabulary.

C(2)QU

Teachers can involve students in a process approach to using context at the same time they present specific vocabulary (Blachowicz, 1993). A process formulated in several middle-grade classrooms is **C(2)QU** (or See-Two-Cue-You, in homage to *Star Wars!*). As a mode of presenting new vocabulary, the purpose of C(2)QU is to present both definitional and contextual information about new words to students in a way that allows them to hypothesize about meaning, to articulate the cues that lead to the hypothesis, and to refine and use what they have learned with feedback from the group and from the teacher if necessary.

Teaching Idea File 2.3

Vocabulary Self-Selection Strategy

(Haggard, 1982)

1. Students bring two words to class that they have found in reading, or listening, etc.
2. Each student presents words to the group.
3. The group votes on five to eight words to be learned for the week.
4. The teacher leads a discussion to clarify, elaborate, and extend word meanings. Discussion is critical.
5. Students enter their words into personal word logs and create some sort of memory and meaning aid (chart, diagram, picture, mnemonic, definition frame, etc.).
6. Students may create writing assignments, activities, games, and tests for practice.

From Blachowicz & Fisher, *Teaching Vocabulary in All Classrooms*, p. 30.

C1: (First example in context)

My new stepmother moved into our house after the wedding.

C2: (Second example in context)

When my father married again, his new wife became my stepmother.

Q: (Question involving interpretation)

Can a person have a mother and a stepmother at the same time? (Open to multiple interpretations in the discussion. It depends on whether or not the father is a widower or divorced.)

U: (Teacher asks students to give examples of word use or give attributes)

Figure 2.6   C(2)QU Example

Prepare for the process by composing a transparency on the words you wish to examine. (See Figure 2.6 for an example with the word *stepmother.*) The strategy has four steps:

- C1: Present the word in a broad but meaningful context, such as a word selected from a story or chapter. Ask students to form hypotheses about the word's meaning; to give attributes, ideas, or association; and to "think aloud" to explain to the group the sources of their hypotheses.
- C2: Provide more explicit context with some definitional information. Ask students to reflect on their initial ideas and to reaffirm or refine them again in a "think-aloud" mode.
- Q: Ask a question that involves semantic interpretation of the word. At this point, you can also ask for a definition or give one if necessary. Discuss as needed with group members, using each other's cues and explanations as more data.
- U: Ask students to use the word in a meaningful sentence. Go back into the C(2)QU loop as needed.

Words suitable for this process are any that appear in reading material in a context that provides some information for hypothesizing. Most productive are new labels for already-known concepts or partially known words for which the context adds a new twist or further rich information. C(2)QU is also a good process for cooperative reading groups where one role is that of "vocabulary director." Teachers can model the process for the vocabulary directors and then let them choose words from a chapter for their group's focus. They use the process with their groups and come back together to evaluate how the process worked. C(2)QU helps students develop a context-use process that involves rich discussion and self-monitoring. A summary of this technique is shown in Teaching Idea File 2.4.

C(2)QU—Teaching Words in Context

Choose a word to be taught.

C1: Present the word in a broad but meaningful context, such as a word selected from a story or chapter. Ask students to form hypotheses about the word's meaning; to give attributes, ideas, or association; and to "think aloud" to explain to the group the sources of their hypotheses.

C2: Provide more explicit context with some definitional information. Ask students to reflect on their initial ideas and to reaffirm or refine them again in a "think-aloud" mode.

Q: Ask a question that involves semantic interpretation of the word. At this point, you can also ask for a definition or give one if necessary. Discuss as needed with group members, using each other's cues and explanations as more data.

U: Ask students to use the word in a meaningful sentence. Go back into the C(2)QU loop as needed.

From Blachowicz & Fisher, *Teaching Vocabulary in All Classrooms*, p. 32.

The Sentence Game

A similar process can be made into a game for student guessing (after Gipe, 1979–80, as interpreted in Barr & Johnson, 1990). Prepare a question and three-sentence context for each word that follows this pattern:

- *Question.* Uses the meaning of the word
- *Sentence 1.* A broad but meaningful context
- *Sentence 2.* Adds more detailed information
- *Sentence 3.* An explicit definition

For example, if you wanted students to learn the word *aeronaut:*

- *Question.* What is an aeronaut's job?
- *Sentence 1.* The aeronaut was getting the hot air balloon ready for flying.
- *Sentence 2.* The aeronaut told her helpers to let go of the ropes so she could fly the hot air balloon.
- *Sentence 3.* An aeronaut is a person who flies a hot air balloon.

Student teams are shown the question first and shown sentence 1. Any team that can correctly answer the question after this first clue wins 2 points. If the students need more help, the second sentence is shown. Correct responses after two clue sentences win 1 point. The definition is used for checking or for instruction if no group comes up with the right answer. For more difficult words, any number of sentences can be used with clues. Students often enjoy setting up a TV game show process for this game and can form teams to compose contexts as well.

Create a Personal Context

Creating personal contexts helps students learn and remember new words. These contexts can take several forms. Written personal contexts can describe a word's importance to a book, an event, or an individual. For example, for the word *wardrobe* a student created the following in his word journal:

> When I read *The Lion, the Witch and the Wardrobe,* I imagined this really big closet with doors on both sides. There was a picture in my book, and it looked bigger than any closet in our house. When I was little, I used to like to make a cave in my closet and pretend it was my tent, with all the clothes hanging down. So I had a good feeling for that wardrobe. I saw the movie *Shadowlands* which is about the author of the Narnia books, and they showed a wardrobe in his attic. I was surprised because the one in my imagination was so much bigger.

Another student used personal visual contexts to help her establish and remember the meaning of the word *scabbard*. See Figure 2.7. ESL students often draw and label in two languages. These visual descriptions are powerful aids for memory and meaning.

Looking Back and Looking Ahead

Since context is one of the most important aspects of all word learning in all types of classes, it was our first instructional focus. In this chapter, we have described several

Figure 2.7   Student's Use of Personal Visual Context to Remember the Word *Scabbard*

different ways in which context can aid vocabulary learning—from its use as a teacher presentation method to a process for developing metacognitive context-use strategies for students. In the next chapter, we look at the place of word learning in reading strategy instruction.

For Further Learning

Blachowicz, C. L., & Zabroske, B. (1990). Context instruction: A metacognitive approach for at-risk readers. *Journal of Reading, 33,* 504–508. (Describes a discussion process used with remedial middle schoolers to learn to infer from context)

Buikema, J. L., & Graves, M. F. (1993). Teaching students to use context cues to infer word meaning. *Journal of Reading, 36,* 450–458. (Describes an instructional unit for seventh and eighth graders)

Feitelson, B., Kita, B., & Goldstein, A. (1986). Effects of listening to stories on first graders' comprehension and use of language. *Research in the Teaching of English, 20,* 339–356. (Describes storybook reading in first grade. Vocabulary learning is a major outcome of the process.)

www.vocabulary.com

This website can be used by both teachers and students in middle school and above. It appears to be completely free to use, with puzzles that change regularly. The site contains leveled puzzles that ask visitors to guess words based on a given definition and a common root word. After visitors submit their answers by e-mail, answers are given. These puzzles are called "rooty-hoot-hoot" puzzles.

All other puzzles on the site have answers at the bottom of the screen, so they may be better for teachers to use by printing out the screens. The same words used in the first puzzle are also used in three other printable exercises: fill-in-the-blank, crossword, and definition matching. The same general format is used for themed activities, such as "Election 2000," "Football 2000," and "Thanksgiving." Again, multiple activities are used to reinforce the definitions of words that share the same root words. Especially helpful for a teacher looking for enrichment activities is an archive of the last 10 or so puzzle sessions.

The rest of the website may be best for teachers at the high school level or students trying to improve their vocabulary for taking the SAT. There are vocabulary lists and related activities for novels commonly used in high school, a set of activities focused on Shakespeare, and activities using words commonly found on the verbal portion of the SAT.

CHAPTER 3

INTEGRATING VOCABULARY AND READING STRATEGY INSTRUCTION

☑ Prepare Yourself

Prepare yourself by evaluating your own knowledge. Rate your ability to answer some of the key questions for this chapter. Check the boxes that best describe your prereading knowledge.

Key concept questions	Well informed	Aware	Need ideas
1. *What is strategic reading and how is it developed?*	❏	❏	❏
2. *How do you integrate vocabulary and reading strategy instruction?*	❏	❏	❏
3. *What are some classroom-tested examples for connecting vocabulary and reading strategy instruction —through graphic organizers? —through writing? —through drama? —through student self-evaluation?*	❏	❏	❏

☑️ Strategy Overview Guide

This chapter presents background, ideas, and strategies to help you understand how vocabulary learning can be integrated with reading instruction that focuses on strategy development. Strategies such as prediction, verification, self-questioning, previewing, and other metacognitive processes naturally incorporate and build vocabulary knowledge. This type of instruction typically takes place in guided reading and involves teacher modeling and scaffolding. In this chapter, we'll introduce strategies using graphic organizers, writing, drama, and student self-evaluation that develop word knowledge at the same time they build effective reading strategies. The following chart can help you choose suitable instructional strategies for your classroom.

Instructional strategy	Goal—use when you want to . . .	Comments
Story structure (p. 47)	*Identify and classify selection vocabulary.*	*Useful for both teacher and students.*
Vocab-o-Gram (p. 48)	*Organize vocabulary from a narrative selection and make predictions.*	*Can be used by "vocabulary directors" in literature circles.*
Story impressions (p. 52)	*Have students write before reading.*	*Great nudge for creativity.*
Word plays (p. 54)	*Involve the kinesthetic in learning.*	*Useful for creating comprehensible input for ESL students.*
Knowledge rating (p. 55)	*Have students do their own evaluation.*	*Works best with expository selections.*

DEVELOPING STRATEGIC READING

What Is Strategic Reading?

A major goal for all classrooms is comprehension development. Teachers want to help their students not only understand specific content materials, but also develop independent strategies for comprehension. For example, imagine a student reading this passage:

> Jesse was dressed in her best party dress and carrying a brightly wrapped package. When she reached Tracy's front door, she rang the bell and waited. . . and waited . . . and waited. After 10 minutes of waiting, she ran home, sobbing.

For most students, this passage is composed of familiar, easy words. However, comprehension involves more than just decoding the words: The reader needs to call up prior knowledge and to make some predictions and inferences to comprehend this simple passage. Prior knowledge of "dressing up" and carrying wrapped packages suggests that some sort of celebration, such as a birthday, is taking place. Making a cause and effect connection across the sentences in the passage suggests to most readers that Jesse is crying because she expected a party and there isn't one. Using prior knowledge of cause and effect and motivation, several scenarios can be suggested: Jesse got the date wrong; Jesse is at the wrong house. These are only two of several options, none of which is explicitly stated by the author. If we predicted that Jesse got the date wrong, we might have to change our predictions when we read the next sentence:

> As she left, Tracy and the other kids snickered behind the door.

We'd have to change our predictions, based on our knowledge of motivation and behavior, to one involving Tracy and the other kids playing a trick on Jesse.

Research on good readers reveals that they use what they already know, and they understand that reading is more than just "getting the words." They recognize that reading also involves reasoning and adding information from their own knowledge. Good readers make predictions based on their prior knowledge and their first impressions from surveying something they are about to read. They use titles, pictures, headings, vocabulary, and other cues from the author to ask themselves questions or make predictions ("I think she came on the wrong day.") As they read, good readers collect new information. This information combines with what they already know and allows them to make inferences about what the author doesn't tell them explicitly ("Hmmm, presents, dress up—it might be a birthday").

Good readers also monitor their reading. They keep track of their hunches, change them when needed ("If they snickered, they must be playing a trick"), and seek help when they can't resolve difficulties. This process of monitoring their own thinking is called **metacognition.** Lastly, good readers respond personally to what they read. They make personal judgments ("That was mean to do to Jesse" or "Maybe she had done something mean to Tracy"), respond personally ("I'd never do that"), and relate reading to their own lives ("Something like this happened to me once"). Their personal response makes the reading experience richer and also enhances comprehension. These actions that assist the reader in interacting with the text are referred to as **reading strategies,** comprehension strategies, or the hallmarks of strategic reading. They are also the components of problem solving.

How Is Strategic Reading Developed?

Instruction aimed at developing these strategies in young readers actively involves them in the actual strategic processes while the teacher provides models and scaffolds learning as needed (see Figure 3.1). The idea is to support students by calling on them to survey the selection, activate prior knowledge, make predictions, gather data from reading, make inferences, and monitor their understanding to refine or change their predictions as they go forward, respond to, and use new information. This process is cyclical and takes place repeatedly during reading.

> *Survey/Activate.* To get a basis for prediction, the reader's prior knowledge is activated by something in the text—a title, picture, vocabulary word, or something known about the type of book or the author.
>
> *Predict.* Make some hypotheses about the topic, the structure, and the content of what will be read based on survey information and what is already known.
>
> *Gather data.* Read, research, and think to gain information.
>
> *Monitor/Refine.* Use data, knowledge, and inferences to decide if you are on the right track. Should you change predictions, rethink, or continue with the same ideas?
>
> *Respond.* Take a personal view. What does this mean to me?
>
> *Repeat the cycle.*

Figure 3.1   Integrative Reading Strategies Used by Good Readers

The teacher's goal is to support the development of these processes in readers by asking questions, providing examples and models, and directing attention with questions or cues. Though the teacher is active in providing these guides and cues, the goal is to lead students through the actual processes, much as a parent helps a child get the "feel" of riding a bike by running alongside and providing support and guidance. Many types of instruction can help to develop students' abilities to read strategically. The directed reading-thinking activity, or DR-TA (Stauffer, 1969), the know-want-learn, or KWL (Ogle, 1986), and reciprocal teaching (Palincsar & Brown, 1984) all involve students in these activities and have been shown to develop good reading strategies. The literature on instruction from the past 15 years is rich with ideas for developing strategic readers in the classroom (see Tierney, Readence, & Dishner, 1985, for example). These strategic approaches to reading instruction offer new ways of approaching vocabulary as well.

Why Connect Vocabulary and Strategic Reading Instruction?

Vocabulary instruction is "naturally" connected with strategic reading instruction. For starters, as you can see by connecting what you read in Chapter 1 with what we've said about developing strategic reading in this chapter, the problem-solving processes for learning new vocabulary are directly related to the processes of strategic reading. Using what you know (prior knowledge), making initial predictions about meaning, and gradually refining that meaning are essential processes in gaining new word meaning and reading strategically.

Secondly, vocabulary itself can often drive prediction. Those things that help readers cue up prior knowledge are often particular terms and vocabulary. For example, in the sample passage at the beginning of this chapter, the words *brightly wrapped package* and *party dress* may have cued up the prediction *birthday* for many readers. Analyses of classroom comprehension instruction have suggested that prereading attention to developing and activating prior knowledge is critical to good comprehension (Beck, McKeown, McCaslin, & Burkes, 1979; Durkin, 1978–79). Good instruction emphasizes that talking, thinking, and planning before reading enhance comprehension as they aid readers in developing strategic approaches. Vocabulary stimulates prereading thinking and is an excellent initiator of the prediction process.

Lastly, important instructional benefits can be gained by connecting vocabulary with reading strategy instruction. Making vocabulary instruction an important part of the prereading component of the lesson provides for a more integrated lesson. Traditional lesson organization that has a vocabulary presentation separated from the start of the lesson is time consuming and fragments the lesson. "Collapsing" vocabulary and the prereading segment of the lesson not only saves time, but also makes sense. Using vocabulary as a "reading starter" also allows the teacher to quickly assess students' prior knowledge. Knowledge of vocabulary is a key indicator of prior knowledge and can help a teacher determine when more prereading concept development is needed for a particular selection, chapter, or book.

In conclusion, we can say that the same processes that are useful for developing a strategic approach to vocabulary are also useful for learning new words. And considering vocabulary as a part of strategic reading lessons not only results in good learning, but provides assessment information and makes efficient use of instructional time. In Chapter 5 on content reading, we will present specific ideas for developing content vocabulary which can be used when you want students to master a specific body of words related to some chapter, selection, or textbook they will be reading. This chapter will focus on developing vocabulary in the context of independent reading strategies.

VOCABULARY IN STRATEGIC READING INSTRUCTION

There are many different starting points for developing good predictive strategies. The teacher can start with graphic organizers, writing, dramatization, self-assessment, or any other strategy that suits the selection, the needs of the students, and the teacher's purpose. No matter what format or modality is chosen, lessons integrating vocabulary with strategic reading instruction share the characteristics of strategic reading:

- Select vocabulary that is important to students' comprehension and ability to make predictions.
- Encourage students to survey vocabulary before they read to activate their prior knowledge. Encourage students to make predictions from vocabulary.
- Remind students to gather data to evaluate their predictions and build knowledge.
- Set up postreading discussions so students can practice making inferences necessary for monitoring and refining vocabulary meaning.
- Arrange for activities that allow students to respond and use vocabulary (discussion, reading, writing).

The sections that follow will provide some specific ideas for implementing these strategies in the classroom.

```
┌─────────────────────────────────────────────┐
│ Characters:                                   │
└─┬───────────────────────────────────────────┘
  │    1. Sonia, loves animals so much; dresses like a **vet** (short for veterinarian); asks people
  │       to call her "Dr. Ackley."
  │    2. Richard = dad
  │    3. Annette = stepmother
  │    4. Max, **abandoned, stray** dog
┌─┴───────────────────────────────────────────┐
│ Setting:                                      │
└─┬───────────────────────────────────────────┘
  │    Sonia lives with mom during week, dad and **stepmother** during weekend.
┌─┴───────────────────────────────────────────┐
│ Problem:                                      │
└─┬───────────────────────────────────────────┘
  │    •Sonia wants to keep dog.
  │    •Richard doesn't want **responsibility** of dog during week and feels all pets **abuse**
  │     him. Wants to send dog to **pound.**
  │    •Annette is empathetic with Sonia but doesn't feel she has much say in **decision.**
┌─┴───────────────────────────────────────────┐
│ Resolution:                                   │
└─┬───────────────────────────────────────────┘
  │    Annette asserts herself as someone who has **responsibility** for Sonia and can be
  │    part of **decision.**
  │
  │    Note: Phrase **hopped a freight** is important to Annette's story and her feelings.
┌─┴───────────────────────────────────────────┐
│ Possible "big ideas":                         │
└─────────────────────────────────────────────┘
       1. What is a stepmother and stepmother's relationship to stepchildren?
       2. How do decisions get made in a family?
       3. Genre — reverses stereotype of stepmother.
```

Figure 3.2   Map of *No One Is Going to Nashville* with Target Vocabulary Italicized and Boldfaced

Select Important Vocabulary.   First of all, when choosing vocabulary to use for reading strategy instruction, focus on words that are important to the selection and can be used in discussing, explaining, summarizing, or responding to the material. For example, for the book *No One Is Going to Nashville* (Jukes, 1983) used in a fourth-grade classroom, the teacher first constructed the story structure map of the selection shown in Figure 3.2. Then she identified vocabulary that related to understanding the selection and would be useful for the students in discussion or response as well. From this trade book she chose to focus on *vet, veterinarian, stepmother, abandoned, stray, responsibility, abuse, dog pound, decision,* and *hopped a freight.*

Have Students Survey for Activation and Prediction.   Design an activity that will activate what kids already know and will help them make predictions about the selection. These activities can include writing, drama, mapping and charting, or other experiences—several classroom examples will follow this section. These prereading activities should use vocabulary to get students both to think about what they already know and to make some hypotheses. Discussion, either whole class or in cooperative groups, is critical. Students need to talk about and experiment with the words.

It's also essential that some of the vocabulary be familiar to give students a topic or other conceptual peg on which to begin to make predictions about the other words they know less well or not at all. Too often, students are faced with a large list of unknown words without any way to begin to classify or relate the terms. For example, consider these words:

mandan
casa colonica
trullo

It would be difficult for most adults to make any predictions about these words in the context of a list. Consider the same list when embedded with a few more familiar terms (as we will see in a classroom example later in this chapter):

mandan	manor
high rise	villa
casa colonica	cá d'oro
tipi	

Even though *high rise, manor,* and *villa* are not overly familiar words to most readers, students can begin to make predictions about these words as "dwelling related" and begin asking some questions as will be fully explored in the classroom example on knowledge rating.

These activation and prediction activities are useful for cooperative groups because the sum of the knowledge of the group is greater than the knowledge of each individual in the group. The group members can begin to learn from each other before reading. This activity helps the teacher preassess the class's level of prior knowledge. If their knowledge level is low, the teacher can do some concept building at this point rather than going directly into reading.

Remind Students to Gather Data.   Remind kids to gather data as they read. This can be as simple as paying attention to words that were unfamiliar or might involve jotting down a page number or some bit of relevant information. If a graphic organizer is used to start the process, it can provide a framework for jotting notes during or after reading.

Design Postreading for Drawing Inferences, Monitoring, and Refining.   Come back to vocabulary in postreading discussion. If the vocabulary is chosen sensibly, this will happen naturally. For example, for *No One Is Going to Nashville* (Jukes, 1983), a fourth-grader's summary looked like the following:

> Sonia wanted to be a *veterinarian* and loved animals. Max was a *stray* dog and she wanted to keep him. her dad didn't like animals much, 'cuz they always *abused* him, like biting him. He wanted to send Max to a dog *pound* but her stepmother helped her dad make a *decision* to keep the dog.

As is frequently the case when words are chosen to reflect the story line or key concepts of a selection, students must use them when responding after reading.

Another teacher using the same trade book planned postreading questions using the vocabulary that required students to refine and monitor their predicted meanings. She asked: "Who was the *stray*? Why wouldn't Sonia want Max to go to the *pound*? Would Sonia be a good *vet*?" In asking these questions, she gave her students practice in interpreting and using these keywords based on the supporting information in the selection. The questions also gave her a means of assessing their knowledge after reading. Then she could decide if they needed to gather more information or if she needed to use direct instruction.

Use contextual "look-backs" and semantic analysis to help students refine and monitor their understanding of words that are still unclear after prediction, reading, and discussion/response. Research suggests that most vocabulary instruction occurs before reading, with little attention to word learning after reading (Blachowicz, 1986). Since our focus is on developing students' problem-solving abilities, it is critical that time be devoted after reading to help students flesh out and consolidate their knowledge of words and to make inferences based on what they knew before they read and on the information provided by the author. This should be done in a format where they can experiment with the words and receive feedback on their learning.

For example, one teacher using the trade book *No One Is Going to Nashville* thought that student responses suggested they still were unclear about the meaning of *pound* as used in *dog pound*. She asked students to locate and read the parts of the selection where the author used the word *pound* and to analyze what information about the word meaning they could abstract. They found and analyzed

> Richard wanted to send Max to the *pound*.
> (A *pound* is a place.)

> "We'll keep the dog as long as the *pound* would. . . ."
> (A *pound* keeps animals.)

> Richard called the *pound*. They only kept dogs 5 days.
> (There's a time limit on how long animals are kept.)

From these examples, the teacher led the students to conclude that an animal *pound* is a place that keeps unwanted animals for a limited time. They then discussed why this was so distressful to Sonia. Alternatively, the teacher could pose, or have students pose, a series of questions that would have readers respond on the basis of their understanding of the semantic features of the word. For example, a teacher might ask, "Does a *pound* need walls? Explain." "Would a dog want to go to the *pound*? Explain."

Set Up Activities for Meaningful Use and Response. Use the words in integrated experiences. By this point in a lesson, the readers would have seen, heard, read, and used the vocabulary in many ways. Because the selection integrates what would otherwise be an unrelated set of words, a teacher might let the use of the words emerge in response activities. For example, in a dramatization of this trade book, Richard, the father, explains, "Those animals all *abuse* me. One bit my foot. The other tore up my slippers. And the worst is that *stray*, Max." Another teacher has students make a silent video with explanatory title cards. Characters were labeled, "Sonia, a would-be *vet*." "Max, the *stray*." Before the final scene, the title card read "The *Decision*." These five guidelines are critical components of vocabulary development integrated with reading strategy instruction. Most often, when words are well chosen, these processes happen naturally in reading strategy lessons so that few words need major attention after reading. In any event, teachers should view these components as guides to be used when instruction doesn't flow naturally rather than rigid guidelines for instruction. The following examples from classrooms can give a clearer picture of how some lessons might look.

CLASSROOM EXAMPLES

Starting with Graphic Organizers: Vocab-o-Grams

There are many types of **graphic organizers,** or visual and spatial formats for classifying or relating words, with which teachers can work with vocabulary. In Chapter 5 on content reading, we will discuss maps and webs, which have great utility in content area classes where content classification, relationships, or hierarchies provide an organizing principle. Because so many teachers use narratives as the bases for reading strategy instruction, we will talk about a type of organizer that uses the structure of narratives as its organizing principle—story structure.

Story Structure. Many narratives, stories, and descriptions of real events share the same basic elements. They have settings and characters, the characters have a problem they want to solve or a goal they want to reach, some actions take place, and there is a resolution. These elements often constitute what is referred to as a **story structure** or **story grammar**, the elements of a well-formed story in Western literature. Narratives of other cultures also have structures that share some, but not all, of these characteristics. When developing comprehension, one productive strategy is to use our anticipation of such structures and our knowledge of other stories to help us predict what the author might be likely to tell us. For example, for a story that begins "Once upon a time," a reader might make these predictions:

Setting:	A fairy tale land with castles.
Characters:	Princes, princesses, magical characters.
Problem/Goal:	A task, a quest.
Actions:	Some sort of magic will happen or something not like real life.
Resolution:	Happily ever after!

Story structure is also a good conceptual peg to help students organize and remember vocabulary that might not fall into nice, neat classifications (Blachowicz & Leipzig, 1989). A basic sense of story is usually fairly well developed by the upper primary grades.

Many suggestions for making story structure visible to students involve story maps or webs, which we discuss at length in Chapter 5. The first technique we'll discuss works off a graphic form and may help develop vocabulary as well as a sense of structure.

Vocab-o-Gram. A **Vocab-o-Gram** (Blachowicz, 1986) is a generic classification chart that reflects the categories of story structure. It is used with a charting process that asks students to organize vocabulary in relationship to the structure of the selection. To use a Vocab-o-Gram, place the story framework on the board or on a transparency (see Figure 3.3) and have each student construct a work copy. Then place the vocabulary words on the board and ask students, working in pairs or groups, to share what they know about the words and to classify them according to their predictions of how the author might use them. For example, for the trade book *Greyling* (Yolen, 1993), the teacher placed the following on the board:

greyling	wail	stranded
fisherman	baby	townsfolk
roiling seas	shallows	joyously
sandbar	grief	slough off
selchie		

She then asked the students to work in teams to share what they knew about the words and to classify them according to the clues they gave about the upcoming selection. Working as a team, Jim and Monica produced the Vocab-o-Gram shown in Figure 3.3.

The contents of the Vocab-o-Gram became their predictions about the selection, and the question was a purpose-setting one. Each team brought its Vocab-o-Gram to a large-group session where the teams shared their ideas, placements, and reasoning. At this point, all predictions are acceptable and the initial discussion helps the teacher to gauge the state of class knowledge so that more direct instruction can be used if it is appropriate. After groups shared their knowledge of individual words and their predictions, the teacher decided that their level of word knowledge was sufficient for them to jump right in to reading *Greyling*.

After reading and the comprehension discussion following the selection, the teacher asked the students to refine their Vocab-o-Grams in another color pencil. Jim and Monica's revision looked like the one shown in Figure 3.4. They had refined their knowledge of *wail*, built knowledge of *slough off*, and confirmed knowledge of the other words. The teacher decided that no further work with the words was necessary and, as an extension activity, had them use their Vocab-o-Grams as keys to write a summary of the book. Teaching Idea File 3.1 provides a summary of the Vocab-o-Gram strategy.

Vocab-o-Gram	
Use vocabulary to make predictions about . . .	
(May be used more than once)	
The setting townsfolk roiling seas sandbar	What will the setting be like? little town by the sea
The characters fisherman greyling baby wail townsfolk	Any ideas about the characters? There's a big wail. Maybe the fisherman is related to baby. Greyling is a fish.
The problem or goal	What might it be? Somebody gets stranded on sandbar.
The actions	What might happen? Fisherman saves baby. Fisherman is saved.
The resolution	How might it end? Joyously or sad (grief) both sad and happy; bittersweet
What question(s) do you have?	What happens to the baby?
Mystery words: selchie, slough off	

Figure 3.3 Jim and Monica's Initial Vocab-o-Gram

Vocab-o-Gram	
Use vocabulary to make predictions about . . .	
(May be used more than once)	
The setting townsfolk roiling seas sandbar	What will the setting be like? little town by the sea Wail was sound of wind
The characters fisherman greyling baby wail townsfolk	Any ideas about the characters? ~~There's a big wail.~~ Maybe the fisherman is related to baby. Greyling is a ~~fish.~~ selchie.
The problem or goal	What might it be? Somebody gets stranded on sandbar.
The actions	What might happen? Fisherman saves baby. ⓡ Fisherman is saved.
The resolution	How might it end? Joyously or sad (grief) both sad and happy; bittersweet
What question(s) do you have?	What happens to the baby? return to the sea

Mystery words:
selchie,   slough off
  ↓   ↓
seal child   what the seal child did with skin

Figure 3.4 Jim and Monica's Revised Vocab-o-Gram

Teaching Idea File 3.1

Vocab-o-Gram

(Blachowicz, 1986)

1. Select a vocabulary list from a narrative selection that reflects story grammar and present it to students by writing the words on the board or using an overhead projector.
2. Have students, working in teams, decide which words give clues to setting, characters, problem/goal, resolution, and feelings. Include a "?" category as well.
3. Discuss placement. Words may typically be placed in more than one category. Share knowledge about words.
4. Make predictions.
5. Have each student formulate a personal question to answer.
6. After reading, refine vocabulary. Go back to the selection to clarify or use references.
7. Use in further oral or written work. Students may use Vocab-o-Gram as an organizer for summarizing.

From Blachowicz & Fisher, *Teaching Vocabulary in All Classrooms*, p. 47.

Vocab-o-Grams are excellent for use with cooperative groups because the sum of the group's knowledge is always greater than individual knowledge. Some teachers also use them with large groups or whole classes. In these cases, the teacher might place the words on the board and use the Vocab-o-Gram on a transparency to guide supportive questioning and to facilitate direct instruction. For example, one teacher in a bilingual sixth-grade classroom first had students provide Spanish synonyms for some of the words (grief = dolor) before asking them to make predictions about the selection based on the vocabulary. As they predicted, the teacher used their Vocab-o-Grams for assessment and realized that several keywords were unfamiliar. As a result, the teacher worked with definitional and contextual information for the words *stranded* and *sandbar* before letting the group begin to read. After reading and comprehension instruction, the teacher decided that *stranded, sandbar, grief,* and *wail* were still confusing to a small group of students. So she had the students locate these words in the book, did reader's theater on the sections in which they were located, and did some visualizing experiences as well. **Reader's theater** involves the oral interpretation of scripts by two or more readers (Tierney, Readence, & Dishner, 1985). Interpretation, not memorization, is the goal. Vocal and facial expressions and gestures are used to suggest character as the readers interpret the script. Scenery and costumes are typically not used; the audience must "fill in the blanks" as the readers create the scenes. The students ended by illustrating key scenes related to *stranded, sandbar, grief,* and *wail*. Vocab-o-Grams can also be used individually once students are familiar with the process, but it is critical that prereading and postreading discussion, monitoring, and refinement of meaning take place.

Starting with Writing: Story Impressions

Connecting reading and writing is an important concern in all classrooms. We know that reading and writing develop together and that they are mutually enhancing as students gain proficiency. We often think of writing *after* reading, but writing *before* reading can engage students more completely in reading, and it can give them another way to make predictions. These can help the teacher gauge what they already know and point out strengths as well as misconceptions. Writing before reading can also help students think about how a well-formed story might develop and give them a basis for later comparison of their choices and author choices.

Story impressions (McGinley & Denner, 1987) is a technique that calls on students to survey a set of vocabulary words and get some general impressions about the setting, characters, problems, and actions that might be described. Then they write their own version before reading. Thus their version becomes their prediction or possible selection. For example, before students read the trade book *Saint George and the Dragon* (Hodges, 1984), the teacher placed the following words on the board:

legend	princess	bellowed
noble knight	hermit	ancient spring
foe	patron saint	severed
dragon	in vain	victorious

Then students were asked to work alone, in pairs, or in groups to give their impressions of the story they were to read. They could do this either by writing a story suggested by the vocabulary or by listing what their separate impressions were.

David and Jake wrote:

> Our impression is that this story takes place in the past and is a famous *legend*. A *noble knight* has to fight a dragon. A small *hermit* crab sits on his shoulder and acts as his *patron saint*. But the knight falls, stabbed by an *ancient spring* with poison on it and the dragon is victorious.

Jesse and Jeni wrote:

> Once upon a time there was a noble knight who loved a princess who was scared by a dragon. But the knight is a *hermit* and doesn't want to come out and fight the dragon. The dragon is vain and lives *bellowed* an *ancient spring*. When he comes out to look at his face several times each day, the princess cuts off his head and is victorious.

After groups prepare their stories or impressions, they compare and contrast. The similarities between these stories were:

The setting—times of knights and ladies.

The characters—a knight, a princess and dragon.

The problem—someone has to fight the dragon.

Teaching Idea File 3.2

Story Impressions

(McGinley & Denner, 1987)

1. Choose vocabulary words from the selection that give an impression of some of the aspects of story grammar: setting, characters, problem/goal, actions, resolution, and feeling. Place the words on the chalkboard or overhead projector.
2. Ask students to use the words to write the story they would write if they were the author. For unknown words, they can take a guess, ask a friend, or put them aside.
3. After writing, share stories as a group. Compare and contrast across student stories to look for similarities and differences.
4. Read the selection to compare the author's choices with students' choices.
5. After reading, refine vocabulary. Go back to the selection to clarify or use references.
6. Use in further oral or written work. Students may use knowledge rating as an organizer for studying.

From Blachowicz & Fisher, *Teaching Vocabulary in All Classrooms*, p. 49.

The resolutions differed, as did the students' predictions about the words they weren't sure about: *ancient spring, patron saint, bellowed,* and *severed.*

The teacher then had all of the students read *Saint George and the Dragon* as retold by Margaret Hodges (1984) and come back and compare their stories with the text. The setting and characters were the same, but the actions and resolutions were quite different. First, students completed a comprehension discussion for the selection. Then, as a vocabulary follow-up, the teacher asked them to compare, in their vocabulary journals, what they learned about the terms *hermit, spring, bellowed,* and *patron saint* as they were used in the book. Some of the students wrote:

> The *hermit* in the story was some person who lived high in a mountain all by himself.
>
> The *ancient spring* wasn't a metal *spring* but a *spring* of water, like a bubbling stream.
>
> *Bellowed* is a loud sound the dragon made when wounded.

Patron saint remained the most elusive, and the teacher did a short lesson on this concept using St. Patrick as an example. Teaching Idea File 3.2 provides a summary of the story impressions strategy.

For some students, simpler brainstorming techniques may be useful (Allen, 1999). But for most, Story Impressions is an excellent technique for involving writing, vocabulary, and strategic reading where working with story structure is required, and it is appropriate for all ages.

Starting with Drama: Word Plays

Rather than beginning with writing or graphics, you might like to start with oral language activities, especially for younger students. Using drama is an excellent way to motivate learners to make predictions about the possible use of words in an upcoming selection (Duffelmeyer, 1980). For students for whom English is a second language, such dramatization gives them chances to experiment with using words in their own speech and in vignettes of their own creation before having to comprehend them in print. Drama activities are also excellent choices for cooperative group work.

To do a word play, select your words in the same way you did for any of the previous activities and place them on word cards, preparing one set for each group. Having several groups do the same sets of words provides the fun of comparison as well as the possibility of seeing similarities suggested by the same sets of words. Students are given a specified length of time to discuss the words and to prepare a play using them. Each student must speak, and each word must be used at least one time. The teacher, a reference book, or other groups can be consulted about the meanings or pronunciation of any of the words.

For example, for a simple first-grade selection, the teacher chose four keywords: *quack, drip, mother,* and *hole.* Then he set simple directions with some story grammar questions: "You should describe a story. I want to know what kind of day it is, whom the story is about, and what the main character's problem is. How does it all work out?"

The first graders took the cards back to their groups and first pronounced and discussed what the words meant, though the teacher had pronounced them as he presented them. Then they planned a drama suggested by the words. One sounded like this:

> CHILD 1: Once upon a time, there was a little duck who loved to quack.
> CHILD 2: It was a rainy day and the rain was falling "Drip, drip, drip."
> CHILD 3: The duck's mother said she had to go to the store and reminded him not to go outside.
> CHILD 4: But as soon as his mother left, the duck decided to go outside and play anyhow.
> CHILD 1: Right when he walked out of the door, he fell into a big deep hole.
> CHILD 2: The rain went drip, drip, drip on top of him.
> CHILD 3: The duck went, "Quack quack," to call for help.
> CHILD 4: His mother got him out, but she was mad and made him stay in the rest of the day.

A second group also had a duck (the quack gave that away), but this duck's problem was a hole in his rubber boots that made his feet all muddy so that when he came in he dripped all over the floor, resulting in another mad mother. Group 3 had the duck with the problem of a hole in his umbrella and so forth.

After their performances, when the groups compared the dramas, which the teacher had videotaped, they noticed that the setting of a rainy day was shared by all their dramas, as was the mischievous duck and the angry mother (stereotypes in kids'

Teaching Idea File 3.3

Word Play

1. Choose a short list of vocabulary words (three to five words) from the selection that gives an impression of some of the aspects of story grammar: setting, characters, problem/goal, actions, resolution, and feeling. Place the words on index cards. Make a set of cards for each group of students.
2. Give each team a set and ask them to construct a 3-minute skit based on the vocabulary. As they plan, circulate to provide information and clarification as needed.
3. Share the skits. Compare and contrast across student skits to look for similarities and differences.
4. Read the selection to compare the author's choices with students' choices.
5. After reading, refine vocabulary. Go back to the selection to clarify meaning or use reference works.
6. Use the words in further oral or written work.

From Blachowicz & Fisher, *Teaching Vocabulary in All Classrooms,* p. 50.

---

drama as well). Not only had they been able to predict a possible story, but they had each heard, used, and encountered the words many times in meaningful settings. See Teaching Idea File 3.3 for a summary of how to use word plays.

Word play can be varied in many ways. Students can pantomime words for another group who holds the word cards. They can videotape scenarios that suggest, but don't use, a particular word on the class list and play them back for class guessing. In all these approaches, it is then important to compare their uses and interpretations of the words with the author's choices and uses after reading.

Starting with Student Self-Evaluation: Knowledge Rating

Another way to integrate vocabulary with reading strategy instruction is to use student self-evaluation as a starting point for learning. This process follows the same strategic model as presented earlier in the chapter. Vocabulary is surveyed to activate prior knowledge. Some preliminary predictions are made, with the teacher's supplying some focusing questions. Students gather data while reading and then monitor and refine their insights after reading. Take the following example from an eighth-grade social studies class getting ready to read a chapter with this vocabulary:

tipi	dascha
villa	trullo
casa colonica	mandan
apartment	lean-to
high rise	yurt

Table 3.1   Knowledge Rating Sheet

Check your knowledge level for each of these terms:

Term	3 Can Define/Use	2 Heard It	1 Don't Know It
tipi			
villa			
casa colonica			
apartment			
high rise			
dascha			
trullo			
mandan			
lean-to			
yurt			

Table 3.2   Prediction Transparency

Term	Where?	Used Now?	Looks Like?	Who?
tipi				
villa				
casa colonica				
apartment				
high rise				
dascha				
trullo				
mandan				
lean-to				
yurt				

The teacher and class went through the following process:

Survey Words to Activate Prior Knowledge.   The teacher gave each student a Knowledge Rating Sheet (see Table 3.1) and asked each student to rate his or her level of knowledge about each term. Students were asked to rate the terms as very familiar ("I could give a definition or use in an illustrative sentence"), somewhat familiar ("I have seen or heard this word before and may have some association with it"), or unfamiliar ("I don't know anything about this word"). The teacher had placed the students in small groups and encouraged them to talk to each other about the terms as they worked. As the groups talked and worked, the teacher circulated to get a sense of the students' knowledge before going further.

Make Predictions.   After giving the students adequate time for self-evaluation, the teacher encouraged students to share their knowledge and predictions about the words with the larger group. She used an overhead transparency to record notes. (See Table 3.2.) For this group of students who lived in a suburb of a large city, *tipi, apartment,* and *high rise* were well-established terms. *Villa, lean-to,* and *dascha* were somewhat familiar, and the rest were unknown.

The teacher then asked some focusing questions related to the structure of the chapter. She wanted to get students to think about the topic (in this case, dwellings) and what the author might logically want to tell readers about the topic (location, description, people who used them, time of use). The goal was to get the students to make predictions about the words and the chapter that would form the purposes for reading. The class dialogue looked like this:

> T(EACHER): OK, you know something about several of these terms, but let's see if we can use all the terms to get some ideas and predictions about the chapter we're going to read. Looking at these terms, what do you think the topic of the chapter is?
>
> S(tudents): Houses, homes
>
> T: OK, all in the United States?
>
> S: No.
>
> T: Why not?
>
> S: Well, there are some here that sound kind of foreign.
>
> T: Like what?
>
> S: Like *dascha* and *illa*.
>
> S: And *trullo* and *casa colonica*.
>
> S: *Mandan*.
>
> S: I think *mandan* is from here because I remember it from something about the Native Americans we studied.
>
> S: There's a mandan house in the museum . . . you know, that big earth lodge.
>
> T: Well, interesting. It seems as if we think some are not in the United States, but let's put a question mark next to *mandan* and watch for that especially (puts a red question mark next to *mandan*). Do you think all of these are dwellings people live in now?
>
> S: No, people don't live in tipis now.
>
> S: I don't know about that. When we went to Mt. Rushmore, we saw tipis.
>
> S: Yea, but that was probably just tourist stuff.
>
> S: No, I think they lived in them.
>
> T: Let's put another question mark next to *Used now* and *tipi*. What about the other terms?
>
> S: (Many suggestions concluding the class is not sure. They place a question mark next to the question "used now?")
>
> T: Before we read, let's try to think like a textbook author. If you were going to write this chapter about types of dwellings, what would you tell about each one?
>
> S: Who lives in them.
>
> S: What they look like.
>
> S: Where they are.
>
> S: When they were lived in.
>
> T: OK, we've got some good ideas about these and some predictions about the chapter. Let's read, thinking of these issues and questions, and come back after reading to talk about them.

Teaching Idea File 3.4

Knowledge Rating

(Blachowicz, 1986)

1. From the selection, choose a list of vocabulary words that cluster in some way. Place the list on the chalkboard or overhead projector.
2. Ask students to copy the list and to rate their knowledge of the words as : 1—Don't know anything. 2—I've heard or seen this word but I'm not sure what it means. 3—I know this word well enough to use it or define it. Students may share their knowledge as they work.
3. Use the ratings for group discussion. Lead students to make appropriate predictions (e.g., who, what, where, what the author will include).
4. Read the selection, watching for the vocabulary.
5. After reading, have students rerate themselves. Then refine vocabulary. Go back to the selection to clarify words or use reference books.
6. Use the words in further oral or written work. Students may use knowledge rating as an organizer for studying.

From Blachowicz & Fisher, *Teaching Vocabulary in All Classrooms*, p. 54.

Gather Data.   The students then read their chapter so that they could encounter terms in their "natural" environment. Though the students did not know specifics about each word, they had a topic to help them organize their thinking and several questions to answer about each word. They recorded their data during and after reading on a personal record sheet that looked like the transparency the teacher used to focus predictions with the addition of the questions they added.

Make Inferences to Monitor and Refine Predictions and Knowledge.   After reading, the teacher used the transparency version of their record sheet to record student findings about the terms. She followed up on some of the questions from the pre-reading discussion. Students reflected on their earlier hypotheses to find that the dwellings were not, indeed, all located in the United States. However, they were all in current use as dwellings, a fact that surprised students.

Respond and Use.   The students were called on to use the words in their summary of the chapter and subsequent projects on dwellings.

When students still lack information to refine their hypothetical meanings, the teacher sends them back to the text to reread or refers them to reference works. In the case of the word *mandan*, for example, students looked back in their social studies book from the previous year. Students can then "claim ownership" of the terms by using them in the normal social studies activities that extend a lesson. See Teaching Idea File 3.4 for a summary of knowledge rating.

All these techniques for integrating vocabulary instruction into reading strategy lessons reflect a similar philosophy for learning. Using an approach stressing hypothesizing and hypothesis testing is consistent with general problem-solving models of learning. As such, both vocabulary knowledge and useful strategies are developed simultaneously. Secondly, techniques such as these do "double duty"—both for vocabulary introduction and for reading preparation. Lastly, all techniques such as those presented in this chapter inject fun into learning at the same time strategies are being developed.

Looking Back and Looking Ahead

In this chapter, we described strategic reading, an important component of the reading curriculum, and we discussed the ways in which it connected to vocabulary instruction. Several classroom examples integrating vocabulary and reading strategy instruction were shared, including those focusing on graphic organizers, writing, drama, and student self-evaluation. Along with strategy reading, reading instruction has a strong emphasis on literature-based reading. Many teachers are using literature circles, novel units, or cooperative literature groups in their classroom. The next chapter focuses on vocabulary learning in literature-focused instruction.

For Further Learning

Allen, Janet. (1999). *Words, Words, Words*. Portsmouth, NH: Heinemann. www.CIERA.com (Website with many early literacy documents relevant to strategies).

Blachowicz, C. L. Z. (1986). Making connections: Alternatives to the vocabulary notebook. *Journal of Reading, 29,* 643–649. (Describes Vocab-o-Gram and other predictive vocabulary activities)

Duffelmeyer, F. A. (1980). The influence of experience-based vocabulary instruction on learning word meanings. *Journal of Reading, 24,* 35–40. (Good ideas for dramatizing vocabulary)

McGinley, W. J., & Denner, P. R. (1987). Story Impressions: A prereading/writing activity. *Journal of Reading, 31,* 248–53. (A clear description of story impressions with good examples)

CHAPTER 4

LEARNING VOCABULARY IN LITERATURE–BASED READING INSTRUCTION

☑ Prepare Yourself

Prepare yourself by evaluating your own knowledge. Rate your ability to answer some of the key questions for this chapter. Check the boxes that describe your pre-reading knowledge.

Key concept questions	Well informed	Aware	Need ideas
1. *What are some strategies for teaching vocabulary when all students read or hear the same core book?*	❏	❏	❏
2. *What are some strategies for teaching vocabulary when students read different books around a common theme in a literature unit?*	❏	❏	❏
3. *What are some strategies for teaching vocabulary when students choose and use their own books for individual reading?*	❏	❏	❏
4. *How can figurative language be a part of vocabulary instruction?*	❏	❏	❏

✓ Strategy Overview Guide

In this chapter we present background, ideas, and strategies to help you understand vocabulary instruction that is appropriate in different classroom settings where literature (primarily fiction) is used as a focus of the literacy curriculum. A contrast is drawn between methods of teaching that are useful when students all read the same book (core book), when students read books around a common theme in a literature unit, and when students all read books of their own choice. Finally, we suggest ways of using the rich figurative language found in literature (metaphors, similes, idioms) to develop vocabulary. The following chart can help you choose suitable instructional strategies for your classroom.

Instructional strategy	Goal—use when you want to . . .	Comments
Big books (p. 65)	*Introduce students to new words in the context of a story.*	*Other emergent literacy skills may be the primary focus of the activity.*
Character mapping (p. 67)	*Have students understand the attributes of story characters.*	*By refining their understanding of words (such as brave), students understand how or why the character has that attribute.*
Comprehension Court (p. 68)	*Have students examine text closely for clues to meaning.*	*Useful after group reading assignments.*
Semantic Analysis to Writing (p. 69)	*Have students develop essay writing skills in relation to important themes.*	*Asks students to think carefully about word meanings in different contexts.*
Making alphabet books (p. 72)	*Have students learn words related to a theme.*	*Useful as an ongoing activity during a unit.*
Vocabulary research in cooperative groups (p. 73)	*Have students recognize, learn, and teach words they do not know in literature.*	*Only one of the rotating tasks in cooperative groups: can take different forms.*
Book contracts with vocabulary logs (p. 77)	*Allow individual choices in the learning of new words.*	*Children do not spend time learning already familiar words.*
Illustrating or acting out idioms (p. 81)	*Have students explore figurative language.*	*Fun activity.*

The movement to literature-based reading instruction in the schools has meant that teachers are confronted with teaching vocabulary or having students learn vocabulary without the guidance of teacher's manuals that describe which words to select or how best to teach the meanings. Some of these issues have been addressed in Chapter 1, but let us contemplate the task of a teacher who previously was using a 10-page story with her students in fourth grade. Even if vocabulary was not preselected, it was a fairly easy task to review the story for possible words the students might not understand. Having identified those words, the teacher could decide how central they were to the story and how much time she wanted to spend teaching them. In a literature-based classroom, if all students are reading the same book, the teacher may be confronted with selecting words for a 180-page novel (although this could be done over two or three weeks) where the vocabulary levels are not controlled. If students are reading different books, the task is even more complex if the teacher wants to maintain control of the selection process. Scharer (1992) has argued that teachers find it difficult to organize for literature discussion and are uncertain of their roles when a class discards the basal. In this chapter, we will explore possible options for teachers at different grade levels and in a variety of situations in which they may want to use literature. Some of the strategies we suggest not only are applicable for literature-based reading, but could also be used in other ways. Similarly, strategies we described in the previous chapter, such as C(2)QU, and others (such as the keyword method) that we will describe in subsequent chapters could be (and have been) used with literature. However, most of the strategies in this chapter focus on vocabulary that is important to exploring characters and themes in literature.

LITERATURE-BASED READING INSTRUCTION

Teachers choose to organize their classrooms in different ways for literature-based instruction. Three common ways are used in elementary classrooms: the core book, the literature unit, and individual reading that incorporates self-selection and self-pacing (Courtland, 1992; Zarrillo, 1989). Table 4.1 shows these options in a graphic form. When teachers use a core book, all students read the same novel or have it read to them. In kindergarten and first grade, this novel may be a big book. Teachers develop activities and assignments that spring from the book itself or from the topic of the book. In contrast, a literature unit has a unifying theme, which might include a particular author, a genre (such as animal fantasy), or a theme from social studies or science (such as communities). In the primary grades, the unit may include a basic set of books on the same theme that are read to all the children. In the elementary grades, there may be one or two "read-alouds," but students can select books either individually or from a short list. Zarrillo (1989) argues that "successful implementation of a literature unit involved the teacher finding a balance of common activities and student-selected options" (p. 25). For the third option, individual reading (including self-selection and self-pacing) is used as the main form of instruction rather than as a supplement to a core book or as part of a literature unit. The key factors in successful implementation may be access to a large number of books, consistent standards,

Table 4.1   Possible Strategies for Types of Literature-Based Instruction

Core Book	Vocabulary Selection	Possible Strategies
	Teacher selection/instruction	Character mapping
	Teacher selection/ student instruction	Comprehension Court
	Student selection/instruction	Semantic Analysis to Writing
Literature Unit	Teacher selection/instruction	Cooperative groups
	Student selection/instruction	Vocabulary logs
Individual Reading	Student selection/instruction	Book contacts
		Vocabulary notebooks

and record keeping. Personal conferences about reading and group discussions are also common elements. Most teachers will use three forms of organization over the period of a year, depending on the grade levels of the students. Vocabulary instruction obviously needs to be adapted for situations in which students share the same reading experience and for those in which they do not. We will outline some teaching strategies and organizational options for each type of situation.

The Core Book Approach

As noted earlier, a **core book** is one that is shared by all students in a classroom. In some school systems, there are lists of core books that every child at a particular grade level is expected to read. Teachers may have all students read the core book or, sometimes, may read it to them. The advantage of using a core book is that all students share the same literary experience and can talk about it together, and the teacher can use it to demonstrate some point in the literature curriculum (e.g., how an author develops a particular character). The disadvantage of a core book is the same as any other shared experience—it will appeal to some students more than to others. The choice of which books to use as core books will be influenced by curriculum demands, the availability of multiple copies, and the students themselves. In an ideal situation, to increase interest, students should participate in selecting which books will be so used. For example, a teacher may want to have students vote on which book she will read aloud, after having introduced three or four books to the class through book talks. With lower grade levels, where a book may be read in one session, this participation may be less important as a motivator than for higher grades.

Core Books in the Primary Grades.   When children are in the beginning stages of learning to read, the term *vocabulary instruction* can be used to include both the teaching of word meanings and the teaching of sight vocabulary. The traditional rationale for controlled vocabulary in readers was primarily so that children would not be confronted with too many difficult words in terms of their decoding ability (i.e., words were included in the readers for their common usage and regularity of sound-symbol correspondence). However, controlled vocabulary also meant that the books included words that were part of the students' speaking or listening vocabulary. The move into literature-based instruction in the primary grades has meant that students are now hearing words being read, and reading words on their own, that they have not previously encountered or that may have unfamiliar meanings.

Big Books.   In kindergarten or first grade, a big book experience will normally include the teacher's previewing the book in some way, her reading the book to the students while pointing to words in the text, talking about the story and illustrations, asking and answering questions, and several rereadings of the book either from the big book itself or from small versions of the book. By doing this, students are learning directionality, concepts of word, sight words, story structure, and other early literacy skills, depending on their stages of reading development.

If we take the example of *What Do You Do With a Kangaroo?* (1973) by Mercer Mayer, we can see that students may also be confronting words that are unfamiliar in terms of meaning. In that book, the child may encounter the terms *opossum,*

Big books help students learn directionality, concepts of word, sight words, and story structure.

llama, finger bowl, gold-plated, sassafras root, and *Bengal tiger* for the first time. The teacher may use the pictures to explain what an opossum, a llama, and a Bengal tiger look like, or students may infer the nature of the animal from the pictures. Children in the early stages of literacy can learn many terms by labeling items or actions in illustrations, by asking questions such as "What's that?" or "What's he doing?", or by responding to adult inquiries such as "Where's the brown yak?" Certainly, they will learn from Mayer's story, incidentally or through instruction, that there *are* such animals as opossums, llamas, and Bengal tigers. Will they learn how to decode the words? Possibly, depending on the extent of their literacy development. However, consider the terms *finger bowl, gold-plated,* and *sassafras root.* These concepts are not central to the story line, and the teacher may read them without explanation. If she does so, the story does not suffer. If students ask what they are, she can explain them. If not, students may still be learning something about the terms in case the students ever encounter them again (e.g., that a sassafras root has something to do with cleaning teeth).

In reading instruction in the early grades, therefore, students may learn vocabulary primarily from books read aloud to them and from discussions about them. Books they can read themselves are most likely to contain mainly vocabulary that is already part of their listening or speaking vocabulary. Some teachers will also use **language experience stories** with their students. These are stories that are dictated by the student(s) and written down by the teacher. The purpose of the activity is to make plain to students that writing is speech "written down." It is important, therefore, that the stories are the same words that were spoken. Consequently, the teacher uses the language of the children. When working with an individual child, this activity will therefore be of little or no help in vocabulary development. However, in a group setting, children have an opportunity to learn new words from their peers. Since a good language experience story draws heavily on the students' own experiences, many of the new words introduced will relate to the children's backgrounds and will be easily accessible in terms of their understanding. A group or class language experience story is, in a sense, a core book.

At all grade levels, students will be learning vocabulary in the literature/literacy curriculum, but it is important to remember that they will also be learning important concepts through other forms of instruction (e.g., colors through art, spatial relations such as *under* and *over* through movement). However, their greatest learning in vocabulary at this level may be through listening.

Core Books in the Elementary and Upper Grades.   Some of the vocabulary instruction we have described earlier is appropriate for use with older students who are reading the same book. Any children's novel will contain many words that are unfamiliar to students. Commonly, the child (in the same way we do as adults) will skip any unfamiliar word unless not knowing it compromises understanding of the story line. It is through multiple exposures to unfamiliar words in context that we all learn most of our vocabulary, so literature-based instruction also encourages the growth of each student's vocabulary in an incidental way. However, particular instructional strategies may be appropriate for use before reading, during reading, and after reading.

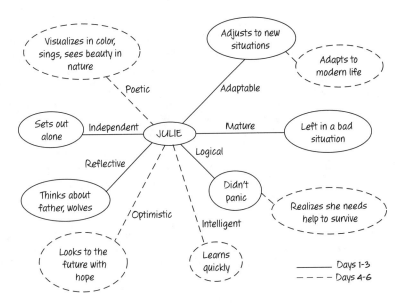

Figure 4.1 Character Map for *Julie of the Wolves*
*(with thanks to Sheila Shapiro)

Character Mapping. Semantic mapping will be covered in detail in Chapter 5, but it is also included here because it is so useful in developing students' understanding of characters while a story is being read. Character development is such a central component of good literature for children and young adults that facilitating students' understanding of the author's craft in this area is also an important component of literature instruction. Many teaching techniques relating to understanding character development focus on possible words to describe characters, which are then supported by incidents and illustrations from the story. **Character mapping** is a way of graphically displaying words that describe characters and makes word relationships apparent.

Older students usually read a core novel over several class periods. Teachers can help students develop and extend a map for characters during this time, displaying it in some fashion during each lesson so that new characteristics of the person and incidents that support each characteristic can be added as the character develops. A map for Julie in *Julie of the Wolves* (1972), by Jean Craighead George, is shown in Figure 4.1 in various stages of its development.

After the students had read the first few chapters, the teacher asked them (sixth-grade students) to suggest some adjectives that they thought appropriately described Julie. They chose *independent, mature, logical, spiritual,* and *reflective,* using incidents from the story to support their suggestions. In doing so, they provided examples and nonexamples, which we suggested in Chapter 1 was an important component of how vocabulary knowledge develops. Two days later, students were able to add additional characteristics, and by the end of the book they were able to add another, as well as a further reason for Julie's adaptability. Using this technique, the teacher was also able to make clear how an author uses the plot to develop our understanding of characters and the changes that they go through.

Comprehension Court.   Character mapping is appropriate before and during the reading of a story or novel. Another technique emphasizing the vocabulary that authors use to create characters is Comprehension Court (Sentell & Blachowicz, 1989), a process that can be used after students have finished reading a story or a novel. As with character mapping, **Comprehension Court** requires students to justify descriptions of a character by drawing on information and clues the author supplies throughout the text. The process also encourages students to reread, make inferences, and construct arguments.

After students have read a chapter or a section of the novel, the teacher hands out an evidence sheet centered on descriptive character words. For example, for the chapter "The Case of the Whistling Ghost" in *Encyclopedia Brown Gets His Man* (Sobol, 1967), the teacher asked questions about three characters—Fabius, Rocky, and Encyclopedia (see Figure 4.2).

The procedure for Comprehension Court involves having students look over the questions, reread the text, and jot notes on the evidence sheet whenever they find information that helps them answer a question. The evidence need not be in sequence. Students may find information relevant to one question, then to a second, more on the first, and so on. Close reading and rereading are encouraged because readers know they may not go back to the text for more information once the "court is in session," but must rely on the evidence that they have gathered. They record the page location to help with the next phase, the Comprehension Court itself.

After students have prepared their evidence, the teacher calls the Comprehension Court into session. The teacher, a designated student, or a student team can direct the discussion. The purpose is to come to a consensus on answering the questions and to identify all the relevant information, reasoning, and the question-answering processes that were used. The whole class may participate, or the teacher may structure teams, each taking a turn in responding. Another group may act as the jury to decide whether a question has been adequately answered.

Students become models for others as they discuss the author's clues that helped them respond to the descriptive vocabulary words. Difficult terms often become resolved through the group's cooperative effort in amassing evidence. For example, for discussion of the phrase *master of deduction,* the students consulted the dictionary about the meaning of *deduction,* used the context of the story, and made allusions to prior knowledge of the phrase *master of . . .* (the universe, deception, etc.). Use of transparencies can help students record and discuss their views of the questions.

The teacher may take many roles in Comprehension Court: (a) *model*—by being a participant, providing relevant evidence, and showing her location and reasoning processes; (b) *prober*—by requesting clarification or more evidence or by posing refocusing questions; or (c) *judge*—by sending readers back to the text. Further, by

Questions:
1. Do you agree that Fabius is a bug expert? Give support for your answer.
2. Which of these words describe Rocky?

honest	liar
benevolent	friendly
mean	funny
shy	criminal

   Justify your answers with evidence.
3. Was Rocky a thief? Give evidence for your answer.
4. Would you say Encyclopedia is a "master of deduction"?
   Give reasons for your answer.

Evidence Summary:

Question	Page	Paragraph	Evidence (key words and explanation)

Figure 4.2 Sample Comprehension Court Evidence Sheet for *Encyclopedia Brown Gets His Man*

choosing descriptive terms that invite reflection and that need multiple sources of evidence, the teacher engages the students in reflection about characters and their traits. After students have used Comprehension Court at least twice, a group can construct its own evidence sheet for a story or book for use by other groups in the class.

Semantic Analysis to Writing. With junior high and high school students, when writing a thematic essay may be a class requirement, **Semantic Analysis to Writing** is a technique that incorporates vocabulary development (Beyersdorfer & Schauer, 1989). The focus of the instruction is having students develop their understanding of key vocabulary terms to respond to an essay question about a text, for example, concerning whether one of the characters displayed courage. Beyersdorfer and Schauer suggest 11 steps in using this instructional technique.

Prior to Class Presentation

1. The teacher composes an essay question that demands that students examine the theme of the literary work just read. Such a question might be: "Define *prejudice* and determine whether the State's rules regarding equality in the story 'Harrison Bergeron' are based on prejudice. Identify specific events from the story that demonstrate that the State exhibits the essential characteristics of prejudice. Explain why you think the State's rules show or do not show prejudice."

2. The teacher selects five to seven words for the framework of the essay by consulting a dictionary, glossary, or thesaurus and compiles a list of pronunciations, parts of speech, and definitions. These words are incorporated on the Semantic Analysis to Writing Thinksheet (see Figure 4.3). The teacher should consider words that students will encounter again in their studies and should choose synonyms that highlight subtle connotative differences to expand the theme and antonyms to allow students to define by opposition.

During the Class

3. The students define the theme based on their current level of knowledge.
4. They brainstorm words related to the theme and categorize them.
5. They discuss each word listed on the Semantic Analysis to Writing Thinksheet.
6. They select the "essential characteristics" of the theme from the thinksheet.
7. They add essential characteristics from the brainstormed list.
8. Then they write and revise the definition of the thematic word, modeling a topic sentence.
9. After they revise, they analyze the essay question and search the text for evidence of the theme; they record the data.
10. They organize the evidence by ranking it in chronological order, spatial order, or order of importance.
11. Finally, they write a draft in response to the essay question posed.

This instructional strategy enables students to explore fine distinctions in word meaning and goes beyond the learning of specific words to provide a model for thinking about vocabulary and how meanings develop and change.

All these techniques are appropriate where the class has shared a literary experience. They all require students to discuss the meanings of words with teacher guidance. Discussion is also an important component when not all students have read the same book.

The Literature Unit Approach

Many teachers are now using literature units to integrate the language arts across the curriculum. This enables them to develop vocabulary using techniques suggested in Chapter 5 on content area reading, but also allows for a wide range of reading in a

Name: _____

Extended Definition: *Prejudice*

Question:
Define *prejudice* and determine whether the State's rules regarding equality in the story
"Harrison Bergeron" are based on prejudice. Identify specific events from the story that
demonstrate that the State exhibits the essential characteristics of prejudice. Explain why
you think the State's rules show or do not show prejudice.

Step 1:
What is prejudice? _____

_____

Step 2:
Consider each of the following words as you extend your definition of *prejudice* and determine if the State's rules were prejudicial. Add two words (#7 and #8) from the list of
words from the group discussion. Locate evidence from the story that supports your opinion about whether the rules were prejudicial or not.

Definition	Essential Yes No	Illustration from the Story (page #)
1. *coercion* (kō r' shən) to force someone to do something.		
2. *discrimination* (dis krim´ ə nā shən) attitudes about a group become actions against that group or members of the group.		
3. *scapegoat* (skāp´ gōt) person or thing that suffers or bears the blame for the faults, misfortunes, or errors of another.		
4. *advocate* (ad´ və kit) a person who publicly supports or pleads the case/cause of another person or group.		
5. *bigot* (big´ ət) person who is unwilling to accept or permit differences of opinion or actions because they differ from his own.		
6. *intolerance* (in tol´ ər əns) unwillingness to permit or endure differences of opinion or action.		
7.		
8.		

Continue listing words, definitions, and illustrations on loose-leaf paper.

Figure 4.3 Semantic Analysis to Writing Thinksheet

variety of texts. Typically when older students (second grade and above) read around a theme or a topic in a literature unit, they will read individually (for example, as they research some aspect of the topic in the library or find out about a particular author); read the same books as other students; and either read, or listen to, stories and text that all students share. As a whole class or in groups, younger students may have a variety of books read to them from various genres (e.g., modern realistic fiction, fantasy, folktales, poetry, and information books about "friends").

The themes and topics that teachers select for instruction depend heavily on grade level and the curriculum of the school district. The advantage of thematic instruction in vocabulary development is that many of the words that are new to the students may have some relation to each other. Thus a unit on immigration may include words such as *passport, customs officer, import, visa,* and *alien,* which may all be unfamiliar to students or only partially understood. Since many of the words are related, students may find it easier to remember them (rather than a similar number of unrelated words). Additionally, teaching a unit will probably give the students more than one exposure to the same word in different contexts, which contributes to better learning and understanding.

Literature Units in Primary Grades. An excellent way to develop vocabulary around a topic for younger students is to make a class alphabet book. Many authors of alphabet books select objects that relate to a theme. Some examples are *The Halloween ABC* by Eve Merriam (1987) and *On Market Street* by Arnold Lobel (1981). Constructing a class alphabet book can be an exploration of new words that students learn in a unit and can also be a wonderful culminating activity for the class. One way is for each child to be responsible for a letter and to find one or two words from the unit that begin with that letter. Better, perhaps, is to have small groups responsible for two or three letters. This avoids the problem of finding words for the "difficult" letters and promotes group exploration and collaboration, ideally with heterogeneous groups. Students may define the words with pictures or words or both, depending on the word and the students' writing competency.

Literature Units in Elementary and Upper Grades. Teachers in elementary and junior high schools have also used class alphabet books to organize study around a topic. Similarly some first-grade teachers are already using literature circles, although they are more commonly seen with older students. **Literature circles** are groups in which students meet to talk about the books they are reading. They can take a variety of forms but, when the teacher is included, can become a series of teacher-student dialogues (J. D. Marshall, 1989). Scharer (1992) has contrasted teacher-led discussions that are mainly low-level questioning and those that are more open-ended and allow students a voice. When teachers are involved, they can incorporate, in a fairly informal way, vocabulary instruction through, for example, discussion of character development, as we outlined more formally earlier. When teachers are not part of the discussion group, it can be helpful to have more formal organizational patterns. These are most appropriate with older students.

Cooperative Literature Discussion Groups. Cooperative groups have been used in various areas of the curriculum and with some success for literature study in elementary classrooms. Johnson, Johnson, and Holubec (1986) have argued that cooperative learning groups promote participation and can be used with any academic task. Our own students have told us that working in cooperative groups, where each group member is assigned a different task, has helped them approach a book from different perspectives. In cooperative literature discussion groups, vocabulary is typically selected by a student in the group, assigned by the teacher, or chosen by a combination of these methods. While not much work has been done concerning the processes of vocabulary learning in these student-directed groups, our research (Fisher, Blachowicz, & Smith, 1991) suggests that students are effective in choosing and learning vocabulary.

The use of cooperative grouping may require the teacher to help students develop skills in cooperative learning. It is beyond the scope of this book to suggest appropriate ways of doing this, and we refer readers to Johnson, Johnson, and Holubec (1986) for a discussion. In our experience, students can be assigned roles for discussing literature without extensive training in cooperative techniques, although some work on process is always necessary.

How then do cooperative groups for literature discussion operate? The basic configuration requires the teacher to assign certain roles to students. The number of these roles depends on the number of students in each group, but three or four is typical. The only role that is always necessary is that of a discussion director, although those of vocabulary researcher and literary leader are also commonly used (if sometimes with a different designation).

The **discussion director** is responsible for preparing questions to lead the group's discussion. Sometimes teachers must show students how to ask open-ended questions or even provide question starters, such as "What do you think about . . . ?" or "What happened when . . . ?" It is the discussion leader's responsibility to make sure that questions are asked clearly, that only one person talks at once, and that time is allowed for discussion. Obviously, in any group, some students will be better at leading discussions than others. However, it is important that everyone has a chance to be a leader.

The **vocabulary researcher (developer)** chooses four to six words that will be unfamiliar to the group. The words are introduced to the group by locating them in the story, discussing possible meanings, and providing a dictionary definition if needed.

The **literary leader** is responsible for selecting a passage for oral reading that may illustrate some literary language that the teacher wishes to emphasize (e.g., figurative language, metaphors, or good character descriptions). The final role can be that of a **secretary-checker.** This student ensures that group members come prepared, keeps track of time, and collects and distributes any logs or work that the teacher requires. The roles in the groups can, and should, rotate daily (the discussion leader becomes the vocabulary researcher, then the literary leader, etc.). A possible scheme for operating cooperative discussion groups over a six-day period is shown in Figure 4.4. This schedule can be adapted for longer (or shorter) periods.

In addition to preparing their roles, all students can be asked to summarize the chapter(s), write a personal reaction to the reading, and predict what will happen next. The log sheet for Linda, a fourth-grade student who was reading *The Castle in*

Day 1: Form groups, distribute books and journals, and explain procedures. Each group decides on the number of pages to read for each class to complete the book in four sessions. Each person in the group is responsible for taking a different role on each of the four days.

Days 2, 3, and 4: Each group member is responsible for coming to class having completed the reading and prepared to fulfill his or her role for the day.
Procedures (20- to 30-minute sessions):
1. Discussion leader reads a summary of the action.
2. All group members read their reactions.
3. Each member completes the assigned daily task, beginning with the discussion leader, vocabulary researcher, literary leader, and secretary-checker.
4. Group members share their predictions for the next reading.
5. Complete and discuss self- and group-process evaluations and assign roles for the next day.

Day 5: Same as days 2, 3, and 4. Additionally, each group needs to develop a plan for sharing its novel with the class on day 6.

Day 6: Each group shares its novel with the whole class.

Figure 4.4   Daily Procedures for Cooperative Groups

the Attic (1985) by Elizabeth Winthrop, is shown in Figure 4.5. The role definitions can be seen at the top of the sheet, with her vocabulary selections below that. At the end of the three weeks spent on the book, the teacher stapled each student's sheets together with a cover, which became the record of the student's reading.

A typical discussion in such a group might be as follows. Seventh graders Lisa, Julia, Susan, and Shari are reading *Prairie Songs* by Pam Conrad (1989). They are talking about the meaning of *warily* which Lisa has chosen, and using a dictionary to confirm their predictions.

> L: It's on page 66. The sentence says, "He wound his fingers around it and applied them warily to the inside cover of the book."
> S: I think that would mean like *cautiously* maybe. (Reads it again.) Maybe like really hard or soft.
> Sh: I think *cautiously*. Let's look it up.
> J: There it is—*in a wary manner, carefully, cautiously.*
> Sh: I told you!

In this example, students use the sentence context to predict the meaning of the word, and then they confirm one of their predictions. This is a much more powerful learning experience than if the teacher had given them the word as a dictionary exercise or just told them the meaning.

	Chapter **15** Name **Linda**
	Date **March 10, 1994**

My preparation for this chapter is ...

○ Discussion Director
5+ questions asking why
. . . how . . . compare

✓ Vocabulary Researcher
6+ words and definitions
using context, dictionary

○ Literary Leader
4+ examples of comparisons
simile/metaphor, good description

always include page numbers

1. p. 149 1st audience -- people watching
2. p. 149 2nd various -- different
3. p. 150 1st gyrations -- turning around a center of a room
4. p. 150 3rd taskmaker -- a person who assines work
5. p. 150 4th crone -- old woman
6. p. 151 4th churlish -- a unpleasant

Well done +

Summary of this chapter...	My reaction...
William had to do lots of things to entertain the Wizard so much that when he goes back he will ready for the meet. William defeated Alaston and broke the mirrow.	If I were William I would be so proud that I defeated Alastor.
How?	✓x

My prediction for the next chapter... and why...
He will go back and change Mrs. Philips and himself back to normal.

Figure 4.5 Reading Log Sheet for a Fourth-Grade Student

Teaching Idea File 4.1

Peer Teaching of Self-Selected Words

1. Each student selects one word from a book to teach other students.
2. Each student prepares for the discussion group by writing on three index cards the word and the sentence in which the word appears. The student confirms the word's meaning by consulting a dictionary.
3. Students meet in groups of three. Each student reads his or her chosen word in the sentence context from the card.
4. The other students discuss possible meanings of the word.
5. A meaning is decided on in consultation with the person who brought the word to the group.
6. All the students write the meaning on the index cards under the sentence in which the word appears.
7. The index cards become part of each student's word box.

From Blachowicz & Fisher, *Teaching Vocabulary in All Classrooms,* p. 70.

Cooperative literature discussion groups can, of course, be used when all students are reading the same book. However, they are ideally suited for situations in which different groups of children are reading different books around a common theme. They promote vocabulary learning in context and include the motivating factor of student self-selection of words to be learned.

A Note on Student Self-Selection of Words. When teachers (or publishers) select words that they think should be taught to students, there will always be some words that nobody in the class has come across before, words that some students know, and even words that everyone knows to a certain extent (Haggard, 1982). One advantage of having students select their own words is that they have the opportunity to develop their vocabulary knowledge genuinely. Our own research had indicated that, when asked to do so, students will generally select difficult words to learn and to teach each other. In one fifth-grade classroom, students chose words that were above their grade level 100% of the time (Fisher, Blachowicz, Pozzi, & Costa, 1992). These students met in vocabulary discussion groups to teach each other words prior to meeting in a larger group with the teacher to discuss the books they were reading. Each student brought one word to the group to teach the other group members. In the group, they followed a context and definition procedure similar to that outlined for cooperative groups (see Teaching Idea File 4.1). In addition, they attempted to generate new sentences for each word.

Many interesting discussions resulted as students grappled with attributes and boundaries of meaning. The best discussions involved identifying attributes of the word that helped with the definition (e.g., "Can a dog get trachoma?"). Similarly, in a fourth-grade class, students selected words that were at or above grade level over 85% of the time. Teachers need not necessarily be concerned that students won't select difficult words if given the chance.

The Individual Reading Approach

Most teachers include some individual reading choice in their reading/language arts program. This may take the form of **sustained silent reading,** where all students read a book of their choice silently for some time (such as 15 minutes a day). Some teachers operate a **reading workshop** (Atwell, 1987) in which the silent reading of personal choices is the main part of the program.

The strength of a program that allows students to select their own books is that they are more likely to read and to become involved in their reading. Although teachers may wish to set certain parameters (e.g., one nonfiction book per marking period or at least one book that is above grade level), a reading workshop approach to the literature curriculum allows students individual freedom and can encompass a wide range of abilities in the classroom. Students at all levels enjoy knowing that it is OK to reread favorite books—what better way to develop sight vocabulary in the primary grades and meaning vocabulary in the upper grades? Atwell (1987) has shown how using literature logs can facilitate this process. However, some teachers prefer more structure.

Book Contracts with Vocabulary Logs.   A book contract is negotiated between each student and the teacher. The student agrees to complete the work designated in the contract. This arrangement allows students to work on things that interest them, while allowing the teacher to help students monitor and be responsible for their own learning. By working with individual students, the teacher can focus on particular strengths and weaknesses in literacy that need to be developed or addressed. A contract for a particular student with a particular book might include

- A reading record of what is read each day
- Personality descriptions of the main characters
- A vocabulary log
- Journal questions to respond to
- Author study questions
- Extension activities through art, drama, or further reading

The vocabulary log component might be very traditional—to write the word, a definition, and a sentence that shows its meaning. An example of a partially completed traditional vocabulary log for *Tom Sawyer* is shown in Figure 4.6.

However, since we know that different levels of understanding meanings are appropriate, it may also be appropriate to allow students to choose their own level of learning and to design a more personal log. For example, based on his level of learning, a student could negotiate to select four words for which he wanted to learn a definition, four words that he wanted to be able to use appropriately, and six words for which he found some meaning that made sense in the story. For the first four words, he would probably use the dictionary, for the last six he might use context clues and a friend (or a parent), while for the middle four he would probably have to use multiple sources. The student might also wish to design his own type of log. Some options could be to draw a picture to represent the word, to use a schematic or diagram

Name _____Rachel_____		BOOK _____Tom Sawyer_____
WORD	PAGE	DEFINITION AND SENTENCE
inarticulately	69	not like regular speech The man, who was very scared, talked inarticulately.
shingle	72	thin piece of wood The shingle cut Rob's hand.
lugubrious	75	very sad She is lugubrious because her hamster died.

Figure 4.6   Traditional Vocabulary Log for *Tom Sawyer*

to show the meaning, to make a list of synonyms, to collect various uses of the word from books and conversations, or to use a keyword method (see Chapter 8). An example of this type of contract for *Dogsong* (1985), by Gary Paulsen, is shown in Figure 4.7.

Within the book contract there are, therefore, many options that could be appropriate for vocabulary learning. A similar idea, but not related to a particular book, has been used by teachers in schools for years—vocabulary notebooks.

Keeping Track of Vocabulary: Vocabulary Notebooks.   Vocabulary notebooks can be just notebooks in which students record the vocabulary the teacher expects them to learn for a quiz. While this may be appropriate in some settings, a more useful function is for students to use the notebooks to keep interesting words and phrases that appeal to them. They can then use these words in their own writing. The advantage of this system is that students not only select their own words, but do so in the expectation of *using* them. The organization of the notebooks can be simple, for example, alphabetic, or more complex, e.g., by categories, depending on the grade level and function of the book. For example, primary-grade students might keep a book in which they record interesting words relating to size, words of motion, or happy words. Older students may have more sophisticated categories, such as interesting adjectives relating to age, thinking verbs, or amazing alliterations. The notebooks then become a resource that students and teachers can use. When the note-

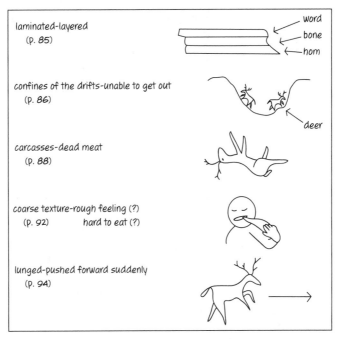

laminated-layered
(p. 85)

confines of the drifts-unable to get out
(p. 86)

carcasses-dead meat
(p. 88)

coarse texture-rough feeling (?)
(p. 92)   hard to eat (?)

lunged-pushed forward suddenly
(p. 94)

Figure 4.7   Nontraditional Log as Part of a Contract for *Dogsong*

books are used in this way, it encourages students to "play" with language. This objective manipulation of language encourages students to become interested in words *as words* and so focus their attention on vocabulary.

FIGURATIVE LANGUAGE

One of the characteristics of good literature is the high incidence of figurative language, which is a special consideration in vocabulary instruction. Authors of good books want us to reflect on the world and view it in different ways as a result of reading their work. Figurative language uses comparisons, contrasts, and unusual juxtapositioning of words to draw our attention to aspects of the world in which we live. But figurative language is also part of our daily lives. Petrosky (1980) calculates that an adult may use over 500,000 figures of speech a year (admittedly the majority being clichés). He argues that "figurative language is a natural and necessary part of how we construct the world and reality" (p. 153).

While there are many types of figurative language, Riccio (1980) suggests that all figures of speech may be viewed as types of metaphor, "in that words and phrases are not only used figuratively but also express their meaning in representative terms" (p. 195). Thus, although hyperbole, metonymy, and synecdoche are all types of figurative language, we will focus on metaphors (and similes) and one other type that can be fun instructionally but can cause problems for some students—idioms.

Metaphors and Similes

Most of us have had students who are confused by metaphors such as, "After two weeks of sun, the garden was a desert." However, most children understand, "Your room is a pigsty." How can it be that they understand and use some metaphors (think of some of the derogatory remarks you hear during recess, such as *pigface*), but be confused by others? In the first example, students may take the phrase literally, that is, fail to recognize the language as figurative. In the second example, children understand that their room and a pigsty have an attribute in common, messiness. Readence, Baldwin, and Head (1986) have suggested that there are three possible reasons for a reader's inability to understand a metaphor. First, the reader may fail to recognize the metaphor as figurative (nonliteral). Second, the reader may fail to identify the attribute that is the basis of the comparison. Third, the reader may have insufficient word knowledge, in that he does not know (rather than cannot identify) the necessary attribute. For example, to say that the man was "like a lion" does not make explicit which attribute of a lion is being used—for instance, kingliness, wildness, or sleepiness. A reader must infer the appropriate attribute from the context of the passage. Not knowing that a lion is a sleepy creature would make incomprehensible any metaphor using that as an attribute, which is a failure in word knowledge about lions.

To address problems with metaphors, we need to instruct students at all three levels. First, we need to ensure that they understand the nature of figurative language and practice identifying it in the context of literature. Second, we need to enable students to use a process of identifying possible attributes in any comparison. Third, where appropriate, we need to supply vocabulary instruction of specific words for specific metaphors. Poetry is the genre where metaphors are most common, so an example can be best drawn from that source.

Poetry as a Source of Metaphors.   The titles of two of the most popular books of light verse for children are metaphors—*A Light in the Attic* (1974) and *Where the Sidewalk Ends* (1974), both by Shel Silverstein. Poetry is a wonderful source of metaphors and similes, and a great source of interesting vocabulary. The high density of new or "difficult" words and unusual metaphors can, in the hand of a poor poet, create problems of interpretation or understanding that turn children off to poetry. However, if poetry is approached in the right way, students can learn not only new ways of looking at the world, but also new words for exploring their own experiences of the world.

If a class read the poem "Dreams" by Langston Hughes, it would be appropriate first for them to hear it (preferably read by the teacher, who is the best reader in the room), then to read it, and then to discuss it in some form. During the discussion, it would be appropriate to ask students to identify some of the figurative language. They might select the line "life is a broken-winged bird," a metaphor. To explore the meaning of Hughes's poem, it is necessary to identify some of the characteristics of a bird that he might want us to know in relation to life (beyond the nonflying aspect of this bird). Students can brainstorm some of these. With a different poem, a more lighthearted poem, it might be appropriate to explore some of the characteristics he probably *didn't* have in mind! Much poetry becomes understandable only when these relationships are made more explicit, and what we are doing in exploring the relationships is developing understandings, not just of the meaning of the poem, but of the meanings of the words themselves.

Idioms

Have you ever *paid through the nose* for something? Perhaps you can remember some *slips of the tongue* that have embarrassed you as a teacher. **Idioms** such as these are phrases or expressions that have meanings different from the literal. These two examples illustrate how idioms are typically types of metaphor, but they are also "accepted phrases" or expressions that have accepted meanings. Idioms are not the same as clichés or slang. **Clichés** are expressions that are trite or overused (e.g., *as white as snow*), whereas **slang** is a colloquialism that may be used briefly by a particular group (e.g., *groovy*). Idioms are fun to work with because they are part of everyday vocabulary, but students enjoy working with possible literal meanings for the expressions.

Bromley (1984) has some suggestions for teaching idioms. She suggests defining them, using them, and applying them. Students can define and explain idioms when they encounter them in context. Some students become fascinated with the origins of such expressions. Our favorite source of this information is *2107 Curious Word Origins* (which includes *A Hog on Ice and Other Curious Expressions*) by Charles Funk (1993), but other sources are also available (see Appendix B). We have found that *using* idioms by having students act out or illustrate literal interpretations of particular idioms for other students is great fun (see Teaching Idea File 4.2). This activity, a form of charades, is fun for all grade levels—it varies only in the sophistication of the idiom and the interpretation.

Finally, identifying idioms in literature, on TV, and in conversations with parents and friends is a form of application. Peggy Parish's books about Amelia Bedelia are great favorites among second and third graders who love the way Amelia interprets idioms literally.

Teaching Idea File 4.2

Dramatizing Idioms

1. Have students in groups identify idioms in recent stories that they have read.
2. Students select an idiom that they think might be easy to act out, for example, "Don't pull my leg."
3. Students write a short episode or skit in which the literal meaning of the idiom occurs. For example, a person selling shoes might pull someone's leg when trying to get off a tight-fitting shoe.
4. Other students in the class try to guess what idiom is being acted out by the group.

From Blachowicz & Fisher, *Teaching Vocabulary in All Classrooms*, p. 75.

Looking Back and Looking Ahead

The old reading curricula, which relied on basal readers, controlled the introduction of vocabulary in an attempt to make learning to read easier. The move to the use of literature in the classroom has ensured that students will be exposed to new and exciting words every day. This chapter has introduced some ways of helping students learn those words, especially as relating to literary analysis. However, many teachers are using literature across the curriculum, especially in social studies. The next chapter introduces techniques that may be used in the content areas, sometimes in conjunction with literature.

For Further Learning

Readence, J. E., Baldwin, R. S., & Head, M. H. (1986). Direct instruction in processing metaphors. *Journal of Reading Behavior, 18,* 325–339. (Includes several teaching ideas)

Tompkins, G. E., & McGee, L. M. (1993). *Teaching reading with literature: Case studies to action plans.* Englewood Cliffs, NJ: Merrill/Prentice Hall. (Full of excellent ideas for literature-based reading instruction)

Zarrillo, J. (1989). Teachers' interpretations of literature-based reading. *Reading Teacher, 43,* 22–28. (Provides a framework and guidelines for implementing a literature-based approach to reading instruction)

http://rhyme.lycos.com

This website contains a rhyming dictionary and thesaurus program developed by Datamuse. After typing in a word, visitors can choose to find rhymes, synonyms, definitions, quotations, pictures, words with similar spellings, homophones, and related words. Results are plentiful and seem to be helpful, especially the listings of simple rhymes. Searching for more pictures, on the other hand, was time consuming and never produced any pictures when we tried it.

The database of famous quotations, which can be searched by person and by certain words, is interesting, but it does not say where and when these quotes were first spoken or written. Visitors can also access "great works," including Mother Goose rhymes, many of Shakespeare's works, the Bible, American historical documents (e.g., the Constitution), and various submissions by other site users.

CHAPTER 5

LEARNING VOCABULARY IN THE CONTENT AREAS

☑ Prepare Yourself

Prepare yourself by evaluating your own knowledge. Rate your ability to answer some of the key questions for this chapter. Check the boxes that describe your pre-reading knowledge.

Key concept questions	Well informed	Aware	Need ideas
1. *What are some strategies for teaching new meanings for known words in the content areas?*	❑	❑	❑
2. *What are some strategies for teaching new words for new concepts in the content areas?*	❑	❑	❑
3. *What are some strategies for teaching new words for known concepts in the content areas?*	❑	❑	❑

☑ Strategy Overview Guide

In this chapter we present background, ideas, and strategies to help you teach vocabulary in the content areas, where the focus and purpose of instruction may be different from those for the language arts. We draw a contrast between learning new meanings for known words, new words representing new concepts, and new words for known concepts. The nature of vocabulary learning in the content areas focuses on the first two of these. The following chart can help you choose suitable instructional strategies for your classroom.

Instructional strategy	Goal—use when you want to . . .	Comments
Typical-to-technical meaning (p. 87)	*Teach a new meaning for a known word, and the new meaning is an important concept.*	*Time consuming. Better with older students.*
Illustrating differing meanings (p. 87)	*Teach new meanings for known words, but the concepts are not central to the topic.*	*Fun to do. Good with all ages of students.*
Vocabulary-focused K-W-L (p. 89)	*Teach words that may have new meanings or extended meanings as part of a unit.*	*Encourages further student research.*
Clarifying misconceptions (p. 90)	*Introduce new meanings where students are likely to have misconceptions that interfere with learning.*	*Requires students to think metacognitively about what they know.*
Frayer model (p. 92)	*Teach new words for new concepts, and the concepts are central to the topic.*	*The most complete way of teaching a new word.*
Semantic feature analysis (p. 93)	*Help students decide what features discriminate one word from another.*	*Most useful when doing extended work on a topic or theme.*
Possible sentences (p. 94)	*Have fun playing with the contexts in which newly learned words can occur.*	*A reinforcement exercise.*
Semantic gradients (p. 95)	*Teach how synonymous or antonymous adjectives and adverbs relate to known words.*	*Useful for generating group discussions.*

Instructional strategy	Goal—use when you want to . . .	Comments
Maps (p. 96)	*Show the relationships between words.*	*Good way of beginning and ending vocabulary instruction in a unit.*
Structured overviews (p. 98)	*Show the hierarchical relationships among important concepts.*	*Useful as an overview or a summary of a chapter.*
Knowledge rating (p. 100)	*Encourage students to examine what they know about words they will encounter.*	*Best used when the whole class is reading the same text.*
Concept guides (p. 101)	*Have students read the same text to explore the hierarchical relationships among concepts.*	*Time consuming to prepare. Good for discussion.*
Analogical study guides (p. 102)	*Make an analogy between new concepts and familiar ones.*	*Great when the analogy is easily accessible to the teacher and the students.*
Vocabulary overview guides (p. 103)	*Teach students to monitor their own understanding as they read texts.*	*Definitely for older students.*
Keyword (p. 106)	*Teach new words for known concepts.*	*Often used for the superficial learning of definitions.*

"What does matrimony mean?" asked seven-year-old Cathy of her mother last week at a rather formal wedding.
"It's just another word for marriage, darling," answered her mother.
"So, what does consummate mean?" asked Cathy.

The ease with which Cathy's mother responded to the first question and the problems she had with the second demonstrate one of the differences between learning a new word for a concept that is already known and learning a new word for a new, or only partially understood, concept. As children begin to learn vocabulary for the content areas, they encounter more and more words that are both new words and new concepts. Less commonly, as with the word *matrimony*, they are also learning new words for familiar concepts. In addition, they face a complication in relation to what they already know—new meanings for familiar words.

Let us imagine a second-grade student working on a unit about space exploration. As she works on information about space probes to Mars, she encounters three new terms—*rocket stage, asteroid,* and *adhere.* She knows the word *stage,* but only in relation to her class performance in the school presentations at Christmas. She now has to learn a new meaning for the word. As she reads about asteroids, she is learning not only a new word, but also a new concept—one she has never encountered before. She may be familiar with the word *adhere* as a concept—like how a stamp sticks to an envelope. This makes the learning of the word *adhere* relatively easy. The amount of learning that has to occur can vary, therefore, depending on which of the three categories the word falls into. The nature of the instruction may also have to change with respect to each category.

A teacher in the content areas is often facing different task demands in vocabulary instruction. In reading and writing instruction, a child may need only a superficial knowledge of the meaning of a word to comprehend a text. For example, the text might read, "He lay down to sleep on the pallet." The reader needs to recognize only that a *pallet* is some form of bed; it is not necessary to know the defining characteristics that differentiate a pallet from other types of bed. It may not be important for a student to remember the meaning of the word after reading the book or passage. In contrast, when writing, a student may need to know only a particular meaning to use a word effectively. The literacy teacher may be concerned with developing a student's vocabulary in *general,* rather than knowledge of *particular* words. In contrast, in the content areas, certain words and concepts may be central to understanding a whole topic. For example, it would be difficult for a science student to understand a unit on light without having a clear understanding of the concept of "refraction." It may be vital that the child remembers a word's meaning in order to understand subsequent instruction. For example, a math student would have difficulty in more advanced geometry without an understanding from earlier instruction of the concept of a "diameter." The instruction designed for such key concepts must, therefore, require some deep processing on the part of the student. A student may need to know several definitions of a word to fully understand the subject. For example, in literature study, a student may need to know that the word *character* refers not only to a particular person in a book or play, but also to the way the author represents that person (as in "Jones is a master of character development") or in the sense of having a reputation, such as in having a good or bad character.

As we suggested in Chapter 1, "knowing" a word is a continuous process. We constantly refine and extend our knowledge of a word's meanings through different encounters with the word. Students in the content areas continually refine and extend their understanding of key concepts. After all, think how your knowledge of the concept of vocabulary instruction has been extended as you read this book!

TEACHING NEW MEANINGS FOR KNOWN WORDS

Sometimes common words have technical meanings in the content areas. Students may have developed comprehensive understandings of a word, only to be confronted with a new meaning. Occasionally, students can become confused when applying a familiar meaning for a word, which does not match its use in the subject. For example, students may know the term *product* as being something manufactured by a company. However, a *product* in mathematics is the number resulting from the multiplication of two other numbers. All three strategies described in this section help students contrast what they already know with what they need to know.

"Typical-to-Technical" Meaning Approach

The **typical-to-technical meaning approach,** outlined by Pearson and Johnson (1984), requires students to be engaged in discussion to clarify the differences between the earlier known meaning of the word and the new meaning. Although this discussion can be time consuming, the benefits of a clear understanding of keyterms justify the time spent. The technique has three stages:

1. Discuss the common meaning of the word and then introduce its technical definition.

2. Have students do word-to-meaning exercises in which they match the word with both the common and the technical definitions (for example, Exercise 1 in Figure 5.1).

3. Develop maze sentences, which require students to fill in the blanks where the word is used in both technical and common ways (for example, Exercise 2 in Figure 5.1).

Welker (1987) published an account of this technique as it was used with a junior high school mathematics class studying the words *acute, complementary, angle,* and *supplementary.* Examples of the exercises he used after discussion are shown in Figure 5.1 The example shows how Welker developed both definitional and contextual knowledge, as suggested by Stahl (1985). In this instance, contextual knowledge would also be understanding developed from seeing, drawing, and labeling the appropriate angles.

Illustrating Differing Meanings

Searls and Klesius (1984) identified 99 primary-level multiple-meaning words that had four or more different definitions. Some examples are *about, color, head, mean, right,* and *will.* They suggest several strategies for teaching such words, including the use of sentence context (as described earlier in Chapter 2), semantic maps (as described later in this chapter), picture dictionaries and concept books, and illustrations of the different definitions. Illustrations include not just pictures, but also objects, models, actions, and pantomimes. For example, the word *paper* could be illustrated by showing writing paper and wrapping paper or by drawing someone papering a wall or reading the newspaper. Searls and Klesius (1984) suggest that the teacher can lead a discussion about the different meanings of the word and give students a chance to share an experience that they have had with that word.

A further extension that they suggest is to have a target "word for the day." After instruction in its various meanings, children can be encouraged to bring in pictures showing different meanings to post on a bulletin board (see Teaching Idea File 5.1).

Exercise 1

Select the correct common and mathematical definitions for each term. Write the letter of each definition in the appropriate column for common or technical meaning.

Definitions

A. Point of view
B. Making whole; completing
C. Supplying what is lacking; additional
D. Space between two lines or surfaces that meet
E. Having a sharp point
 F. Either of 2 angles that combine to equal 90 degrees
G. An angle that is less than 90 degrees in value
H. Either of 2 angles that together form exactly 180 degrees

Terms	Common Meaning	Technical Meaning
acute	_____	_____
supplementary	_____	_____
complementary	_____	_____
angle	_____	_____

Exercise 2

Select the best word to complete each sentence below. Each word will be used twice.
Words: complementary, acute, angle, supplementary

1. The sword had a very _____ cutting edge.

2. The _____ angle for a 50-degree angle is a 40-degree angle.

3. Our reading textbook comes with _____ materials such as workbooks and ditto sheets.

4. If an angle is 55 degrees, it is called a(n) _____ angle.

5. A black tie with a white shirt would be considered a _____ match.

6. Now that I have given my thoughts on the subject, what is your _____ (or opinion) on the matter?

7. A pie can be sliced into pieces with many different _____.

8. Two angles that go together to equal 180 degrees are _____ angles.

_____

Note. From "Going from Typical to Technical Meaning" by W. A. Welker, 1987, *Journal of Reading, 31,* 275–276. Reprinted by permission.

Figure 5.1 Typical-to-Technical Meaning

Teaching Idea File 5.1

Illustrating the Word for the Day

1. The teacher selects one word from previous vocabulary instruction that has multiple meanings.
2. Students are asked to bring pictures or items that show one particular meaning of the word.
3. On "the day," students share what they have brought and describe the meaning that it shows.
4. Pictures or items are displayed around a poster of the word and the various definitions.

From Blachowicz & Fisher, *Teaching Vocabulary in All Classrooms*, p. 83.

Searls and Klesius note that students could then play charades, where the class tries to guess which meaning of a word is being acted out.

Vocabulary-Focused K–W–L

Using the **K-W-L procedure** (Ogle, 1986), students write what they know about a topic (K), what they want to know about it (W), and what they have learned (L). When a selection or a topic contains several words that may take on new meanings or where there are several familiar words with extended meanings, a vocabulary-focused K-W-L may be appropriate. In this strategy, the teacher selects vocabulary words from a topic or selection and guides students to discuss what they know about the words. Students then develop questions based on their own knowledge and on the selected vocabulary. After students read about the topic, the teacher may ask them to categorize the words and describe what they have learned. The steps in the process are:

1. Select words from the text or topic that have unfamiliar meanings or are new words for the students.
2. List the words.
3. Lead a discussion of the words and the meanings that the students know.
4. Introduce the new meanings for the topic in question.
5. Have students develop questions based on the words and their own knowledge of the topic.
6. Read the text or texts.
7. Ask students to write answers to the questions that were asked in step 5.
8. Have students cluster or categorize the information that they have learned, including meanings for all the words presented.

A fourth-grade teacher was going to ask her students to read about giraffes as part of a unit on Africa. Included in the selection were the following words: *mirage, cow, bull, parasite, muzzle, thickets, calf, hide, predators, suckles, prehensile tongue, pacing, browsing, herd,* and *hyena.* Several of the words would require the students to extend their knowledge of the meanings (such as *herd, tongue, browsing,* and *muzzle*), and others would focus on new meanings (such as *cow, bull, calf, pacing,* and *hide*). Still other words might be totally new (such as *thickets, predators, suckles, parasite, mirage,* and *hyena*). The teacher wrote the words on the board and elicited meanings from the whole class. Where their definitions did not match the meaning of a word in the text, she told them the new meaning or asked them to look at how it was used when they read. The students then developed their own questions including (among others):

> What do giraffes eat and how do they use their tongue?
>
> What are the giraffes' enemies/predators?
>
> How tall are full-grown bull giraffes?
>
> How long do calves suckle?
>
> How many calves can a cow giraffe have?
>
> Why does a giraffe's hide have spots?
>
> How does a giraffe defend itself?

After reading the selection, students answered their questions and wrote them and the words in categories relating to:

1. How a giraffe looks
2. A giraffe's habitat
3. A giraffe's eating habits
4. The life of a baby giraffe
5. A giraffe's predators
6. Other aspects of a giraffe's life

This vocabulary-focused K-W-L drew students' attention to new meanings for familiar words, exposed them to the words in context, and had them use the words in relation to the rest of the topic. However, sometimes it is not so easy to develop students' knowledge and understandings of new meanings or new concepts.

Clarifying Misconceptions

Some students come to learning in the content areas with misconceptions about certain word meanings. They may "know" a meaning of the word, but while that meaning may make sense in the normal world, in the content area this misconception may prevent the development of good understanding. Some research in this area suggests that confronting students with their misconceptions and changing them is necessary. If this does not occur, students can cling to a misunderstanding that interferes with their learning (Alverman & Hynd, 1989; N. Marshall, 1989). For example, in a science unit, students' naive conceptions of the concept of "reflection" (in relation to the way light helps us see) included the idea that the sun illuminates an object rather

Teaching Idea File 5.2

Confronting Students' Misconceptions

1. Ask students to explain or demonstrate what they understand about a concept. For example, for the concept "reflection," ask students to draw a diagram including the sun, a tree, and a boy to show how light is reflected to enable the boy to see the tree.
2. Examine students' alternatives, asking them to justify their interpretations to each other.
3. Raise questions that encourage students to explore different options. For example, "When I see my own eyes in a mirror, how does light work?"

From Blachowicz & Fisher, *Teaching Vocabulary in All Classrooms*, p. 85.

than that light is reflected from objects. Even when they had been *taught* that light is reflected from objects to our eyes, this misconception remained and limited their understanding of the rest of the unit on light (Nussbaum & Novick, 1982). McKeown and Beck (1989) argue that instruction "must consider not only what the students lack, but also the character of the knowledge they already have and the role it may play in representations of new information" (p. 36). Extensive examination of social studies texts (Haas, 1988) revealed that they present a large number of concepts with very little review or reinforcement. Thus, students who attempt to merge prior understandings with new meanings in the texts are not given an opportunity to check whether ideas are accurately assimilated before new concepts are introduced.

Research (N. Marshall, 1989) suggests that students' misconceptions may be addressed in two ways. The first is to modify the texts they read to directly confront the misconception and contrast it with accurate information (Maria & MacGinitie, 1987). The second is confrontation and contrast in some form of instruction (N. Marshall, 1989; Nussbaum, 1979). Nussbaum suggests a six-stage procedure, that can be reduced to the three steps shown in Teaching Idea File 5.2. As part of a unit on the plains, one teacher was exploring the concept "winter wheat" with her fourth-grade class. She elicited some conceptions of what it was—wheat that grew in the winter in the plains, wheat grown in the winter in another part of the country, wheat that was planted in the winter. She asked students in groups to explain which of these alternatives was best and why. After a short time, she asked the students if they knew of any plants that grew in their gardens in the winter, or if they knew of any plants that were planted in the fall but that grew in the spring. Many students mentioned daffodils and tulips. The groups then talked again, referred to the concept in their textbooks, and reported their decisions. Most students arrived at a correct understanding of winter wheat being planted in the fall to allow for an early harvest, but that it did not *grow* in the plains in winter. This problem-solving approach encourages students to develop their own understandings when the teacher is not present to help them.

We should remember that low knowledge of a particular topic is not just a lack of knowledge. Low knowledge can also be characterized as poorly organized knowledge. Perkins and Simmons (1988), in addition to noting how individuals may have misconceptions about concepts in a domain, suggest that faulty knowledge may also reflect "malprioritized concepts." That is, low-knowledge students may fail to understand the difference in importance of various concepts in a domain. Further, they argue that knowledge can become garbled when new understandings in one domain are applied incorrectly to another. Thus, any instruction that relates new meanings to old meanings needs to address how these meanings are related, if at all, and how they are related to other concepts in the domain under study. This is also particularly important when new concepts are represented by new words.

TEACHING NEW WORDS FOR NEW CONCEPTS

The second grader who is learning about asteroids was described in the introduction as exploring a new word for a new concept. As her understanding grows, it may become clear to her how an asteroid differs from a planet. This basic idea of discriminating features characterizes the first set of strategies in this section. As her knowledge of space exploration develops, our second grader may come to understand how asteroids, planets, stars, moons, and galaxies not only differ, but are interconnected. This aspect of connectedness is addressed in the second set of strategies. Finally, both features—discrimination and interconnection—are examined in relation to strategies that are particularly useful when students are reading from textbooks.

Strategies That Focus on Discriminating Features

The Frayer Model. Dorothy Frayer and her colleagues at the University of Wisconsin designed a model to provide a thorough basis for understanding new words (Frayer, Frederick, & Klausmeier, 1969). The procedure has seven steps:

1. Define the new concept, discriminating the attributes relevant to all instances of the concept.
2. Discriminate the relevant from the irrelevant properties of instances of the concept.
3. Provide an example of the concept.
4. Provide a nonexample of the concept.
5. Relate the concept to a subordinate concept.
6. Relate the concept to a superordinate concept.
7. Relate the concept to a coordinate term.

An example of this method is shown in Figure 5.2.

You can tell that this procedure is rather complex and could be time consuming. It may be justifiable to spend so much time only if the concept is central to the work in the classroom. It is important when presenting the examples and nonexamples to explain *why* they are examples or not. For example, with *treasurer,* it may be important to explain why an accountant is not an example, although accountants often serve in such a role. An extension of the procedure is then to ask students to gen-

Word: *Treasurer*

Step 1. The discriminating attributes of *treasurer* are membership in an organization and responsibility for the accounts.

Step 2. The amount of money the treasurer is responsible for is an irrelevant attribute.

Step 3. The "treasurer of the school board" and the "treasurer of the school book club" are examples of the word.

Step 4. The "chairman or secretary of the board" and "a banker" are nonexamples of the concept.

Step 5. Examples of subordinate concepts would be particular generic instances of a treasurer, such as the treasurer of a country club or boys' club.

Step 6. The superordinate concept is "people who deal with money."

Step 7. A coordinate term is *bookkeeper.*

Figure 5.2 An Example of the Frayer Model

Table 5.1 Semantic Feature Analysis for People Who Deal with Money

	Cash	Checks	Accounts	Daily	(Other Features)
Treasurer	?	+	+	−	
Purser	?	+	+	+	
Cashier	+	+	+	+	
Banker	−	−	+	?	
Accountant	−	−	+	?	
Croupier	+	−	−	+	
Stockbroker	−	−	+	?	
(Others Who Deal with Money)					

erate examples and nonexamples and to explain their choices. In Chapter 6 we will present a similar technique to the Frayer model called **concept of definition,** a graphic form with similar features that shares the characteristic of the Frayer model of helping students know when they know a word. Thus, if students know the seven steps of the model, they can test their own knowledge of unfamiliar concepts by seeing if they can complete all seven steps.

Semantic Feature Analysis. Another technique that focuses on discriminating features is semantic feature analysis. Using the previous example of the word *treasurer,* we could ask students to complete a grid that lists people who deal with money on one axis and discriminating features on the other axis (see Table 5.1). Semantic feature analysis requires students to complete the grid with positive, negative, or possible attributes.

Table 5.2   Semantic Feature Analysis for Pets

	Fur	Tail	Feathers	Gills	(Other Features)
Cat	+	+	−	−	
Dog	+	+	−	−	
Canary	−	+	+	−	
Fish	−	−	−	+	
Snake	−	−	−	−	
Tortoise	−	+	−	−	
(Other Pets)					

The students may then be asked to add features that discriminate one example from another. Thus, in Table 5.1 they would have to add features that distinguish between a *banker,* an *accountant,* and a *stockbroker.* Students could also generate further examples of people who deal with money and complete the features that discriminate them from the examples already on the grid. Obviously this exercise is especially useful if you are teaching a unit that requires students to understand the distinction between various related concepts. Our example might be used in a unit on business. Some teachers keep such a grid on chart paper on the wall and allow students to add to it as they develop their understanding. Pittelman, Heimlich, Berglund, and French (1991) provide many examples of how semantic feature analysis can be used in the classroom in all the content areas.

A common semantic feature analysis in primary-grade classrooms is on pets. Students complete the grid for the various pets that are owned by members of the class. In doing so, they learn the distinguishing features of the animals. An example is shown in Table 5.2.

Possible Sentences.   Children love to play nonsense games. The strategy of **possible sentences** capitalizes on that motivation by asking them to decide whether a sentence is possible or not.

> The *staunchly* built house collapsed in a storm.
>
> The *treasurer* gave a report to the board meeting.
>
> The *canary* breathed slowly through its gills.

Asking students to say whether sentences such as these are possible focuses them on discriminating features of a new word. To construct such sentences, the teacher must choose some feature of the new word to highlight, a feature that may show how one concept in a category is different from another. The sentence about the canary is an example. Alternatively, a sentence may require students to remember a particular feature, such as *strength* being a part of *staunchness.* The sentences can be as ridiculous or as sophisticated as the teacher wishes—from "The *dog* flew to the moon" to "The runner *devoured* the miles." Beck and McKeown (1983) report using this technique

---

Arrange these words from the coldest to the hottest: *cool, hot, lukewarm, boiling, freezing, tepid, chilled, warm*

HOTTEST

_____

_____

_____

_____

_____

_____

_____

COLDEST

Figure 5.3 Semantic Gradient

with fourth graders. They used words from particular semantic categories, such as people, and asked "Could a *virtuoso* be a *rival?*" and "Could a *philanthropist* be a *miser?*" (p. 624). Students in this task must decide whether the features of the two words are mutually exclusive. Some teachers have had students develop their own "possible sentences" for other children to respond to. As with most vocabulary production activities, the ability to produce a "possible sentence" requires good understanding of the target word. Students enjoy the play aspect of the task and can produce some wonderful nonsense sentences.

A related activity was called "Yays and Boos" by Beck and McKeown (1983). Students were asked to respond "yay" or "boo" depending on how they felt about someone who could be called a word from the people category, for example *miser* and *virtuoso*. This activity could be extended to any group of words that had connotative meanings and that could elicit an affective response.

Strategies That Focus on Interconnected Concepts

Semantic Gradients. Teachers often focus students' attention on synonyms and antonyms in vocabulary instruction because it is easier to define some words, particularly adjectives and adverbs, in this way. For example, *little* is easily defined as *small* or *not big*. However, antonyms are not all of the same kind. Powell (1986) draws attention to the fact that *polar antonyms* are dichotomous (single/married), whereas *scalar antonyms* allow for gradations (hot, warm, tepid, cool, cold). Teachers who are dealing with terms that fall into this latter category may want to have the students develop semantic gradients.

A semantic gradient allows students to make connections between known words and new vocabulary. Asking children to arrange the words in Figure 5.3 in a **semantic gradient** allows them to see the relations between them in a graphic form.

As students arrange the words in the list, they can discuss and justify their ordering. They can also expand their list to include other words related to temperature (e.g., *steamy, scorching, raw, balmy,* and *glacial*). What they will discover is that some of the words generated apply only in particular instances. For example, a day can be *balmy,* but a dinner cannot. This type of distinction can lead to activities that focus on discriminating features (see the previous section).

Older students might apply semantic gradients in relation to characters in novels along dimensions such as *courage/cowardice* or *pride/humility.* Social studies students could explore terms on a scale of *democracy/dictatorship* or *wealth/poverty.* While semantic gradients clarify the distinctions between scalar antonyms and close synonyms, they cannot be applied to all related concepts. A freer form of showing relationships may be required.

Maps.   Mapping of words is now a common activity in many classrooms. A **map** can be any form of graphic representation that shows the relationships among and between words or concepts. Students may engage in mapping for a variety of purposes, such as organizing information after reading a selection from a text. This section deals primarily with mapping to show relations between words. Three main ways of using maps will be explored: for brainstorming, for showing semantic relationships and associations, and for showing structured relationships.

Brainstorming Maps.   A brainstorming map is a good way to get students to think about the extent of a new important concept. For example, at the beginning of a new unit on cities, a teacher asked a fifth-grade class to develop maps about the topic. In groups, the students thought about things that they saw in their city and that they knew about cities. They developed subcategories of things they thought were important and brainstormed lists around those subcategories. One group produced the map shown in Figure 5.4.

As can be seen, a brainstorming map can have a variety of subcategories that may not be of equal importance. Since the aim of the activity is to have students think about vocabulary and concepts they know in relation to a topic, the interconnections are not important at this stage. A teacher may choose to do one large brainstorming map for the whole class.

Once students have shared their maps, the teacher will help the class to develop more structured subcategories from the information they generated. The new organizational map for the cities is shown in Figure 5.5. This map is not meant to be a complete representation of the concept of cities, but to impose a better organization on the information that the students have provided. Where certain superordinate concepts were not part of the originals, the teacher may provide them, for example *performing arts.* This map can then form the basis for the class's work on cities. New subcategories can be added as needed, and students can put information that they learn in each category. Some teachers use a large map on paper on a wall for students to write on. Some would like students to make an individual copy of the map. Some teachers prefer to begin with a more structured map.

Semantic Maps.   Often the term **semantic map** is used broadly for any graphic that draws attention to the relationship between words. However, we are going to use the term for a map in which:

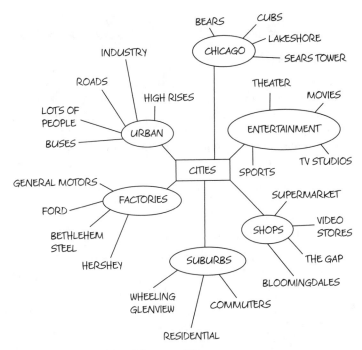

Figure 5.4 A Brainstorming Map on Cities

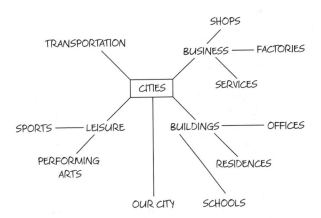

Figure 5.5 More Organized Class Map for Cities

Teaching Idea File 5.3

Developing a Semantic Map

1. The teacher selects a keyword and target words.
2. The keyword is written at the center of the map; the target words are listed at the side.
3. Students generate words related to the keyword and target words.
4. Relationships between the keyword, target words, and student words are discussed.
5. The map is constructed (or copies of an incomplete map are handed out for completion).
6. The students add to the map or maps as they read or work on the topic.

From Blachowicz & Fisher, *Teaching Vocabulary in All Classrooms*, p. 92.

1. A major theme or concept is at the center of the map.

2. Other important ideas, concepts, and terms are highlighted in some way (boxes, circles, colors).

3. Lines are used to connect related ideas.

4. The farther from the center of the map, the more specific the information.

5. The interrelated concepts are not hierarchically ordered (see the section on structured overviews).

The difference between a semantic map and a brainstorming map, for us, is that in the former the teacher determines the major vocabulary terms and concepts that will appear, while the students generate examples. Often a copy of an incomplete map is handed to the students to fill out. Otherwise, the procedures are similar to those outlined here (see Teaching Idea File 5.3).

While a semantic map addresses the relationships between words, it allows students to generate new information based on their reading and learning. In this way, it expands their understanding of central concepts in the content areas. An example of a map for population growth is shown in Figure 5.6.

Structured Overviews.   Structured overviews work best when the teacher is presenting concepts that are directly related through subordination and superordination. They work well in relation to the concepts presented in a text, but should not be limited to this. The basic pattern is presented in Figure 5.7, but variations can occur. The two advantages of **structured overviews** are that they present a graphical representation of the whole domain under study and that they show hierarchical relationships among the concepts.

As with other maps, structured overviews may be presented only partly completed (as in the math example in Figure 5.7). Students are required to fill in the missing terms after reading or learning in other ways. The advantage of a structured overview is that it presents information in a way that formalizes the hierarchical relationships between concepts. The graphic form allows students to examine these relationships in a way that no other format can.

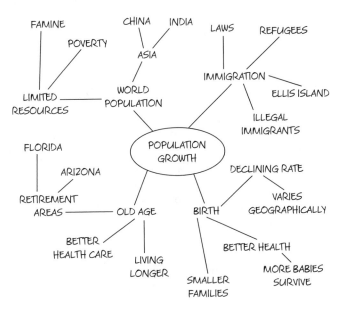

Figure 5.6   Semantic Map on Population Growth

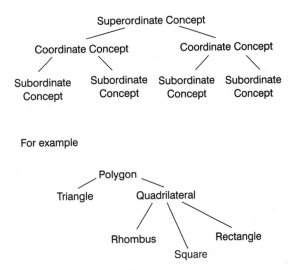

Figure 5.7   The Relationships in a Structured Overview

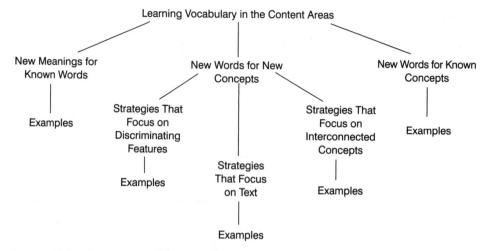

Figure 5.8   A Structured Overview of This Chapter

Strategies That Focus on Textbooks

A structured overview can also be useful in showing the organization of the content of a chapter of a textbook, and many publishers of content area texts use them for such a purpose. The overview in Figure 5.8 shows the organization of this chapter.

This section addresses other strategies that can be used best in conjunction with texts.

Vocabulary Knowledge Rating.   Knowledge ratings (Blachowicz, 1986) emphasize to students that knowing the meaning of a word is not something that happens all at once. It demonstrates that word knowledge develops along a continuum, from not knowing anything about the word, to knowing something (features) of the meaning, to a rich understanding. We all differ in our understandings of words depending on our experience with them. (The authors acknowledge that their understanding of the concepts of "men" and "women" differ!) However, our knowledge of words does accrue over time, so that we know some words well, some vaguely, and many not at all. For **knowledge rating,** students are presented with a list of words and asked to rate their understanding of each (see Figure 5.9).

Once students have completed the rating sheet on their own, the teacher has them share their ideas about the words and leads a discussion that focuses on the particular words or features of words that she or he is interested in highlighting. In addition, the teacher can have students make predictions about the content of the chapter that will be read. In the example from Figure 5.9, the teacher might ask:

1.   What do you think the topic of this chapter will be?

2.   Are these all contemporary U.S. dwellings?

3.   Can you predict some of the things the author will tell about each of these dwellings? (such as location, characteristics, or occupants)

Rate your knowledge of these words.			
Word	Know Well	Seen/Heard It	Don't Know
apartment	✔		
villa		✔	
geodesic dome		✔	
tipi	✔		
trullo			✔
yurt			✔
high rise	✔		
lean-to		✔	

Figure 5.9   Knowledge Rating (Blachowicz, 1994).

Having read the text, students can then go back to their rating sheet and complete the ratings in a different color or with a different symbol. This rating makes students more aware of whether they know the important concepts in the text. Developing this metacognitive understanding is an extra advantage to using knowledge ratings.

Concept Guides.   **Concept guides** utilize specific information from texts to have students categorize information hierarchically. The steps in preparing and using a concept guide (adapted from Barron, 1969) are:

1. List the major concepts that you want students to learn from reading the chapter. These will be Part II of the guide (see Figure 5.10).

2. Reread the chapter and select statements that underlie the concepts you have chosen. These statements form the basis of Part I of the guide.

3. Write some distractors that look and sound like the text *but do not actually appear.* Mix these with the statements from the text to form Part I of the guide.

4. Have students complete the guide while reading by:

   a. Indicating which statements actually appeared in the chapter

   b. Categorizing the statements from Part I under the major concepts that appear in Part II

5. Provide students with feedback. This should preferably be in the form of discussion.

An example of a concept guide is shown in Figure 5.10.

The purpose of using a concept guide is to help students read and understand the text effectively. Other types of guides do a similar job.

I. Write true (T) or false (F) for each of the following statements. Some may be statements which the author made, some may be paraphrases of what the author said, and some are made up.

_____ 1. Proteins are nutrients.
_____ 2. Carbohydrates are nutrients.
_____ 3. Starch is a nutrient.
_____ 4. Sugars are proteins.
_____ 5. Molecules are easy to see if you look closely at a plate of food.
_____ 6. Molecules are always in motion.
_____ 7. Food digested by your body must eventually get to all your cells.
_____ 8. Digestion begins in your mouth.
_____ 9. Enzymes slow down digestion.
_____10. There are enzymes in your saliva.
_____11. Food remains in your stomach for several hours.
_____12. Saliva is made in the small intestine.
_____13. Food goes through the large intestine before reaching the small intestine.
_____14. Villi are on the inner and outer surfaces of the intestine.
_____15. No digestion takes place in the large intestine.

II. Fill in the blanks. After reading the complete list, put the correct word in each blank.

digestion   digestive system   nutrients
diffusion   pylorus   large intestine
small intestine   molecules   enzymes

1. _____ explains how molecules move into or out of cells.
2. _____ is when large food molecules are broken into smaller ones.
3. A _____ makes digested food available to the bloodstream.
4. The _____ is a sphincter that opens to let food into the stomach.
5. The _____ absorbs water from undigested food.
6. _____ are substances in food that are used by our cells to keep us alive.
7. Some special _____ used in digestion to break down food are called _____.
8. The _____ is where food molecules diffuse into the bloodstream.

III. Take each **correct** statement in Section I and place it in one of the following categories.

1. Substances Found in Food
2. How Food Gets Into Cells
3. Digestive Systems of Large Organisms

Figure 5.10   Concept Guide for Seventh-Grade Life Science on Digestion

Analogical Study Guides.   An **analogical study guide** works by comparing new concepts and ideas to some with which students are already familiar. The teacher prepares a guide that draws analogies for the major concepts that students will encounter in the text (Bean, Singer, & Cowen, 1985). An example for teaching cell structure is shown in Table 5.3.

Table 5.3   Analogical Study Guide

Structure	Main Functions	Analogy (comparing a cell to a factory)
cell wall	support, protection	factory walls
cell membrane	boundary, gatekeeper	security guards
cytoplasm	site of most metabolism	the work area
centrioles	cell reproduction	?
chloroplasts	photosynthesis	snack bar
endoplasmic reticulum	intracellular transport	conveyer belts
Golgi bodies	storage secretion	packaging—storage and shipping
lysosomes	intracellular digestion	clean-up crew
microfilaments	movement	?
nucleus	control, heredity	boss's office, copy machine
ribosomes	protein synthesis	assembly line
vacuoles	storage	warehouses

Note. Reprinted with the permission of Simon & Schuster, Inc., from the Merrill/Prentice Hall text *Content Area Reading and Learning* by D. Lapp, J. Flood, and N. Farnan. Copyright © 1989 by Prentice Hall, Inc.

The advantage of using analogies in this way is that it helps clarify very difficult concepts. However, the difficulty of developing appropriate analogies means that constructing such a guide may be appropriate only for concepts that students have problems learning.

Vocabulary Overview Guides.   **Vocabulary overview guides,** suggested by Carr (1985), teach students to monitor their own understanding of vocabulary as they read texts. These guides are particularly useful for older students. A vocabulary overview guide is a self-monitoring checklist that uses a 10-step procedure. Students are required to select the words that they think are important, find definitions for them, and then study and learn them. These are the steps for the students as outlined by Carr (1985):

Defining the Vocabulary Through the Use of Context

1. Survey/look over the material (title, headings) to see what it is about.

2. Skim the materials to identify unknown vocabulary words and underline them.

3. Try to figure out the meaning of the words from the context of the sentences around it. Ask someone or use a dictionary to check the meaning.

4. Write the definition in the text (use pencil) or on paper so that it will be available when you read the text.

5. Read the passage with the defined vocabulary to ensure comprehension.

Completing the Vocabulary Overview Guide

6. Fill in your Vocabulary Overview Guide. Write:

   (a) the title of the passage,

   (b) the category titles—decide on the categories you need by asking yourself the topics the vocabulary described or discussed,

   (c) the vocabulary word,

   (d) the definition underneath the vocabulary word (you can use synonyms here—make sure you leave room to add a few more synonyms as your vocabulary increases),

   (e) a clue to help you connect the meaning to something you know or have experienced.

Studying the Vocabulary

7. Read the title and categories to activate background knowledge and recall words associated with each aspect of the text.

8. When you study the word in each category, cover the clue and the word meaning—uncover the clue if necessary. If the clue doesn't jog your memory, then uncover the meaning.

9. Review your words frequently (each day) until you know them well. Review them once a week or periodically as you learn more words.

10. Add synonyms to old vocabulary words as you learn them—in this way you will connect the old with the new words and that will help you remember them. (p. 686)

An example of a completed vocabulary overview guide is shown in Figure 5.11.

The metacognitive aspect of these guides is an advantage for older, less able students. It gives them a basis for studying that the other guides use implicitly, but do not make explicit for them.

Teaching the Use of Aids in the Book. Many students fail to use the aids provided by book publishers and authors to learn new vocabulary. Our experience in working with older students suggests that they fail to use even the most obvious clues that information is important. We recommend teaching such students why books have the following features:

1. *The use of boldface type and italics.* Some students fail to pay special attention to text that is highlighted in this way. They read the words at the same speed and assign the same amount of attention as for regular text.

2. *Glossaries.* Although most students know about glossaries, some consistently fail to use them, partly because of the poor information sometimes provided.

3. *Pronunciation guides.* Few students use pronunciation guides effectively, and yet we are constantly amazed by students who say, "Oh, I know that word" when *we* pronounce it for them.

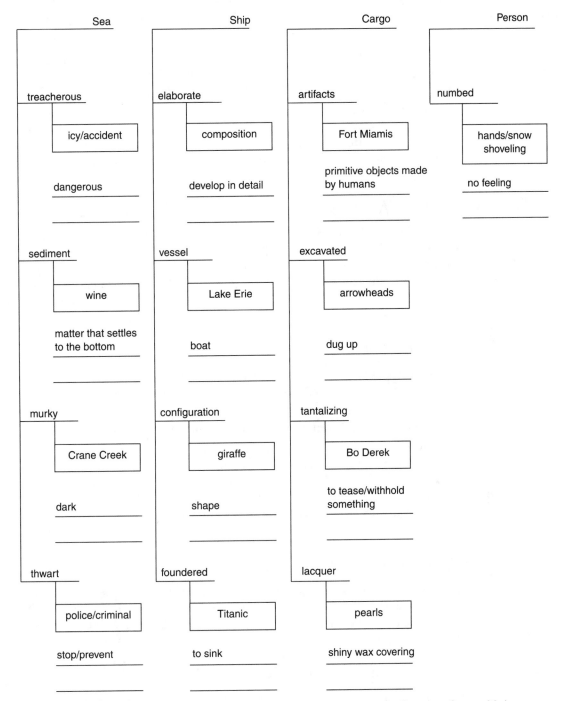

Figure 5.11 Sample of Vocabulary Overview Guide: A Fourteenth-Century Cargo Makes Port at Last

Note. From "The Vocabulary Overview Guide: A Metacognitive Strategy to Improve Vocabulary Comprehension and Retention" by E. M. Carr, 1985, *Journal of Reading, 28,* 688. Reprinted by permission.

4. *Words defined contextually.* Content area texts are one of the few places where words are often defined contextually (as in "Pollution, the soiling of the air and water, is an increasing threat to wildlife in the Gulf region").

5. *End-of-unit exercises.* Many students do not look at these exercises until *after* they read the chapter or unit. (We even know graduate students who admit to this!) Teaching that these exercises provide evidence of what concepts are important is not the same as teaching to the test.

TEACHING NEW WORDS FOR KNOWN CONCEPTS

The easiest words to teach are those for which students already have the concepts. In the example at the beginning of the chapter, Cathy already knew what marriage was, so learning the word *matrimony* was merely learning to apply another label. Not many words in the content areas are like this. If they were, we would not be teaching students very much. When we teach such words, therefore, we can focus on strategies that encourage students to remember.

Keyword Method

The **keyword method** uses imagery to help students remember the meanings of words (see Chapter 8 for a fuller explanation). The strategy operates in two stages:

1. Choose a part of the keyword to be learned that is recognizable or that sounds similar to part of that word. For example, for *stereotype* choose the word *stereo.*

2. Link the keyword to the definition of the target word with an image. In this instance, make an image of a stereotypical pop singer playing a stereo tape deck. The student who knows the concept of a stereotype will now be helped to remember the new word for that concept. This technique can be particularly helpful with ESL students, who have to learn many new words for concepts that they already possess.

Word Substitution and Matching Exercises

One of the easiest ways to review new words for familiar concepts is with exercises that require students to match meanings to words or to substitute the new words in sentences that contain synonyms. Games can be particularly effective and will be addressed in Chapter 10.

Looking Back and Looking Ahead

One of the major tasks of content area teachers is to introduce students to the vocabulary of their discipline. This chapter has outlined how different techniques may be appropriate for different types of words, depending on the students' existing knowledge. This existing knowledge must be connected to the new knowledge for effective learning to occur. Textbooks play a dominant role in learning in most of the content areas. This is not necessarily to be decried. While many teachers complain that students don't understand what they are assigned to read, if they did so immediately, what would the role of the teacher be? But students may sometimes have to learn words without a teacher's help. The next chapter explores ways to familiarize students with dictionaries and other aids to word learning.

For Further Learning

Ogle, D. (1986). K-W-L: A teaching model that develops active reading of expository text. *The Reading Teacher, 39,* 564–570. (Explains in detail how to do a K-W-L)

Pittelman, S. D., Heimlich, J. E., Berglund, R. L., & French, M. P. (1991). *Semantic feature analysis: Classroom applications.* Newark, DE: International Reading Association. (Explains the use of semantic feature analysis, with many different examples at various grade levels)

Searls, E. F., & Klesius, J. P. (1984). 99 multiple meaning words for primary students and ways to teach them. *Reading Psychology, 5,* 55–63. (Includes a useful list of words)

www.wordsmith.org/awad

A.Word.A.Day (AWAD) is the name of this website, and it's quite simple. Visitors can subscribe to this so that they receive a word each day via e-mail, and they can go through AWAD archives to find interesting words. Most words are difficult, but they offer students a chance to analyze the parts of words in guessing their meaning. For each word there is an explanation of its origin, a definition, a pronunciation guide, and a quote or two using the word. Each week of words has a theme, such as words of German origin or words related to Halloween. There is also a discussion board, which we believe, is of little value.

CHAPTER 6

USING DICTIONARIES AND OTHER REFERENCES

✓ **Prepare Yourself**

Prepare yourself by evaluating your own knowledge. Rate your ability to answer some of the key questions for this chapter. Check the boxes that describe your pre-reading knowledge.

Key concept questions	Well informed	Aware	Need ideas
1. What is *a good definition* and why is knowing how to define words important?	❑	❑	❑
2. What *different types of dictionaries* are available?	❑	❑	❑
3. How can students be taught the various *steps of using dictionaries effectively?*	❑	❑	❑
4. What *other resources* for learning word meanings should students know?	❑	❑	❑

☑ Strategy Overview Guide

This chapter presents background, ideas, and strategies to help you understand the nature of defining and definitions and to understand why dictionaries are as they are. While knowing the meaning of a word does not necessitate being able to define it, a concept of definition is a useful scaffold for metacognition about when we "know" a word. We suggest some methods of teaching students how to use dictionaries, and we outline some ways of familiarizing students with other reference sources for word learning. The following chart can help you choose suitable instructional strategies for your classroom.

Instructional strategy	Goal—use when you want to . . .	Comments
Concept of definition (p. 116)	Have students develop an understanding of what it means to know the definition of a word.	Can be taught in one or two weeks.
Word map (p. 118)	Have students demonstrate full knowledge of certain word meanings.	Useful when certain word meanings are important; easily fits on an index card.
Concept ladder (p. 119)	Help students understand the structural relations in definitions.	Good whole-class activity.
Piquing students' interest (p. 124)	Have students learn parts of a dictionary entry.	Fun activity.
Dictionary game (p. 124)	Have students learn how dictionary definitions function.	Fun activity.
Class dictionary (p. 125)	Have students learn parts of a dictionary entry.	Needs to be used a long time to be effective.
PAVE (p. 126)	Have students practice context and dictionary use.	Best done in small groups.

"A queen is a ruler, like Nancy Raygun."

This was the response when we asked Sara, a fourth-grade student, to define some familiar words (Blachowicz & Fisher, 1989). Children in school are used to playing the "defining game." However, teachers rarely teach them the structure for a good definition. Sara was quite good at defining. In this instance, she gave us a category for the word *ruler* and a charming example. While we may question the connection between a President's wife and a queen of England, Sara was able to demonstrate a good understanding of the word through her definition.

Teachers are often frustrated when they ask students to use dictionaries to demonstrate that they have learned word meanings. Commonly students will be asked to write a definition and then to use the word in a sentence. The definition is copied from a dictionary, for example, "A queen is the wife of a king." The sentence that the student generates is then often generic, for example, "Ann was a queen." Did this student have a good knowledge of English history, or was he just connecting a female name to the term? Did he really learn much about the meaning of the word *queen*? He certainly chose among definitions—he could have chosen from six definitions, including "A female ruler" or "A reproducing female in a colony of bees, ants, etc." We hope to show you that learning a definition is sometimes a good way to learn a word's meaning, that learning a concept of what a good definition is can help in the use of dictionaries, and that some ways of using dictionaries go beyond copying the definition and writing a sentence.

THE NATURE OF DEFINITIONS AND DEFINING

When a student or child asks you the meaning of a word in the course of a conversation, you are unlikely to come out with a full definition. Simon may ask "What's *charcoal?* Your typical response might be, "It's like a black stick and you draw with it" or "It's the black stuff we use to grill our hot dogs." Your response is unlikely to be, "It's a carbonaceous material you get when you heat wood in the absence of air, that is used for drawing, grilling, and producing iron." However, the nature of your response is governed by the context in which the question is asked. If Simon is in school and searching for art materials, then the first response would be effective. If Simon is reading a book with you at home, then the second response might satisfy his curiosity. However, if Simon is writing a science paper, he may need a complete definition, like the third response. In general, we have argued that defining is an unnatural act (Blachowicz & Fisher, 1989). Adults don't often think of telling children word meanings in terms of traditional definitions, and usually such definitions are not the easiest way to convey a word's meaning. The meaning of an adjective or an adverb may be most easily provided with a synonym or an antonym, for example, *big* is *large* or *not small; loudly* is *not quietly*. Some nouns may be best learned by function (as in a *chair* is "something you sit on") and a verb by a description (as in to *jump* is "when you run and leave the ground with both feet") or by demonstration. We do *not* learn the majority of word meanings by hearing their definitions. So what is the role of a definition in learning word meanings?

While defining a word when asked its meaning may be an unnatural act, the ability to define words is an *intelligent* act. As we gradually refine our understandings of a word, we are learning the characteristics that differentiate that concept from another in the same category. As we learn the difference between a *couch* and a *bench*, for example, we learn that a *bench* is a piece of furniture that is normally hard, and narrow, with an upright back (if it has one at all), and is located in places where hard wear from the elements or the user might occur (such as in a park or a stadium). A *couch* is cushioned and comfortable, with an angled back and armrests, and is found in locations where relaxing is important (such as in a home). This ability to list the characteristics that separate a member of a category from other members is the ability to define what something is. It is also a demonstration of knowledge—the more concepts we can distinguish in this way, the more knowledgeable we are. This knowledge is also at the center of what teachers do as they encourage students to learn about a topic—they help students differentiate between concepts in a domain. For example, in science, students may learn to differentiate between clouds based on their appearance and the conditions that give rise to them.

It is important to recognize that we may learn a definition for a word and still not really understand it in terms of being able to use it appropriately. If I hear or read that the definition of *plausible* is "appearing true," I have learned something about the word (a synonym phrase), but I may not understand the meaning sufficiently to use the term in my writing or speaking. However, if I am able to *provide* a definition (without the use of a dictionary), then I probably know enough about the word to use it comfortably. Looking up a word in a dictionary is not, therefore, necessarily the *best* way to teach a word's meaning. Dictionaries are tools that help us learn meanings. The nature of the dictionary and the entries determine what, and how much, is learned about the word.

THE NATURE OF DICTIONARIES

A Brief History of Dictionaries

The first English dictionary was Robert Cawdrey's *A Table Alphabeticall,* published in 1604. It consisted of 2,500 words that were listed alphabetically and defined by other English words (Noyes, 1943). Balmuth (1984) traces the social, technical, and religious changes that led to dictionaries becoming important. It is interesting that the purposes of this first dictionary remain the purposes of most dictionaries today—understanding a word's meaning and knowing its spelling. Among Cawdrey's stated purposes were for his readers to "more easily and better understand many hard English words, which they shall hear or read in Scriptures, Sermons, or elsewhere . . . " and for them to know "the true orthography, that is, the true writing of many hard English words" (quoted in Balmuth, 1984).

In fact, the origin of dictionaries goes back even further. The Homeric Lexicon, compiled in the first century A.D., may have been the first known type of European dictionary. However, after A.D. 200 there were a number of interlingual listings of words (for readers and writers in one language to find words in a second language), with one of the languages usually being Latin, which was the language of scholarship and of the church. By the sixteenth century, a number of modern language interlingual dictionaries were appearing (Balmuth, 1984). Even before Cawdrey's dictionary, therefore, a reader was able to use a dictionary to find a translation from one language to another.

By the publication of Samuel Johnson's *A Dictionary of the English Language* in 1755, authors of dictionaries were drawing on each other's compilations and copying their formats. The role of the dictionary was to provide meaning, spelling, and pronunciation, and these functions were reflected in the components of the entries for the word. The components of an entry in a normal English dictionary have remained much the same, so that this is the role that dictionaries largely play today. The fact that this basic form has remained largely unchanged through the centuries suggests that dictionaries do effectively serve this purpose for most of us. However, other types of dictionaries are used for specific purposes, and students may find it helpful to know some of them as resources.

Types of Dictionaries

Teachers who would like to know more about dictionaries that are available should consult Kister (1992). His comparative guide includes annotations for all of the major types of English-language dictionaries, including a listing by grade level. He notes that four main categories of dictionaries are available for use by North Americans:

1. General English-language dictionaries. These are the type that are generally referred to in this chapter.

2. Special-purpose dictionaries and wordbooks that focus on specific aspects of the language (such as abbreviations, slang, and synonyms).

3. Subject dictionaries that include words about a specialized field (such as engineering) or a particular topic (such as dinosaurs).

4. Foreign-language dictionaries that can be used to translate words into or from English.

Kister deals with the first of these categories. For those who want a shorter and less comprehensive treatment, Karp and Corcoran (1991) provide information about 19 of the most common English-language dictionaries for school-age children. A list of dictionaries of the first three types, suitable for school-age students, can be found in Appendix A.

General English-Language Dictionaries. The largest type of general English-language dictionary is an unabridged dictionary (commonly 300,000 to 600,000 entries) that attempts to be comprehensive in its coverage of standard vocabulary, including derivatives and inflected forms. These dictionaries may be in more than one volume and often are set on dictionary stands in the library. For a teacher, they can be the final resort when a child comes across a word that does not appear in any of the classroom dictionaries. A dictionary such as this would even include the word *interlingual* (see above)!

College desk dictionaries are designed to be more convenient than unabridged versions. They contain fewer vocabulary words, usually between 130,000 and 200,000 entries. The limitations of space mean that each entry also contains less information than in an unabridged version, so that quotations, examples, usage notes, and other extensions of a definition are less common. However, for most adult use, and certainly for school use, a college desk dictionary is usually sufficient. It is a welcome addition to any classroom as "the big dictionary" where students can go to find a word that is not in the class dictionaries. Family and office desk dictionaries, which are usually abridged versions of college desk dictionaries (50,000 to 130,000 entries), generally suffer from having less information in each entry and also from less detailed definitions. This means that, for use with students, the elliptical style of the definitions can sometimes be confusing rather than helpful.

Pocket and paperback dictionaries have little to recommend them for school use other than portability. With fewer entries (commonly 20,000 to 75,000) and difficult-to-read typefaces, these books may not be the bargain they seem. They can be difficult to use because of the paucity of information about each word, including only rudimentary definitions. Teachers are advised not to include these dictionaries in the classroom, because their use may lead to difficulties in interpreting definitions and discourage students from using dictionaries in developing vocabulary.

Electronic dictionaries are also common. These will be discussed in the final section of this chapter.

Special-Purpose Dictionaries.   As the name suggests, **special-purpose dictionaries** are devoted to particular aspects of language that may be useful for a specific purpose. If, for example, you needed to know the meaning of a particular abbreviation, you can find it in an abbreviations dictionary. If you know a meaning that you want to find a word for, a reverse dictionary is just what you need. Four types of special-purpose dictionaries are especially useful in the classroom—a spelling dictionary, an antonym/synonym dictionary, a reverse dictionary, and a rhyming dictionary.

A **spelling dictionary** is organized by common misspelled words. For example, the words *fikal, fikel, fikil, fikol, fickal, fickel, fickil, fickle,* and *fickol* all appear as misspellings for *fickle*. Students decide how a word might be spelled *(fickil)* and look under that letter combination to find the correct spelling. Some spelling dictionaries have the misspelled words and the correctly spelled words in two different colors. This type of dictionary is often more useful to find a correct spelling than a regular English-language dictionary.

A good antonym/synonym dictionary is a godsend to a writing teacher. Writers often struggle to find a different word for the same action or emotion to avoid being repetitive in their writing. In this respect, an **antonym/synonym dictionary** is similar to a thesaurus (see the last section of this chapter), but the organization is alphabetic and good dictionaries of this type also include usage sentences. Students often think these dictionaries are convenient when "they just want to know the meaning" of a word and don't want to work their way through long entries including pronunciation guides, etymologies, and other information. We have found that they soon learn that many words aren't in these dictionaries, and that they can better use their time by consulting a class dictionary in the first place.

A **reverse dictionary** is useful if a student is struggling to find a word that has a particular meaning. You may have had this experience—when you know there is a word but you can't quite remember it. For example, you know that there is a word that means when two things *cut across* each other. A reverse dictionary has an entry that tells you the word you want is *intersect.* Sometimes an antonym/synonym dictionary can fulfill the same function.

A **rhyming dictionary** is especially useful when students are writing poetry that they want to rhyme, or when a teacher is looking for words for word study activities! These dictionaries usually list words by the final phoneme, such as *-ead* or *-ay.*

Subject Dictionaries.   When students become involved in a topic or a subject, they can discover how much fun such dictionaries are. **Subject dictionaries** are devoted to a specific topic, such as sports and games, special days of the year, quotations, classical mythology, or to a specific subject area, such as geography, music, or mathematics. The nature and complexity of the entries vary according to the age group at which the dictionary is aimed and the subject matter. We have found *A Dictionary of Days* (Dunkling, 1988) to be great fun for teachers in the primary grades. Each day of the year can be some special day, and who could resist Fat Tuesday?

Foreign-Language Dictionaries.   These dictionaries are similar to antonym/synonym dictionaries in that they provide readers with a synonym for a word, but in a foreign language. Students whose native language is not English may find that the provision of such a dictionary in the classroom is a valuable aid to their learning (see also Chapter 9).

UNDERSTANDING HOW TO USE A DICTIONARY

General English dictionaries can be used to find a word's meanings, its spelling, or its pronunciation. We will mainly be concerned with the first of these three. Scholfield (1982) makes an analogy between a reader not being able to comprehend a passage because of misunderstanding a word and a mechanic faced with the breakdown of a machine because of a faulty part. He suggests that a mechanic has to determine the part that needs to be replaced, locate the appropriate section of the store, select the right part from a range of options, and then install that part effectively in the machine so that it works. Similarly, a reader has to know that comprehension has broken down because a word has been misunderstood or is not known, locate the word in a dictionary, select an appropriate meaning from a series of meanings, and apply that meaning so that the passage can be understood. Scholfield actually enumerates seven steps in the process of using a dictionary effectively, but we prefer to think of there being just five:

1.   Knowing when to use a dictionary (knowing that you don't know the meaning of a word)

2.   Knowing how to locate a word

3.   Knowing the parts of a dictionary entry

4.   Choosing between multiple meanings

5.   Applying the meaning

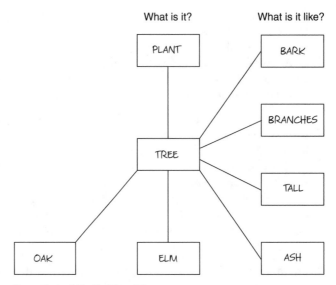

Figure 6.1 Concept of Definition Map

Note: Adapted from Schwartz & Raphael (1985).

Dictionary instruction in schools has not normally included the first of these steps, and instructional materials have emphasized the middle three (Fisher, Kent, & Blachowicz, 1990). However, the conditional knowledge needed to know when it is appropriate to use a dictionary may be one of the most important things we can teach students in relation to vocabulary instruction.

Knowing When to Use a Dictionary

One of the problems that teachers often notice when teaching reading is that students are not certain when they don't know the meaning of a word. To help them develop a clear idea of what "knowing" a word means, we can teach them a **concept of definition**. Students can then compare what they know about a word with what they need to know to determine if they need to use a dictionary.

Concept of Definition.   In teaching a concept of definition, it is most appropriate to use a graphic, similar to a semantic web (Schwartz & Raphael, 1985). Figure 6.1 shows a concept of definition map (sometimes called a word web). The map follows the form of a traditional definition in that it contains the category to which the word belongs, the defining characteristics, and some examples. For younger children, as in this example, the category "What is it?" and the defining characteristics become "What is it like?"

The example in Figure 6.1 demonstrates the various components of a good definition. A *tree* belongs to the category of plants. Some of its differentiating features are that it has *bark* and *branches,* and is *tall.* Notice how these features distinguish it from, say, a tulip. When working with students, it is important to demonstrate that all items that might describe a word may not show how it is different from other words in that category. For example, that a tree has *green leaves* is not a distinguishing feature, nor is the fact that it has *roots*.

The way in which you introduce a concept of definition map to the students will depend on the age of the students and the function you want it to perform. Schwartz and Raphael (1985) outline a four-day program for use with fourth-grade students in relation to using sentence contexts to determine word meaning. As part of instruction about when to use a dictionary, the following sequence might be followed:

1. Introduce a concept of definition map on an overhead projector, using a word that is very familiar to students. Do several examples as a class, using gradually less and less familiar words.

2. Have students complete some maps on their own for familiar words. Share examples with the class. Use their examples for teaching points about the nature of categories and defining characteristics.

3. Model for students how to use the map to write a definition. Have students use maps to write definitions for familiar terms.

4. Model for students how knowing the parts of a definition helps you to "know when you know" the meaning of a word. Use examples from their recent reading.

5. Model with a particular passage how to "know when you know."

6. Have the whole class read a passage with some difficult vocabulary. Have students decide as a group which of the difficult words they "know they don't know."

7. Model how to use a dictionary to complete parts of word maps for the difficult words. Demonstrate that a complete map is not always necessary for comprehension.

8. Have students work in groups to repeat steps 6 and 7.

Steps 1 through 4 are self-explanatory. The following example might clarify steps 5 through 7. The passage that students read is:

> Mastodons are animals that lived thousands of years ago. We have learned about this prehistoric relative of the elephant through **fossil** bones and teeth found all over the world. Some experts believe that mastodons were once as common as buffalo in the western **plains** of the United States. Mastodons lived at the end of the ice age, when **glaciers** were retreating north, leaving many lakes and **bogs** among hills of crushed rocks, sand, and soil. These swamps and bogs were excellent places for mastodons to find the **evergreens** that they fed on, but they were also death traps. The heavy **clay** in soft-bottomed pits clung to them and prevented them from climbing the sometimes steep sides. The trapped mastodons became the fossilized bones that have enabled us to learn about them.

The teacher might read this passage, stopping at each of the boldfaced words and asking, "Do I know the category to which this concept belongs? Do I know some distinguishing characteristics? Do I know some examples?" Some of the words (for example, *plains* and *clay*) can be used to model that enough is known to comprehend the passage. Others (such as *fossils* and *glaciers*) might be used to model that more information is needed and how to use a dictionary to complete more of the definition map.

Using a concept of definition map can also help students recognize when an unfamiliar meaning is being used for a word. They may, for example, read the following.

> One day at school, Jimmy Soames called me a rude name in math. He had been pestering me for weeks. I was so mad that I threw a metal **compass** at him. Fortunately, I missed, but the point stuck in the bulletin board. Before I could pull it out, Mrs. Avery saw it. She advanced toward me with a look that seemed to threaten my future well-being.

Some students may not immediately recognize that the word *compass* here is not the sort of compass that tells you where north is. However, two pieces of evidence reveal that it must be something else—the fact that it had a point that stuck in the bulletin board and the fact that the lesson was math. These two clues give sufficient information about the word, that even if students have not used or seen a compass like this, they can recognize that it belongs to the category of things used in math, and that one characteristic is that it has a sharp point. Fluent readers and good comprehenders may recognize these components without their being made explicit. Poorer readers, however, can be taught (using a similar process to that just outlined) how "knowing when you know" can help them decide when other resources, such as dictionaries, need to be used.

There are several difficulties with the use of a concept of definition map as an aid to word learning. First, it takes some time to fill out. When time is a constraining factor, as it often is in vocabulary instruction, completing such maps for every unknown word is impractical and probably not very useful. Second, concept of definition maps work best with nouns. Adjectives and adverbs can often be more easily defined by synonyms or antonyms. For example, finding a category for the word *angry* can be difficult for younger students. Older students are more likely to misidentify it as an emotion (using the noun *anger*) than as an emotional state, although this does not adversely affect their understanding. Verbs also may sometimes be problematic in this regard. For example, what category does *jump* belong to? Older students may identify it as a verb of motion, but for younger students, asking for a category can be more confusing than helpful. Consequently, some teachers prefer a word map that has more flexibility, like that shown in Figure 6.2.

Word Map.   The components of the word map for *angry* are a synonym, an antonym, an example, and a nonexample. The synonym and antonym work well for most non-nouns. Students must think about some distinguishing features of the word to provide an example and a nonexample. In Figure 6.2, the student chose to give a nonexample that exemplified the antonym.

As compared with a concept of definition map, this word map is simpler to complete, does not take as much time, and is more flexible in some ways. It has elements

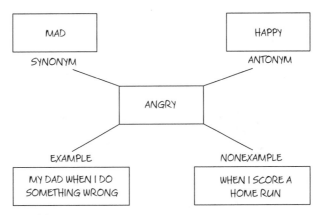

Figure 6.2   Word Map

of the Frayer model described in Chapter 5. Difficulties can arise with nouns. For instance, in our earlier example of *tree,* finding a true synonym and antonym is problematic. Occasionally there may be excellent synonyms but only approximate antonyms. For example, for *jump,* a synonym would be *leap,* but students tend to choose words such as *sit* or *walk* as antonyms. Since both these still demonstrate understanding of the word, you can see that complete accuracy is often not important. This type of word map can also be used (in a way similar to that just outlined) to teach a student how to "know when they know" the meaning of a word.

Concept Ladder.   A final graphic that is useful in teaching students when they know the meaning of a word is a **concept ladder.** This graphic can also be an effective teaching tool for more complex vocabulary, especially in the content areas. Albert Upton, a semanticist, has suggested (1973) that people ask three questions in relation to determining exact meanings for concepts. They are:

1.   What is it a kind of/what are kinds of it?

2.   What is it a part of/what are parts of it?

3.   What is it a stage of/what are stages of it?

Gillet and Temple (1986) have added a fourth question:

4.   What is it a product or result of/what are the products or results of it?

From these questions, Gillet and Temple have devised a concept ladder such as that shown in Figure 6.3. This ladder has similarities to the concept of definition map in using categories, distinguishing features, and examples. The last part of the ladder allows students to recognize that extra information may be relevant to their understanding of a word.

We have found that the third and fourth questions regarding stages and products need to be supplemented with other possibilities, such as "functions of/functions of

Kind of?		
Political ideology		
Part of?		
Not relevant		
Product of?		
Political and economic turbulence and instability		
FASCISM		
Kinds of it?		
1. Neo-Fascism		
2. Germany under Hitler		
Parts of it?		
1. Nationalism		
2. Racism		
Product of it?		
1. Violence		
2. Hatred		
3. Holocaust		

Figure 6.3   Concept Ladder for the Word *Fascism*

Kind of?	Part of?	Function or made of?
Clothing	Winter outfit	Fur or wool
EARMUFF	**EARMUFF**	**EARMUFF**
Not relevant	Two ear covers; Connector	To keep ears warm
Kinds of it?	Parts of it?	Functions of it?

Possible Answers: fur or wool, clothing, connector, winter outfit, to keep ears warm, two ear covers.

Figure 6.4   Concept Ladder for *earmuff*

it," for the ladder to be adaptable to many words. Older students are quite capable of understanding the necessity for changing the questions on the last part of the ladder.

One way to introduce the ladder is to use easy concepts and to provide students with possible answers, as with *earmuff* in Figure 6.4 (we have put the answers in for you). While the concept ladder is a useful device for teaching students how to know how much they know about a word, it can be equally effective for teaching important concepts in the content areas, especially when students complete the ladder as part of a group activity.

One of the hardest things to teach, but one of the most important, is metacognitive understanding of a breakdown in comprehension, either because of processing or because of a lack of word knowledge. No system is perfect. The concept of definition or other structured word maps can help make explicit an understanding about word knowledge that is implicit for many of us.

Knowing How to Locate a Word

Children learn the order of the letters in the alphabet quite early in their school career. This is a prerequisite skill for locating a word in a dictionary, but sometimes a dictionary activity can be used to reinforce it. Even young children can learn how a dictionary uses the alphabet for organization of words by beginning sounds.

Making a Picture Dictionary. A **picture dictionary** is organized alphabetically, with pictures of words that begin with each letter. One way of having kindergarten and first-grade students learn alphabetical order, beginning letter sounds, and the organization of a dictionary is for them to construct their own picture dictionary. (This is similar to the suggestion in Chapter 4.) The basic idea is that students cut out pictures from magazines or other sources and stick them in a "book" under the appropriate letter and write the word underneath. Conversely, they may decide on a word that they want to include and draw (or find) a picture to go with it. Pupils can then use their dictionary as part of writing instruction to find words that they are having difficulty spelling.

The three following points should be borne in mind when having students construct these dictionaries:

1. Use a "book" that is easily expandable. Some sections under common letters get filled very quickly. The teacher cannot control the size of the pictures that the children select, so one child may have one picture per page whereas another has three or four pictures per page. A loose-leaf binder can be useful in this respect.

2. It is better to allow students to work in groups. That is, although they work on their own dictionary, they also work together and talk about it as they do so. Pupils who are having difficulty discriminating beginning sounds can then learn from their peers.

3. Decide whether correct spelling is important. If it is, the teacher or an aide needs to be available to spell the words. If developmental spelling is used in the classroom, then it may be enough that the students are learning about initial sounds and alphabetization. Alternatively, you may not require the students to write the words at all.

Teaching the Use of Guide Words. Once students have mastered alphabetization, they can be taught to use the guide words provided at the top of each double-page spread. Common exercises in workbooks on this topic include having students identify which of a group of pairs of "guide words" would indicate the location of a particular word. For example,

These students are using a picture dictionary.

If you were looking for the word *project,* which of the following guide words would tell you on what page to look?

- pass/patiently
- professional/pronghorn
- pulpwood/purpose
- pleasantly/plush

Exercises can be devised that require students to look to the third or fourth letter in order to make the decision. However, the use of such exercises is questionable. Blachowicz, Fisher, Wohlreich, and Guastafeste (1990) found that some fourth-grade students demonstrated some strange behaviors as a result of isolated exercises such as these. When interviewed as they went about finding a word, they suggested that they were able to use the guide words, but actually found it easier to look across the middle of a page for some general sense of what was on the page. They construed that moving their eyes down the page was somehow "wrong" or "cheating." Other research (Fisher, Kent, & Blachowicz, 1990) suggests that instruction in guide word use is often done with worksheet and alphabetizing tasks, rather than with real dictionary use. We recommend that the teaching of this comparatively simple task be done in relation to real dictionary use, perhaps as whole-class instruction, rather than as an artificial exercise that divorces the utility of the guide words from locating the entry for an actual word.

Knowing the Parts of a Dictionary Entry

Like many of us, you have probably had the experience of reading a dictionary entry and finding it less than helpful. Students often complain that they don't understand a definition, a difficulty that is related to the main constraint on dictionary compilers—lack of space. Brief definitions often require the use of difficult words or complex phrasing. It is important to understand how these difficulties occur so that we are able to help students more effectively.

McKeown (1990) has noted that traditional dictionary entries can be difficult to understand for young readers because of four factors:

1. *Weak differentiation.* This occurs when the distinguishing characteristics the entry writer chooses are insufficient to allow the reader to differentiate a word from other members of a category. For example, *brim* may be defined as "an edge or rim." The definition does not help the student differentiate what types of *edges* or *rims* might be called *brims*. Can a knife have a sharp brim?

2. *Vague language.* Vague wording of the definition has low explanatory power. For example, *gruff* may be defined as "deep and rough-sounding." The wording of the definition gives poor clues as to the possible nouns that *gruff* may qualify. Can a piano be gruff?

3. *Likely interpretation.* Some definitions convey an unintended sense of the words used that is likely to be more familiar. For example, *perform* may be defined as "to carry out; do." A student may focus on the normal meaning of carry and think that the definition has to do with carrying an object.

4. *Disjointed definitions.* Definitions may give multiple pieces of information but not provide a good sense of how to integrate them. For example, *running mate* may be defined as "a person who is a candidate for office from the same political party as another. A running mate is a candidate for the less important of two offices. A Presidential candidate's running mate is the candidate for the office of Vice-President." The final sentence does give an example to elucidate the first two sentences, but it requires that a student know a lot about political offices and political parties.

When a teacher is aware of these problems related to the structure of definitions provided in a dictionary, she or he can provide instruction that can alleviate some of the problems.

Although one way of alleviating such problems might be to provide entries that children can understand more easily, Scott and Nagy (1990) have argued that students still tend to focus on fragments of the definitions that dictionaries provide. Blachowicz et al. (1990) have suggested that students approach entries with certain styles—either to search for a meaning that fits what they want to know, or to try to integrate information from the various entries, or to abstract their own understanding from the various entries.

To overcome these various obstacles to understanding, students need to be taught the nature of dictionary entries and methods for working their way through them to arrive at an adequate meaning for a word. They should learn flexible strategies for finding meaning, rather than step-by-step processes.

Teaching Idea File 6.1

Piquing Students' Interest

(Smith, 1983)

1. Students form groups of four or five members and choose a secretary to record their discoveries.
2. Each student has the same copy of a page of a dictionary.
3. Students are asked to focus on the entry for only one word. The word Smith uses is *pique.*
4. The teacher tells the number of pieces of information she found about the word. (Smith found 16 for *pique*—for example, how to pronounce it, several definitions, and the etymology.)
5. Students list all the information that the entry gives them about the word and anything they notice about the order of the information. They have 10 minutes.
6. Students share the information they found and compare it with that found by the teacher.

From Blachowicz & Fisher, *Teaching Vocabulary in All Classrooms,* p. 116.

Piquing Students' Interest.   Smith (1983) reports a strategy that she has used effectively for interesting students in dictionary study. It focuses on students working together to very carefully observe and analyze an entry for at least one word. The steps suggested by Smith are shown in Teaching Idea File 6.1.

Smith (1983) notes that students easily surpass her 16 pieces of information. They find other words with the same root (such as *piquant* and *piquet*) and learn about what is contained in dictionary entries. She argues that this strategy also engages students who say that they already know all about dictionaries.

The Dictionary Game.   Koeze (1990) uses a game to teach about dictionary entries and definitions. The focus of this game is having students predict which words will appear in a definition of another word. To be successful, students need to be familiar with the organization of their dictionary entries. The steps in the game are:

1. Students play in groups of two to five, sitting in a circle.
2. One person chooses a familiar word that all the students are likely to know, such as *knight.* Articles and prepositions are not allowed.
3. The student to the immediate left of the first student predicts a word that will appear in the definition of *knight,* such as *title* or *sir.* Play continues around the circle until everyone has selected a word. (Each word must be different.)
4. The last person to select a word is the person who chose *knight.* She looks up the definition in the dictionary and awards points to every player who made a correct prediction.
5. After each round, the dictionary is passed to the left and a new word is chosen.

Teaching Idea File 6.2

Making a Class Dictionary

1. Divide the class into homogeneous groups. Each group will be responsible for adding one word to the dictionary one day of the week (or whatever time period is feasible).
2. The group meets briefly to decide on a word each day that should be selected from classroom instruction. As far as possible, it is important that every student should have heard the word.
3. The group writes a definition and a pronunciation. They compare their definition and pronunciation with those in a dictionary and add the derivation if appropriate. Their entry is written on a card and copied on an overhead transparency.
4. The group presents the word and the entry to the class. The card is entered into the class dictionary.
5. After three or four weeks, individual students add words to the dictionary under the teacher's direction. Each student is responsible for one word a week (presentation to the whole class is omitted).
6. The dictionary is available to the class for reference purposes.

From Blachowicz & Fisher, *Teaching Vocabulary in All Classrooms*, p. 117.

Koeze points out that the game can be adapted for whole-class use by having the students write as many words as they can. Students can award points to each other by examining the dictionary together. It may be important to explain that, even though the students' words do not appear in one dictionary, their predictions or guesses are not necessarily poor. In fact, if they could find the word in another dictionary, that could also count.

This game would be an excellent reinforcement after having worked with students on the concept of definition map and having them write their own definitions. Writing full dictionary entries is also an excellent way of having students learn what to look for.

Making a Class Dictionary. The old adage that students learn by doing applies very well to understanding how a dictionary entry is written. Constructing a class dictionary for words with older students is an extension of making a picture dictionary with kindergartners and first graders. Making a word dictionary on an individual basis is similar to a vocabulary notebook (see Chapter 4). Making a class book is a better way for a teacher to control the quality of each entry.

As with any class activity, making a class dictionary can be done in a variety of ways. Whichever method is used, the teacher should try to ensure that the entries are comparable to the entries in the mainstream school dictionaries. In that sense, they should contain the word, a pronunciation, the meaning(s), and a derivation (where appropriate). One way of doing this after whole-class instruction on the parts of an entry is shown in Teaching Idea File 6.2.

Making a class dictionary can also lead to discussion about constructing better definitions. Students often take pride in the fact that their definition is more understandable than that in a normal dictionary. Since there are few space constraints, students *can* make the entry longer and more comprehensive.

Each dictionary will have its idiosyncracies. However, helping students find their way around entries is an important step in developing their effective use of dictionaries.

Choosing Between Multiple Meanings

When students use a dictionary to locate a word's meaning, they sometimes have difficulty choosing the appropriate meaning from among a series of meanings. This is especially the case when the task is not authentic. Familiarity with the parts of an entry will enable students to identify a variety of meanings when they are available, but they need to learn a cross-checking procedure to decide on the appropriate meaning. A **cross-checking procedure** is one in which the reader refers to the context in which the word has been heard or read and checks the possible meanings against that context. An example that requires students to adopt cross-checking is the PAVE procedure.

The PAVE Procedure. The **PAVE procedure** was developed to encourage students to cross-check a word's meaning with the context in which it appeared. It also encourages students to remember meanings by associating words and images and to read a dictionary entry with some expectations of an appropriate meaning (Bannon, Fisher, Pozzi, & Wessel, 1990). PAVE stands for components of the strategy—prediction, association, verification, and evaluation. The idea is that students predict a meaning from the context in which the word appears, verify it by consulting a dictionary, evaluate their prediction, and make an association of the word's meaning with an image. This is done using a template for the student to complete (see Figure 6.5).

The strategy itself consists of six stages:

1. Students write the sentence or context in which the word appears.
2. They write the word again (to emphasize the word on which they are focused) and predict a meaning.
3. They write a sentence of their own that demonstrates their understanding of the word.
4. They check the word's meaning in a dictionary and write its definition.
5. They examine the sentence from step 3 and write a better sentence if this one is inadequate.
6. They draw an image to help them remember the meaning of the word by creating an associative link.

Students report that while this method is time consuming, it helps them remember words better, and they enjoy using it (for limited periods). The best way to introduce the strategy is:

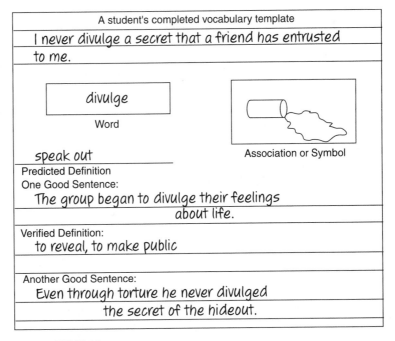

Figure 6.5   A PAVE Map

1. Use a template and an overhead projector to model the six steps with a simple word, emphasizing the cross-checking procedure as part of step 4.

2. Using a more difficult word, repeat steps 1 through 3. Students repeat steps 4 through 6 as a whole class.

3. The whole class does one word together on the overhead projector.

4. Each student does one word. Selected students share with the class.

5. The class works individually or in groups on several more items.

Observations of students working in groups show that excellent reasoning occurs during steps 2 through 5. During step 4, students help each other determine which is the best meaning among any alternatives offered. The strategy also appeals to non-traditional learners who generally find vocabulary learning difficult.

The PAVE procedure is effective in a number of settings. Figure 6.6 shows a template of a student's work while reading *Tom Sawyer*. This sixth-grade class was reading the book for homework, and the teacher was concerned about all the difficult vocabulary. She gave students some words in the context of the sentences from the book and the page numbers for each sentence. For homework, students completed the template as they came to each word that the teacher wanted them to know. The templates were handed in and graded as part of their study of that particular book.

31. The doctor murmured <u>inarticulately</u>. (69)

✓ *Very good, Angela !!*

inarticulately

Word

<u>unclearly</u>
Predicted Definition

Association or Symbol

Blah, Blah Blah Blah Blah !!!!!!!!!! Blah

One Good Sentence:
<u>The man was speaking inarticulately</u>
<u>so we couldn't understand.</u>

Verified Definition:
<u>not distinctly</u>

Another Good Sentence:

32. He picked up a clean pine <u>shingle</u> that lay in the moonlight. (72)

shingle

Word

<u>a tile</u>
Predicted Defintition

Association or Symbol

One Good Sentence:
<u>I have a lot of shingles</u>
<u>on the roof.</u>

Verified Definition:

Another Good Sentence:

Figure 6.6   A Completed PAVE Sheet for *Tom Sawyer*

Part of the effectiveness of the PAVE procedure is that it encourages students to cross-check meanings with the context in which the word is seen or heard. Some junior high and high school teachers have used the PAVE sheets with an activity they call "I Heard a Word." Students can sign up each day to present a word to the rest of the class (during homeroom or some other convenient time). They then use the chalkboard or an overhead projector to go through the following steps:

1. I heard a word and it was *culminated* in this sentence: "The match culminated in a brilliant final set."
2. I thought it meant "finished."
3. I found out it meant "reached its highest point."
4. The sentence I wrote is "The play culminated in a great final act."
5. The association I made is _____ .

All students in the class wrote these words in their vocabulary notebooks. Every student who presented a word received a point for doing so. Students could also receive points for using any of the words and bringing verification from other teachers or parents that they had done so. At the end of the marking period there was a quiz. The top eight students who accumulated the most points from the quiz and other sources engaged in a "play-off" vocabulary game and were awarded candy bar prizes for being in the first three. The teachers reported that students through freshmen in high school were enthusiastic participants!

While PAVE requires students to cross-check a meaning with a sentence context, the final part of effective dictionary use is to apply a meaning as part of connected discourse. In school, this most often means reading.

Applying the Meaning

If students have identified when they "know that they don't know" a word's meaning, located an entry in the dictionary, found their way around the entry, and chosen an appropriate meaning for the context, they still need to apply that meaning to their comprehension of the discourse in which they are engaged. As Scholfield (1982) points out, sometimes none of the meanings offered by the dictionary fits exactly in the sentence context, and a meaning needs to be abstracted or generalized from among the entries. This process is similar to that employed by some of the fourth graders in the study by Blachowicz et al. (1990). Often the most problematic words are parts of idioms, as in "He wouldn't give a *brass farthing* for a ride in the hot air balloon." Even if the dictionary supplies the meaning of *farthing* as "an old coin being one quarter of a penny," the somewhat antiquated English idiom of "not giving a brass farthing" needs to be inferred as meaning "not caring for something." One way of giving students practice in applying meanings is to include vocabulary study as part of literature circles (see Chapter 4). However, teachers should model how to apply meaning for students first, and this may best be done through think-alouds.

A teacher can think aloud as she models any process for learning. Let us assume that the teacher is reading the following text:

> Garth stood at the door of the room that was to be his home for the next year, and looked carefully around. Bright sunlight from the French windows on his left highlighted a small figure sitting motionless on one of the five beds. The boy, about Garth's age, sat hunched, staring into the middle distance. His clothes seemed *middle-of-the-road,* making Garth aware of the fur collar on his own woven jacket.

The teacher would begin by reading the passage aloud from an overhead projector or after supplying all the students with copies. When she came to the term *middle-of-the-road*, she might say:

> "I don't understand this expression, *middle-of-the-road*. It may mean that his clothes are shabby. I need to look this up in the dictionary. The entry says "avoiding extremes, as in politics, editorial policy, etc." Hmm. How can his clothes seem to avoid extremes? Perhaps the author means that they are not at the extreme in some other way. It says that Garth had a fur collar. That might mean that his clothes cost a lot. Perhaps *middle-of-the-road* in relation to the boy's clothes means that they did not cost a lot, but they weren't the cheapest kind either. So the author is asking us to recognize that while Garth is probably from a rich family, this boy is from a family that is neither rich nor poor, but somewhere in the middle."

After several think-alouds of this nature, students may be willing to demonstrate some think-alouds of their own, either in front of the whole class or in groups. Once this is modeled and practiced in situations where selected vocabulary can be highlighted, students will be able to practice applying their "dictionary skills" in the context of normal reading in the classroom.

USING DICTIONARIES IN THE CLASSROOM

So far in this chapter we have ignored a common use of dictionaries in classrooms—as a resource to find a correct spelling. We sympathize with students who cry, "If I knew how to spell it, I wouldn't need a dictionary." We understand that as a spelling tool, a dictionary is really useful only to good spellers. This is because they come to the task with some hypothesis about possible letter combinations. For example, if you are unsure if the word *symbol* is spelled with an *si*- or an *sy*- at the beginning, you can make an effective use of the dictionary because there are only two places you have to look. However, if you are uncertain about whether the word begins *si*-, *sy*-, *cy*-, *ci*-, or *ce*-, and has an *n* or an *m* as the third letter, there are 10 possible places for the entry to appear. This makes looking in the dictionary an overwhelming task. In other words, poor spellers, who usually have poor knowledge of possible letter sequences, are the students who are least likely to benefit from the traditional dictionary as a spelling tool.

Fortunately for poor spellers, there are very compact and comparatively cheap electronic dictionaries and spellers available today. These devices, which can actually be carried around more easily than a pocket dictionary, allow a student to enter possible spellings and have alternatives displayed on a small screen. The more expensive electronic dictionaries will also give a definition of the desired word. The accessibility to word knowledge provided by these electronic devices is a boon to students of all ages.

The second aspect of using dictionaries that we have said little about is the use of a pronunciation key. We were in a classroom recently where some third-grade students were looking up the word *character* in the dictionary. The sentence in which they encountered the word was, "He thought that James was of good character." We watched as students went through the first three entries under the word that talked about qualities and what a person really is. They kept cross-checking with the sentence, but it wasn't until one of them read the fourth entry that referred to a character in a book that someone said, "Oh, it means James is an okay guy." What had been the problem? They had been mispronouncing the word—as in *char*. However, none of the students thought to first examine the pronunciation guide. In our experience in watching students use dictionaries, the pronunciation guide is the last part of the entry they consult, if at all. Yet we have frequently noted occasions on which students would have recognized the meaning of the word if they had pronounced it correctly. When teaching the parts of a dictionary entry, therefore, it may be important for students to learn the notation used in the pronunciation guide. Making a class dictionary that includes a pronunciation guide, as suggested above, is an excellent way of encouraging the use of all parts of a dictionary entry.

For students to make effective use of dictionaries in the classroom, two other factors also need to be considered—location and levels. We feel it is important for dictionaries to be located in convenient places for students to be able to use them when they are needed as part of their normal schoolwork. We have been in many classrooms where the dictionaries are in a cupboard, on a high shelf, or with "those old textbooks that never get used" that seem to be a part of every classroom. The ideal is for every student to have a dictionary in or on the student's desk, but realistically we recognize that this is unlikely. However, having a variety of levels of dictionaries is possible and desirable.

We have suggested earlier that a college desk dictionary is useful as "the big dictionary" for students to consult in lower grades for unusual words. But the students themselves will have differing abilities and different needs. In a typical fourth-grade classroom, for example, students' reading and writing abilities will range from first to seventh grade. It is unrealistic to expect one level of dictionary to serve all of the students' needs in such a setting. Appendix A lists dictionaries at different levels that may be appropriate for your classroom.

Dictionaries are not the only resource for finding words that should be available for students' use. The next section suggests some other resources for word learning.

KNOWING OTHER RESOURCES FOR WORD LEARNING

A brief mention was made earlier in the chapter of thesauruses and electronic dictionaries. The function of a thesaurus is to provide a writer with alternative words for overused words. As such, it contains synonyms, antonyms, and usage sentences (much like an antonym/synonym dictionary) but will also normally contain related words. An entry in a junior thesaurus (Schiller & Jenkins, 1977) for *delicious* contains the words *luscious, delightful, delectable, delicate, appetizing, savory, tasty, palatable,* and *fragrant* and some antonyms. With each of these words is an explanation of how it is used and its relation to the target word. An example of a page from a thesaurus is shown in Figure 6.7. Not every thesaurus is as informative, but

honesty	*Honesty* is acting and speaking truthfully. It is the opposite of deceit and dishonesty. A person shows *honesty* by not stealing, stealing or lying. Salespersons appreciate your *honesty* if you tell them that they did not charge you enough for an item.
truthfulness	*Truthfulness* means being open with people and not trying to hide anything from them. It means always telling the truth. People are respected for *truthfulness* in their dealings with others.
sincerity	*Sincerity* also means honesty. It is saying what you really feel or doing something you really believe in. I promised in all *sincerity* to do my best.
honor	A person of *honor* is honest and fair. If someone is "held in *honor*," that person is greatly respected. To "uphold the *honor*" of something means to defend its name and good reputation. The basketball victory upheld the *honor* the team. You give a person your *word of honor* when you promise that you can be trusted to do something.
integrity	*Integrity* is a strong word for honesty. It means honesty and trustworthiness. A person of *integrity* can always be trusted to do what is right and just. That person would never try to deceive anyone or give someone a false impression

Figure 6.7 A Page from a Thesaurus

Note: From *In Other Words: A Junior Thesaurus* by Andrew Schiller and William A. Jenkins. Copyright © 1982, 1977, 1969 Scott Foresman and Company. Reprinted by permission of HarperCollins College Publishers.

the best ones give readers and writers extensive information about the word and words that are related in a particular domain. For students, this can be an opportunity for an exciting exploration through games and mapping activities. Some of the games in Chapter 10 are appropriate.

All the major dictionary publishers also make electronic dictionaries of varying sophistication and complexity. CD-ROM has allowed massive amounts of information to be stored easily, and no doubt by the time you read this, information available to us will be outdated by new technology. However, to date, the *Franklin Speller* has been a great success, selling over a million units. Some of the electronic dictionaries even pronounce words aloud, making phonetic symbols obsolete. Others allow users to compile glossaries of all the terms in that database relating to a special field, such as astronomy. As students increasingly use word processing to write, they have access to electronic thesauruses, spell-checking programs, and electronic dictionaries as part of the package. However, while the first two may be more convenient than paper versions, we believe that, like books in general, paper versions of dictionaries will be most convenient for a long time yet.

Looking Back and Looking Ahead

This chapter examined the nature of dictionaries and definitions and offered strategies for helping students to understand and effectively use dictionaries and other word resources. But how is a teacher to know if a student has learned new vocabulary? The next chapter looks at ways of assessing how well a student has learned word meanings.

For Further Learning

Grambs, D. (1994). *The endangered English dictionary: Bodacious words your dictionary forgot.* New York: W. W. Norton (A fun resource for wonderful words)

Kister, K. F. (1992). *Kister's best dictionaries for adults & young people: A comparative guide.* Phoenix, AZ: The Oryx Press. (The most comprehensive guide to dictionaries available)

Schwartz, R. M., & Raphael, T. E. (1985). Concept of definition: A key to improving students' vocabulary. *The Reading Teacher, 39,* 198–205. (Describes a program of instruction and research with concept of definition)

www.m-w.com

This is an excellent site from Merriam-Webster with an online dictionary, daily word game, and much, much more.

www.randomhouse.com/features/rhwebsters/game.html

The game on this website is called Beat the Dictionary, and it is basically a version of online hangman. Words appear to be moderately difficult but not uncommon, and this could probably be played over and over without reusing words. It would be nice if visitors could choose a level of difficulty. One other feature of this website is a link to "The Mavens' Word of the Day," which is basically like the A.Word.A.Day site but seems to have more common, simple words. Definitions are written in a longer, essay form that is fun to read but possibly less easy to use then the AWAD site. Like AWAD, past words of the day are archived for convenience. Unlike AWAD, visitors do not have a chance to subscribe to e-mail newsletters.

http://projects.ghostwheel.com/dictionary

Titled "The Exploding Dictionary," this simple website is actually quite useful. It consists of a gigantic database of the contents of a number of different dictionaries. When a visitor enters a search word, the site quickly sends back a number of different definitions, each of which seems to be complete and accurate and includes a citation of the source dictionary. Also helpful is a "technojargon" dictionary, something that teachers may need more than students, to define the ever-growing number of new words having to do with computers and the Internet. Again, results are returned quickly and seem accurate.

CHAPTER 7

ASSESSING VOCABULARY KNOWLEDGE

☑ Prepare Yourself

Prepare yourself by evaluating your own knowledge. Rate your ability to answer some of the key questions for this chapter. Check the boxes that best describe your prereading knowledge.

Key concept questions	Well informed	Aware	Need ideas
1. *How can you assess vocabulary learning **through instruction**?*	❏	❏	❏
2. *What can **standardized tests** tell us about vocabulary knowledge?*	❏	❏	❏
3. *How can we **pinpoint the special needs** a particular student might have for vocabulary learning?*	❏	❏	❏

Strategy Overview Guide

This chapter presents background, ideas, and strategies to help you understand different ways in which vocabulary can be assessed. Ideas are given for assessing vocabulary in the context of instruction, for understanding and using standardized measures, and for thoroughly assessing individual children. The following chart can help you choose suitable forms of assessment for your classroom.

Instructional strategy	Goal—use when you want to . . .	Comments
Word set graphics (p. 138)	*Look at prior knowledge about a topic.*	*Very useful in content classes.*
Word maps (p. 140)	*Examine depth of knowledge about a particular concept.*	*Can be used before or after reading.*
Observation guide (p. 141)	*Watch and record what a student does over time.*	*Good portfolio addition.*
Word journals (p. 142)	*Have students record the growth of their personal vocabularies.*	*Alternative to a standard notebook.*
Word monitors (p. 142)	*Put students in charge of assessment.*	*Useful cooperative group role.*
3-minute meetings (p. 142)	*Monitor vocabulary learning of cooperative groups.*	*Good way to keep in touch with literature circles.*
Yea/nay (p. 142)	*Assess rapid access to new meanings.*	*Can be a good game for class.*
Think-alouds (p. 143)	*Analyze one student more thoroughly.*	*Takes time.*
Teacher-constructed tests (p. 146)	*Make a quick assessment of specific learning.*	*Vary your approach.*
Vocabulary record keeping (p. 149)	*Show growth and change across time.*	*Choose the simplest to fit your class situation.*
IRI probe (p. 160)	*Analyze special needs of one student in a contextual situation.*	*Takes time.*

Assessment is the gathering of information to answer specific questions. What type of information you gather and how you analyze it depend on the nature of the questions you are asking. For example, when you have a medical question, your doctor has different avenues for gathering information. Sometimes she will take a history and sketch out a health profile. At other times, she will gather data on your body and your health and compare the data with typical data from your age group to see if your systems are operating normally. For other questions, she will have blood samples taken and analyzed. In still other instances, she will try a procedure or medication and watch how you respond over time.

Similarly, in schools, assessment varies depending on the question being asked. In school settings, we frequently ask three types of questions that involve vocabulary assessments. One set of questions, ordinarily asked by administrators, focuses on how a school or district compares in broad performance with other schools and districts. This type of assessment helps administrators track the long-term performance of their schools and can signal changes and needs that must be addressed. Within the classroom, teachers ask questions that help them with instruction. They want to know how their instruction is working—whether or not students are learning particular concepts, words, and strategies. A third kind of question is asked when students seem to be having problems. These are diagnostic questions that try to pinpoint some aspect of a student's word knowledge or word-learning strategies.

Like doctors, educators gather different types of data using different measures based on the nature of the questions asked. For formal questions of broadscale performance, standardized group measures are commonly used. These take samples of performance and compare them with the typical performance data of larger groups to look for trends. For inquiries centered on classroom instruction, teachers learn to watch instruction closely and to do diagnostic teaching as part of their instruction. They try procedures and see how their students perform over time. Teachers also construct personalized measures to chart growth. For pinpointing problems, teachers and specialists use a variety of individual measures, such as informal reading inventories and some specialized diagnostic tools. Diagnosticians construct a history of performance and sketch out an individual student's reading profile.

This chapter will look at these three types of questions and the means by which they are commonly answered. First we will start with the classroom and examine the kinds of assessment you can use in your classroom to answer some common questions about your students. Most of these instructionally based assessments will be related to instructional ideas we presented earlier, with some additions concerning constructing teacher-made tests and keeping records. Secondly, we will focus on the type of wide-scale assessment carried out in most schools. For the questions asked about district and school performance, standardized measures are commonly used. We will start with a brief refresher on standardized measures and then focus on what the vocabulary components of these measures can tell us. Lastly, we'll examine the type of diagnosis a teacher or specialist does when there is a question about a particular student's word knowledge or word-learning strategies. This type of assessment typically blends informal, instructional, and standardized information gathering.

ASSESSMENT FOR INSTRUCTION

As a classroom teacher, you ask many different types of questions about vocabulary to help plan and evaluate instruction. Sometimes you might want to know if students have a broad knowledge of a general topic you're studying, with some general associations for new words. For example, in a unit on *crustaceans*, would students recognize that *lobsters* and *crayfish* are related? At other times, you might want to know if students have specific, detailed, deep understandings of domains of knowledge and vocabulary. In a social studies unit on the Civil War, *Union* and *Confederacy* are two words that you would want to be well established and have a strong network of related concepts, meanings, and association. Other issues might be: Can students use particular words flexibly and correctly? Can students use context to help them understand new words? Can students recognize common roots, prefixes, and suffixes for new words? Can students find information on new words to help extend their knowledge? Can students self-evaluate? Do students have a general idea of the meaning of some of the new words we have encountered in class?

Questions like these are best answered by ongoing instructional assessment and by teacher-constructed measures. Many of the techniques we have presented in earlier chapters are diagnostic as well as instructional; that is, the teacher discovers what students are learning as lessons progress.

Assessing Vocabulary Breadth: Word Set Graphics

One way to know what students have learned about a broad range of words is to use and analyze pre- and post-instruction graphic organizers that ask students to work with sets of related words. In earlier chapters, we have presented knowledge rating, semantic mapping and webbing, Vocab-o-Grams, semantic feature analysis, and other graphic organizers that can reveal to a teacher what students have learned about groups of terms. For example, look at the knowledge rating constructed by a group of high school students before and after reading a text chapter about dwellings (see Figure 7.1). Before reading, the teacher asked students to rate their knowledge, a technique discussed in Chapter 3. After reading, she used a similar format for some of the more difficult vocabulary but also included some of the questions about dwellings generated in the prereading discussion: Where are they located? Who lives in them? What do they look like?

By looking at the before and after knowledge ratings, the teacher can see that the students topicalized the words—they started to make distinctions based on the key questions of locale, design, and inhabitants but still had a few misconceptions. She decided to use a map to show the students where the yurt-living nomadic tribes might be located and to find a better description of a Sardinian trullo. These became two research topics for her students. This type of group mapping activity can allow a teacher to keep tabs on word learning without testing and to plan further instruction.

Before Reading-Knowledge Rating

Check your knowledge level for each of these terms:

Term	3 Can Define/Use	2 Heard It	1 Don't Know
tipi	✔		
villa		✔	
casa colonica			✔
apartment	✔		
high rise		✔	
dascha		✔	
trullo			✔
dishambe			✔
lean-to		✔	
yurt			✔

After Reading-Knowledge Rating

Term	Rating	Locale	People	Describe	Questions
tipi	3	U.S.Plains	Native American	⌂	
villa	3	Mediterranean	Rich Romans, Italians	Large House	
dascha	3	Russia	Peasants-Rich	big house	
trullo	2	Sardinia	?	Not Sure	are they like tipis?
yurt	2	?	Nomads	⌒	How can it be felt?

Figure 7.1   Before and After Knowledge Ratings

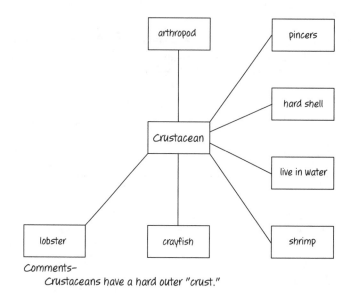

Figure 7.2   Concept Map

Assessing Vocabulary Depth: Word Maps

Sometimes, rather than assessing breadth of knowledge, teachers want to analyze how deeply students understand central terms. Do they see a word in its relationship to other words and placed in a larger domain? Creating a word map for a central word or concept can reveal depth. For example, a teacher wants to know how deep students' knowledge of the term *crustacean* is. In earlier chapters, we discussed such processes as semantic mapping, PAVE, the Frayer concept model, and others. This teacher decided to try a concept of definition map (see Figure 7.2). Like other word mapping strategies, all concept of definition maps require that students look for a class, characteristics, and examples.

In their first concept of definition frame, the students had no knowledge of *crustacean*. When the teacher noted that a *lobster* was an example, they generated *pinchers* (sic) as a characteristic and *sea animal* as a class. After reading, the students had filled out the frame with a class (*arthropod*) and related some other types to this (*arachnid* and *insect*). They also had more examples and characteristics as well as a comment about *crust* that turned out to be accurate when they checked the derivation of the word. The teacher felt that this word map showed that her class had a well-established knowledge of the term *crustacean*. Later in this chapter, we will see a word journal from one student to show how the teacher assessed individual learning.

Assessing Usage

When you want to know about your students' ability to use a new term correctly, flexibly, and richly, assessment through use is the only answer. Rather than a con-

Discussion	Indicate Date, Relevant Vocabulary and Comments
Demonstrates background knowledge	
Uses vocabulary to predict logically	
Uses vocabulary to reason	
Adds to knowledge of a word	
Uses vocabulary to discuss selection elements in summary, retelling, questions, and responses	
In General	
Offers reasonable word associations and word choices in writing	
Can classify words	
Can define words appropriately	
Can infer word meaning from context	
Uses appropriate vocabulary to clearly state ideas	

Note. Adapted and printed with permission. Rathstein, V., and R. Z. Goldberg. *Thinking Through Stories.* East Moline, IL: Lingui Systems, Inc., 1993, p. 64.

Figure 7.3 Vocabulary Observation

trived method, such as, "See how many of this week's new words you can use in one story"—a technique sure to produce distorted and contrived usage—ask students to use vocabulary in meaningful ways in the context of some larger activities. The most direct way to do this is to ask students to incorporate particular words in their responses to questions and in their summaries and retellings. More specific ways to look at vocabulary might be to use an observation guide to record vocabulary learning in any facet of classwork. Some ways in which you might gather data to record on this type of guide, besides the obvious method of reviewing a student writing portfolio, are tracking usage in word journals, having student monitors collect usage information, using 3-minute meetings, or involving students in the yea/nay game. We will describe each in the sections that follow.

Observation Guide.   Observing students' uses of words in discussion, in lessons, and in writing is a means of evaluating their vocabulary usage in the most authentic way. Many teachers compose their own "rubrics," or structured ways of looking at vocabulary and rating usage. For example, you might construct an observation and evaluation sheet like the one in Figure 7.3.

When kept in a notebook with a page for each student, you can pull out sheets for a few students each day to make observations or enter information on the sheet when you notice something in your daily anecdotal records.

In addition to observing students in action in discussion and writing, teachers can observe word usage involved in different sorts of recording processes.

Word Journals.   Students can keep lists of words that interest them and that they encounter in reading and use in writing in a journal that calls on them to tell about how the author used a word and how they might use it. For example, one student's journal page looked like this:

> **shifty:**
> These shifty guys take advantage of many retired and elderly people.
>
> **What it means:** Not being honest; constantly changing
>
> **My use:** In my story about the kids who took my basketball when I was 7. The boy who asked to borrow my ball had a shifty look. I shouldn't have let him have it.

Specific words can be designated by the teacher as journal additions, and teacher review can serve as assessment.

Word Monitors for Discussion.   A student in a discussion group can be designated as a "word monitor" to chart the number of times particular words are used. The monitor for that word can also be charged to survey each student in the group about the word's meaning and ask each to supply a usage for a designated word or words. Records turned into the teacher can be used as assessment (see Figure 7.4).

3-Minute Meetings.   Students can be assigned to construct a collection of new words in a word bank, list, or dictionary or on a word wall or bulletin board. A teacher can have periodic **3-minute meetings** in which she selects 10 words from the collections and asks students to use them in a meaningful way. A simple checklist such as the one in Figure 7.5 (p. 144) can record performance for an ongoing record of word learning. Teachers can choose a few students for meetings each day so that each can have a conference during a 1- to 2-week period. Students can also have 3-minute meetings with one another and work in groups to choose the vocabulary to be discussed.

Yea/Nay.   A game-like activity called yea/nay (Beck & McKeown, 1983) can be used for quick assessment of word knowledge. Students have two different cards, one that says *yes* and one that says *no*. Words are presented in pairs, and rapid questions are asked by the teacher.

> Would a *corpse* be a good *conversationalist?*
> Would a *crook* be commended for *honesty?*

After asking the question, the teacher gives students 15 seconds to think and then asks, "Yea or nay? 1, 2, 3." On the count of 3, students put up their choices and hold them up while a teacher calls on students to explain their choices. Recorders can record initial responses if the teacher wants a formal record.

Name	Paul		Date Oct. 4	

Class	Social Studies			

Chapter/ Book/ Story/ Topic		Ch. 3	

Words	Tally
1. Confederacy	⊬⊬⊬ ⊬⊬⊬ /
2. Union	⊬⊬⊬ ⊬⊬⊬ ///
3. abolition	///
4. Underground Railroad	//
5. carpetbaggers	⊬⊬⊬ //
6. Reconstruction	⊬⊬⊬ /
7. Emancipation Proclamation	//
8.	

Student	Word(s) enter #
Tyrone	OK, all but #7
Blair	OK, all but #5, #7
Jake	OK all
Dave	OK all

Figure 7.4   Word Monitor Sheet

Assessing Independent Word–Learning Strategies

Besides wanting to know if our students have broad or deep meanings for new words and can use them richly and flexibly, we also want to know if students have effective independent word-learning strategies.

Think-Alouds.   Earlier in this book, we discussed extensively the strategies of using context, word parts, and references. In each of these chapters, the approach was

---

The list below shows the words you should have ready for your 3-minute meeting on
_____. Come prepared to use each word in our discussion
or show me how you used it in writing.

Words   **Comments**

1. Confederacy
2. Union
3. abolition
4. Underground Railroad
5. carpetbaggers
6. Reconstruction
7. Emancipation
   Proclamation
8.

Figure 7.5   3-Minute Meeting Record

a strategic one that could also be used for assessment. What is central to the assessment of most strategy development is some process that reveals the students' thinking process. One such process is the *think-aloud* process (Davey, 1983), which asks students to talk about what they are thinking and doing while they are thinking and doing it. In Chapter 2, we used this example of a group thinking through context with their teacher to figure out the term *cellar holes*, which was blanked out of a passage.

> T(EACHER): Remember that for the last few weeks we have been talking about using context clues. Can anyone tell me why we do this?
>
> S(STUDENT)1: When there's a word you don't know, sometimes you can get an idea by looking at the rest of the story for clues.
>
> S2: You can think about what you already know and then see if you can figure out what the new word means or something about it from what the author says.
>
> T: How do we do that?
>
> S3: We look before the word, we look after the word, and we look *at* the word, too, for prefixes and roots and stuff, but we can't do that here because you took that all out (laughter).
>
> T: That's right. I'm making it a real challenge for you. Can you tell me anything about the missing term?
>
> S2: Well, she's outside, so its something outside.
>
> S5: It's something on the ground 'cause she's digging later on.
>
> S1: It says, "Smooth little depressions they were,. . . " but I don't understand that because I know *depressed* and this doesn't make sense.
>
> T: Anyone have anything to say about that? (Students make no response.)

T: Remember to look further on. Is there anything else about depressions?

S4: Later it says that "The shape of the depressions gave a clue," so it's not a feeling. It's something on the ground.

S5: She played in them, so they were holes or like where walls of old stones were left.

T: What made you think of walls?

S5: Well, they keep talking about the houses and said "houses had stood there. . . the doorways had been there," so I think she is somewhere where houses used to be. Like after an earthquake or tornado.

S1: "It looks as if the homes had sunk into the earth," so they must be holes.

T: Would (the *word*) *hole* make sense?

S4: Yea, they could be depressions. She could play in them, and you could dig a spoon out of the hole.

S5: If it's the hole where a house was, then it could be the basement hole, like the hole they dig when they start to build a house.

S1: Basement makes sense; it's a hole for a house.

T: Well, what do you think?

S1: I think we should stop. We know enough.

T: Should we stop or keep thinking? (Students agree to stop and uncover the term *cellar holes*.)

S2: Well, they are holes.

S5: My gram has a fruit cellar in her house, and it's like, it's the same as a basement.

S4: OK, we figured it out. Let's see what this story is about.

T: Good idea.

Think-alouds can be used with groups or with individuals in a conference and provide ideas about independent word use strategy that can be recorded on the all-purpose file such as the one shared in Figure 7.6.

Self-Evaluation.   Along with using teacher-observed introspective methods such as think-alouds to reveal student strategies, another facet of developing an independent word-learning strategy is developing the process of self-evaluation. This type of metacognitive behavior is important to all learning. Currently, with the interest in self-evaluation in the portfolio process, this strategy is receiving major consideration in the assessment process as well. Literature circles often use role sheets for vocabulary directors such as those shared in Chapter 4 (see Figure 4.5). Role sheets ask students to become self-reflective about the words they need to learn and the ways they need to go about learning them.

You might also like to have students include a word strategy evaluation in their word journals. One used by a seventh-grade teacher looked like the one shown in Figure 7.6.

Teaching Idea File 7.1 offers some ideas for assessing vocabulary in cooperative groups.

Word Strategies-1

1. What strategy from the following list did you use today to figure out words that are difficult for you?

   —Thought about what would make sense

   —Went back for something the author said before

   —Read more for more information

   —Used parts of the word (prefix, suffix, root)

   —Used information from pictures and graphs

   —Used a reference (dictionary, encyclopedia glossary, another person, or other)

   —Other (Explain.)

   _____

   _____

   _____

2. Give one example of how you figured out a difficult word. Write the sentence the word was in and underline the word. Then tell how you figured it out. Be specific so someone else can see how you were thinking. Use the back if needed.

   _____

   _____

   _____

   _____

   _____

   _____

   Note. Adapted from *Literacy Assessment: A handbook of Instruments* (p. 48) by L. K. Rhodes, 1993, Portsmouth, NH: Heinemann Educational Books.

Figure 7.6   Word Strategy Self-Evaluation

Teacher–Constructed Tests

Sometimes you want a quick assessment of your students' abilities to associate a new word with a synonym or general meaning. For this type of assessment, short teacher-made tests can work. Teacher-constructed tests can take many forms and usually test recognition (the ability to select an appropriate answer) rather than the more difficult recall (the ability to provide a word from memory). Typical teacher-made tests are types of recall assessment that involve defining a word by:

1. Giving/choosing a synonym (a *diadem* is a *crown*)

2. Giving/choosing a classification (a *shrimp* is a *crustacean*)

3. Giving/choosing examples (*flowers* are things like daisy, rose, mum)

4. Giving/choosing an explanation of how something is used (a *shovel* is a *tool* used to dig holes)

Teaching Idea File 7.1

Vocabulary Assessment Ideas for Cooperative Groups

1. Assign the role of word monitor to one member of the group. Have that student use the chart shown in Figure 7.4.
2. With each group, have a 3-minute meeting in which students must quickly present the vocabulary for you.
3. Have students do word strategy assessments and add them to their portfolios after discussion.
4. Have members plan yea/nay questions and lead the game for another group.

From Blachowicz & Fisher, *Teaching Vocabulary in All Classrooms*, p. 139.

5. Giving/choosing an opposite

6. Giving/choosing a definition

7. Giving/choosing a picture

8. Giving/choosing a word to complete a context

Multiple-Choice Tests. **Multiple-choice tests** can involve picking a choice from a list of choices, matching a word to a synonym or opposite, or choosing a word to complete a larger cloze passage. For example, an item with a list of choices might look like this:

Pick the best synonym for the underlined word in the sentence:

She was a <u>synthesis</u> of the best qualities of her mother and father.

fake   combination   example   daughter

For effective multiple-choice questions, make sure that students have to discriminate among choices that would fit the syntactic context of the sentence. In the example, all of the choices are nouns, though daughter would be an unusual choice for this construction.

Also, you may wish to put in distractors (incorrect choices) related to confusing terms. For example, *fake* might be chosen if *synthesis* is associated with *synthetic*. Just as these make the task more challenging, however, they can mask some constructive thinking on the part of the learner. Many teachers like to have students explain their choices as a way of debriefing exams. Also, the answers you get will be determined by your choice of distractors. Simple, easy-to-eliminate distractors will result in higher "correct" scores than choosing wrong answers that have some subtle or complicated relationship to the target word (Campion & Elley, 1971). You should analyze your tests and debrief with students if your results seem perplexing.

Multiple-Choice Matching.   **Matching tests** call on students to pair words with synonyms. For example,

---

Draw a line between synonyms:

1. paradigm   a. combination
2. synthesis   b. fake
3. synthetic   c. ruler
                     d. example
                     e. dynasty

As in the formats above, the nature of the choices is important. The subtlety of the distinctions involved should be matched to the age and sophistication of the students. Matching is most appropriate when the teacher is interested in the simple ability to associate a term with a suitable synonym. It is important that the list of choices is longer than the number of items to be supplied. Students who are effective test takers will use the process of elimination for those words of which they are not sure.

Multiple-Choice Cloze.   In Chapter 2, we gave several examples of cloze used as a teaching technique. Cloze (in the form called "maze" because choices are given for each deletion) can also be used for assessment and is used for standardized assessment in several standardized tests (e.g., *Degrees of Reading Power,* 1995; MacGinitie & MacGinitie, 1989). Reading a **cloze** passage requires readers to use their knowledge of context to supply appropriate words and concepts to create a meaningful passage. In a cloze used to test vocabulary, choices are supplied such as in the following example:

From the list, choose the best word to fit the context:

He was a _____ of the best qualities of his mother and father. He had his mother's ability to reach out to strangers and his father's habit of being a good listener. He was a genuine, honest human being, with many friends.

synthesis   synthetic   contradiction

When preparing a cloze passage for testing, make sure your students have not seen it before so that they can be called on to use words in new contexts, which is a true test of vocabulary knowledge.

Guidelines for Teacher-Made Tests. Tests that you make for the classroom should be easy and efficient to use. You will also want to ask these questions:

1. Do the items and the process call on students to do the same things you typically ask them to do in class? If your normal question in class is for students to supply a synonym, then asking for an antonym on a test doesn't make much sense.

2. Will answering the item provide useful repetition of vocabulary or make students think more deeply about it? If the test item is an exact repetition of something you did earlier, then it may be testing rote memory rather than more creative or extensive thinking.

3. Will the knowledge you draw on be useful and relevant to the course in which the assessment is taking place? If you are testing aspects of word knowledge not relevant to the topic, your efforts may be counterproductive.

4. Does your test format match your instructional format? If you have stressed usage in instruction, test for usage. If you have emphasized word recognition, test for recognition.

Keeping Vocabulary Records

An important part of all assessment is keeping records to show growth and change. Both students and teachers keep records in the classroom that can record change and growth. Some examples for each are discussed in the following sections.

Student Recording. Student work can be kept and recorded in many ways. Some obvious ways are:

Word Files and Notebooks. From word banks in the primary grades to notebooks kept in middle school and high school, a cumulative record of words encountered and learned can be kept. Some tips for maximizing word files might be:

1. Wherever the word is recorded, include a usage example. This can be from the author or from the student.

2. For easy management, when cards are used, use the front of the card for the word and the back for usage examples. Make sure the student's name or initials are on the card for the inevitable lost cards. Lastly, cards can most easily be kept on a slip ring that runs through the corner of the card. (Shower curtain rings are inexpensive and ideal for this purpose.) Ringed cards are easy to find and don't scatter when dropped, as boxed cards do.

3. For word notebooks, use a loose-leaf format. This allows words to be alphabetized and sorted in different ways. A small loose-leaf notebook allows a word per page and gives plenty of room for illustration and examples.

Student Portfolio Self-Evaluation. A student portfolio is more than just a collection of work. The portfolio process involves students in selecting items to include and reflecting on their choices. Students can be involved in assessment prior to learning, during learning, and after learning. For example, besides the student word strategy of self-evaluation we presented in Figure 7.6, students can be asked to collect prereading,

---

Directions: Choose some item from this unit that shows your growth in vocabulary. Attach this sheet with your reflection and description of why you chose this piece.

What I chose to show my word learning in the unit on sea life is my word map on crustaceans. At first I had never heard of this word and then I found out that it's the name of a family of sea animals like crabs and lobsters. They all have pairs of legs that are jointed. They also have a hard shell, like a crust. Crust actually is related to the word crustacean (but I don't know which came first.)

I thought it was real interesting that crustaceans are related to insects too. When you think about it, an ant sort of looks like a lobster in the shape of it's body. I never heard this word before even though I knew what a lobster was. Now I know a lot more.

Figure 7.7   Seventh Grader's Portfolio Reflection on the Word *Crustacean*

during-reading, and postreading vocabulary information on a particular word or group of words. One of the seventh graders who constructed the word map on *crustacean*, shown in Figure 7.2, constructed the reflection shown in Figure 7.7 to explain his learning and inclusion of the item in his portfolio. This type of self-reflection not only asks students to reflect on their own word learning but also gives them practice in using the terms in meaningful ways.

Teacher Records.   Besides the typical records of test scores teachers might keep, there are other ways teachers can keep records of vocabulary. One of these is the checklist format. For example, the teacher working with the Civil War, described earlier, generated the checklist of important vocabulary shown in Figure 7.8. As she looked at the work of the children in her class, she kept tabs on the words they were learning as her assessment.

Anecdotal Records.   Another form of recording is anecdotal records. Many teachers keep small notes or journals that they file in a daily log. These comments can then be recorded on cumulative sheets for each student at the end of the day or week. For example, one teacher keeps a card file with a card for each student. Each day she picks out five cards and makes some notation about the vocabulary usage of each child. She may decide to have a 3-minute meeting or look at the student's work folder. By the end of the week, she has focused on each child and can start the cycle again.

Another teacher likes to keep notepads and pencils in each corner of his room. When he sees anything of interest during the day, he makes a note on the nearest pad. At the end of the day, he collects the pads, reflects on his notes, and files information in the appropriate place. Large Post-it notes may also be used for this purpose.

In this section, we have focused on the ways teachers do ongoing assessment to help structure instruction. These means were mainly informal and teacher-made. Other types of instruments are used for formal, large-scale assessment and for pinpointing learning needs in a diagnostic fashion.

Word		Paul	Jake	Dave
1.	Confederacy	D W T	D W T	D W T
2.	Union	D W T	D W T	D W T
3.	abolition	D W T	D W T	
4.	Underground Railroad	D W T		D W T
5.	carpetbaggers	D W T	D W T	D W T
6.	Reconstruction	D W T	D W T	D W T
7.	Emancipation Proclamation	W	W	

D = used in discussion
W = used in writing
T = tested

Figure 7.8   Teacher Checklist

STANDARDIZED MEASURES OF VOCABULARY

What Are Standardized Measures?

Five keywords can help you understand standardized measures: They relate performance to some **standard** measure of performance; they try to be **objective;** and they make conclusions from a **sample** of performance that is assumed to be a **valid** and **reliable** predictor of general performance. Let's look at each of these words in turn.

Standard.   There are many different types of standardized measures, but they all share the quality of comparing performance to some **standard** of performance. Tests are called **norm referenced** when they compare the performance of one group with that of the standard performance of a norming group, a large group of test takers from a particular group thought to be typical. Norms help gauge performance in a way that raw scores and percentages do not. For example, a class average of 85% (22 out of 26 correct) on an exam sounds substantial until one learns that all the other classes scored 100% on the same measure. Other tests, called **criterion-referenced tests,** use a particular level of performance on a task as a standard. For example, if the task noted above involved naming the 26 letters of the alphabet, an 85% level of performance (22 letters named) might be very appropriate at first-grade entry with 100% expected at second grade. It's important that the norming group of any standardized measure chosen for a particular school match the school population to get accurate comparisons.

Teaching Idea File 7.2

Tips for Choosing Standardized Measures

1. Check to see that the norming group for the measure is like your school population.
2. Take the test before you give it. This will help you observe appropriate standardized procedure and will alert you to problem points.
3. Analyze the test items. Are they appropriate for your curriculum? How is the validity described and determined?
4. Check the manual. Is the reliability adequate? Are some levels and subtests less reliable?
5. Find out more about the measure in a professional journal or in the appropriate *Mental Measurements Yearbook* (Buros).

From Blachowicz & Fisher, *Teaching Vocabulary in All Classrooms*, p. 144.

Objective. In an argument, when we look for someone **objective** to settle a dispute, we look for someone who will treat each person in the same way and not show favoritism. In the same sense, standardized measures try to be objective. That is, they try to treat each test taker in the same way by having specific guidelines for timing and administration, for dealing with questions, and for evaluating answers. Also, the content and questions are supposed to be equally comprehensible to all students in terms of background knowledge, a point we will discuss further. Because tests are already "error prone," observing standardized procedure is essential when administering any standardized measure.

Sample. When you have your blood tested, you don't need to have all your blood removed and analyzed. The technician works from a small sample and assumes that it will be representative of all the blood in your body. In the same way, standardized tests take a short **sample** of your performance and try to generalize about your larger performance. To do this, a test has to be **valid** (measure what it says it measures) and **reliable** (measure approximately the same way time after time). Reliability can be statistically calculated, but validity is harder to determine. Most standardized measures look for "experts" to attest to validity or to compare measurements with some other measure that "experts" have indicated is valid. It's important that teachers and administrators carefully examine standardized measures chosen for their schools to see that the tasks and items reflect a view of reading that shapes the school curriculum. See Teaching Idea File 7.2 for suggestions on how to choose standardized measures of vocabulary.

Problems with Standardized Tests

A clear understanding of the keywords *standard, objective, sample, valid,* and *reliable* will suggest to many readers some of the greatest problems with standardized measures. We've already noted that poor norming and nonstandardized procedures can give poor information. Further, the formats of many standardized tests have raised some major questions about task validity. The passages are generally short and unrelated, and the tasks are decontextualized and of dubious relationship to real reading (Valencia & Pearson, 1986). For vocabulary, for example, choosing a word to match another in a list of words has very little relationship to actual reading tasks. Because of the power of background knowledge, the question of objectivity can be raised when students of different backgrounds from norming groups take tests. Lastly, because error is inevitable in all assessment, small deviations, for example, a child's feeling unwell on a testing day, may produce a bad sample of a student's regular performance, or guessing may provide a too-optimistic sample. Because of all these possibilities for individual error, standardized measures are meant for large-scale comparisons—district to district, for example, where individual errors in measurement "wash out" when looking at groups composed of large numbers.

Standardized Group Vocabulary Tests

Most standardized group reading tests have sections devoted to vocabulary. Typically, the format involves a multiple-choice selection of a synonym to match a target word. For example:

> From the group below, choose the word with the closest meaning to **discovered**
>
> 1. faded
> 2. concluded
> 3. found
> 4. unwrapped

For a majority of tests, the vocabulary selected is drawn from high-frequency graded word lists that represent textbook words from reading series and science and social studies books (Cooter, 1990). Though separate vocabulary and comprehension scores are given in tests of these types, there is normally a high correlation between the two because vocabulary is an excellent predictor of comprehension (Davis, 1968). In addition to being a general predictor of comprehension and an indicator of prior knowledge, these tests can provide a rough estimate of a student's ability to make broad associations to new words.

We've already noted that standardized measures are meant as group assessment and can have significant error in predicting individual performance. Some other issues to keep in mind about vocabulary measures are:

1. Vocabulary tests are measures of prior knowledge, experience, and culture. For example, a *soda* in New York is a carbonated beverage. In the Midwest, it's an ice cream concoction. Similarly, tests of oral vocabulary using pictures can be most confusing. Look at Figure 7.9. What object is pictured? In parts of the country, this drawing could be a mailbox; in other areas, it's a trash can. In still others, it's a library book return. Often pictures are ambiguous and culture bound, which can cause error.

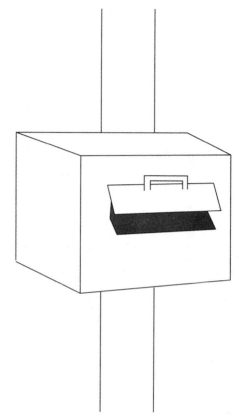

Figure 7.9   Example of Vocabulary Test Item. What would you put in this box?

2.   Vocabulary tests are measures of decoding. In any standardized tests where students must work silently, the students are responsible for analyzing the word before performing the task. Many students with poor decoding skills score poorly on tests of vocabulary even when they have those words in their oral vocabulary.

3.   Students take tests in many ways. Analyzing score sheets will reveal that two students can have the same score, with one answering the first 50 of 100 questions correctly but not finishing and another student answering all 100 but getting 50 correct. Many tests are tests of speed rather than of power. Teachers can allow students to "revisit" a standardized test in an untimed format after the standardized data have been collected to give the teacher a better idea of the student's word power—the performance without time pressure.

4.   All standardized tests measure test-taking skills. Students who know how to guess, how to eliminate answers, how to make the best use of limited time will post scores well beyond their ability. Even measures such as the SAT, which once billed itself as "uncoachable," are now understood to be influenced by test-taking preparation.

5.   Vocabulary tests measure the most superficial aspects of word learning. The ability to make an association or select a synonym is not the ability to use a word richly and flexibly. For bilingual students, in particular, standardized measures can overestimate or underestimate what they know about vocabulary in a second language.

In general, such measures can be used as rough screening devices to assess the general vocabulary levels of your students. Because they so often depend on prior knowledge, they can also be viewed as rough measures of exposure to topics and issues that different vocabulary represents. Later in this chapter, when looking at diagnosis related to vocabulary difficulty, we will discuss ways in which teachers can probe with standardized tests to get more information about a specific student's performance. At that point, we will talk about some specialized standardized vocabulary measures.

Specialized Tests

Peabody Picture Vocabulary Test-Third Ed.   The Peabody Picture Vocabulary Test-Revised (PPVT-R)(Dunn & Dunn, 1997) is a standardized individual test of auditory vocabulary. Each item is pronounced by the examiner, and the examinee selects an appropriate representation from four black-and-white pictures. The PPVT-R is easy to administer, well designed, and standardized. It rules out decoding problems by being an oral test and is well standardized in the school-age versions. Used with probes, ("Why did you pick that one?") that are not part of the standardized procedure, it can be revealing of prior knowledge.

Stanford Diagnostic Reading Tests (1995).   The Stanford Diagnostic Reading Tests are group instruments with interesting subtests that can provide specific types of information.

- *Auditory vocabulary* (Red, Green, and Brown levels). These early levels have auditory vocabulary tests in which the teacher reads the words for selection. The words include various parts of speech and represent three areas of content: reading and literature, mathematics and science, and social studies and the arts.
- *Structural analysis* (Green, Brown, and Blue levels). This subtest measures students' ability to use word parts such as syllables, affixes, and root words.

As with any group test, individual probing often gives a different picture of performance, as does analysis of the same items in contextual reading.

Brigance Diagnostic Comprehensive Inventory of Basic Skills (1983).   The Reading Vocabulary Comprehension assessment consists of three lists of words for each grade level and is used as a rough placement device. Students are asked to indicate which word does not belong in each list. Again, this can be interesting if probed, but the test itself is too short to provide much useful information.

Durrell Analysis of Reading Difficulty (1980).   This test assesses listening vocabulary. The examiner reads a word and students must assign it to a category. For example, a student might hear the word *gigantic* and have to assign it to one of three categories—food, size, or color. The words used in this subtest also appear in a word analysis subtest so that one can compare reading and listening vocabulary.

Woodcock Reading Mastery Tests-Revised (1987). The Woodcock Reading Mastery Tests-Revised has an interesting word comprehension test. It includes three subtests—antonyms, synonyms, and word analogies. For the antonym test, the student reads each word aloud and then supplies a word with the opposite meaning. For the synonym tests, the same process is followed, with the student supplying a word that is similar in meaning. On the analogies subtest, the student reads each word as it is presented and then provides a fourth word to complete the analogy. The words used in the analogies are drawn from content areas of humanities, math and science, social studies, and a general pool. Essentially, this test is a word relationship test and can help you assess students' understandings of the ways in which words are connected and used for reasoning.

The SAT and Other College Entrance Exams. The SAT (College Entrance Examination Board, 1993) and other college entrance tests are heavily weighted toward vocabulary knowledge. Because the SAT is the most widely administered, we will use it as a prototype to discuss this type of test and the type of preparation students can do for it. It was once implied that these were tests of aptitude and, as such, were not influenced by preparation. Now, even the test constructors acknowledge that they are tests of learning and achievement and that students can benefit from preparation (College Entrance Examination Board, 1993).

The verbal portion of the test includes verbal questions with one- or two-blank sentence completion items, verbal analogies, and vocabulary in the context of critical reading (see Figure 7.10 for examples). Though the test can be prepared for, review authorities all suggest a long-term attention to vocabulary works best (Carris, 1993; CEEB, 1993; Robinson, 1993). They suggest keeping word cards on new vocabulary and doing the following:

1.   When you meet a new word in your reading, try to figure it out from context. Write the word on a card and, on the back, write the usage.

2.   Look the word up in a dictionary and add the definitions to your card.

3.   Pay special attention to the usage sentences in the dictionary and add them to your card along with a sentence of your own. Draw a picture if that helps you with the meaning (see Figure 7.11).

4.   When word histories are given, read through them.

5.   Keep a list of common roots and affixes.

6.   Keep a list of common abbreviations.

7.   Do crossword puzzles whenever you can.

8.   Play word games such as Scrabble and Boggle (see Appendix D) with a dictionary nearby. Ask about every word you don't know.

9.   When learning new words, use mnemonics to help you remember. Create a visual image or a sentence to help fix the meaning and usage in your mind.

10.   If you will be taking the new subject area exams, you might want to keep a list of content terms for each of the subjects you might take. They are:

Literature
History: American history and social studies, world history

Foreign Language: Chinese, French, German, Italian,
    Japanese, Latin, modern Hebrew, Spanish

Mathematics:
    Level I: Algebra and geometry
    Level II: Algebra, geometry, and precalculus or
        trigonometry
Science: Biology, chemistry, physics

1-Blank Vocabulary Item

Ravens appear to behave_____, actively
helping one another to find food.
    (A) mysteriously
    (B) warily
    (C) aggressively
    (D) cooperatively
    (E) defensively

2-Blank Vocabulary Item
Both_____and_____, Wilson seldom
spoke and never spent money.

    (A) vociferous . . . generous
    (B) garrulous . . . stingy
    (C) effusive . . . frugal
    (D) taciturn . . . miserly
    (E) reticent . . . munificent

Analogy

ACT: Play
    (A) song: music
    (B) rhyme: poem
    (C) page: novel
    (D) chapter: book
    (E) scenery: performance

Vocabulary in Context
In line 34, "legends" most nearly means
    (A) ancient folklore
    (B) obscure symbols
    (C) history lessons
    (D) famous people
    (E) common misconceptions

Figure 7.10 Examples of Verbal Questions from the SAT

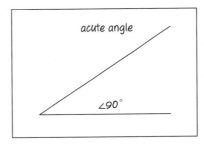

Figure 7.11 Drawing as a Memory Aid

SAT Preparation Guides

Carris, J. D. (2001). *SAT Word Flash*, Princeton, NJ: Peterson's.

College Entrance Examination Board. (1993). *Introducing the New SAT: The College Board's Official Guide.* New York: College Board Publications.

Robinson, A. (1993). *Word Smart: Building an Educated Vocabulary.* New York: Villard Books.

From Blachowicz & Fisher, *Teaching Vocabulary in All Classrooms*, p. 150.

Also, all the preparatory manuals and courses emphasize the need for wide reading and for becoming "word conscious."

You might like to add the excellent guides, shown in Teaching Idea File 7.3, to your student bookshelf if you are a high school teacher.

DIAGNOSIS FOR SPECIAL NEEDS

When a particular student seems to have trouble with vocabulary, you will sometimes want to do an individual diagnosis to help clarify and plan instruction. You have several avenues to pursue. The first frequently involves an **informal reading inventory** (IRI), an individual assessment using passages that reflect the type of work this student is called on to read. Secondly, you can probe the responses from that inventory and from other standardized measures. Thirdly, you can use some of the specialized measures noted above if you still need the type of information they could provide.

Vocabulary Assessment with Informal Reading Inventories

The most commonly used informal diagnostic measure used by teachers is the informal reading inventory. These inventories may be commercially published, produced by the publishers of commercial reading materials, or constructed by teachers. IRIs consist of passages for oral and silent reading, passages to measure listening comprehension, and sets of words used for decoding assessment. Their use is widely described and discussed in books on reading instruction and diagnosis (Barr, Blachowicz, Katz & Kaufman 2001). For vocabulary assessment in IRIs, students read a passage and are asked questions that involve interpretation of preselected words or are sometimes asked direct questions about the meaning of a word in the passage context. Because the assessment is individual, you can probe a student's response in a way that cannot be done in a group measure.

In a high school social studies class, a teacher wondered if Louisa's poor performance might be due to problems with vocabulary. She constructed an informal reading inventory with passages from some of the chapters in the textbooks they would be using. For example, look at the passage about housing shown in Figure 7.12.

Passage

With a few exceptions, environment determines the kinds of shelter people choose. So, houses are usually built from materials that are most readily available in the surrounding areas.

The temporary dwelling, as its name suggests, is not built to last. Nomads, people who are always on the move, build temporary dwellings. For example, Native Americans of the plains developed the tipi, made of buffalo hides. When buffalo were plentiful, they were an important food source. To avoid waste, Native Americans found a practical use for the hides of the animals. When the tribe moved on, the tipis were left behind.

The grass lean-to is favored by the Bush people of the Kalahari Desert. It is made from grasses and sticks found in the area in which they live.

There are two kinds of permanent housing: crude and sophisticated. Igloos, log cabins, and adobe huts are crude permanent housing. They are built to last. The surfaces, however, are rough and unfinished.

The igloo is a dome made of blocks of hard-packed snow. The snow acts as an insulator. It makes the igloo surprisingly warm.

Log cabins were common during America's westward expansion. As settlers headed west, the thick forests provided timber for housing.

Adobe is sun-dried mud. Adobe huts are found in warm, dry areas, such as parts of Mexico and the American Southwest.

Sophisticated permanent housing can be made from many materials. Homes with concrete foundations are built to last from owner to owner. The location of steel mills and ironworks often determines the areas where this housing is found.

Comprehension Questions

1. a. What determines the kind of shelter people choose?
   b. Where do we usually get the materials from which we build houses?
2. What is temporary dwelling?
3. What are the people called who build temporary dwellings?
4. Why do some people build temporary dwellings?
5. What are the two types of permanent housing?
6. What is the difference between crude and sophisticated permanent housing?
7. Name some types of crude permanent housing.
8. What are some materials from which sophisticated permanent housing is made?
9. What determines where sophisticated permanent houses are built?
10. *If you had the choice between living in an igloo, a log cabin, or an adobe hut, which would you choose and why?
11. *Of all the types of housing mentioned in the passage—temporary and permanent, crude permanent, and sophisticated permanent— which type do you live in?
12. *Do climate and environment still govern what materials we use to build houses today?

Vocabulary Knowledge

Key Concept Words

1. environment
2. determines
3. available
4. temporary
5. permanent
6. sophisticated

Contextually Explained

7. insulator
8. adobe
9. igloo
10. nomad

Figure 7.12 Reading Passage and Questions About Kinds of Housing

*These questions require the student to go beyond the information presented in the reading passage.

Louisa made the responses shown in Figure 7.13. She had no problem decoding any of the words in the selection. Of the comprehension questions, she got partial credit on two (items 1 and 9) and missed two items (6 and 8). In her partially correct answers, she gave examples rather than a more classical definition, and she could not define *sophisticated* and *determines*. She was unable to infer that *sophisticated* had to be contrasted with *crude,* perhaps because she did not know what *crude* meant. Because Louisa's difficulty on the comprehension questions seemed to be caused by her limited understanding of some of the vocabulary, her teacher decided to go back and probe her understanding of some of the vocabulary, specifically *sophisticated, crude, determines, plentiful, readily,* and *insulator.*

Probing IRI Responses

The next day Louisa's teacher had Louisa reread the passage, and then the teacher asked her what *crude* meant. She replied that *crude* was a "kind of housing" and gave the three examples from the text. Further probing indicated that she had never heard the words *crude* and *sophisticated.* In the case of *determines,* Louisa seemed to know what it would mean in the context of people making decisions or predicting outcomes, but she seemed unable to grasp the idea that conditions could *determine* something.

> TEACHER: The passage states that environment *determines* the kinds of housing people choose. What does *determine* mean?
>
> LOUISA: If they lived in a cold place, that would show that they lived in an igloo. If it was hot, that would say that they would live in a hut maybe.
>
> TEACHER: OK, then. What would it mean that the environment determined where people would live?
>
> LOUISA: Well, like it would mean they could choose to live in an apartment in the city.
>
> TEACHER: So what do you think *determine* means?
>
> LOUISA: Like a choice. He determined that he wanted to live in a wood house.

So it was not so much the word itself that gave Louisa difficulty but an underlying concept that conditions could set limits on people's choices.

The teacher asked Louisa several other words. She knew *plentiful* meant "a lot." For *readily,* she said, "That it's done, well, ... I'm not sure." As for *insulator,* she thought it was some sort of machine to keep things hot and could not modify that view when rereading the sentence "The snow acts as an insulator" or discussing the fact that a machine of snow didn't make much sense. Louisa knew the word *igloo* but couldn't define *nomad* or *adobe.* She could go back and look at the context and figure out that a nomad was someone who moved around a lot and that adobe was a building material. So, with respect to strategies, when Louisa was allowed to look back and was coached to do so, she could find out the meanings of words that were explicitly cued, but she had trouble when the context was less explicit or when it required her to reason across the selection.

1. a. What determines the kind of shelter people choose? (environment; available materials) RESPONSE: It can be the ground, maybe grass or sand; and like if it's cold or sunny.

   b. Where do we usually get the materials from which we build houses? (environment; surrounding area). RESPONSE: Sometimes we can make it. Like the log cabins, you could get it from the trees around you. The igloos you could pack the snow yourself.

2. What is a temporary dwelling? (one that is not built to last). RESPONSE: It's not built to stay long.

3. What are the people called who build temporary dwellings? (nomads). RESPONSE: Nomads

4. Why do some people build temporary dwellings? (they are always on the move). RESPONSE: They are always moving around.

5. What are the two types of permanent housing? (crude and sophisticated). RESPONSE: Crude and sophisticated.

6. What is the difference between crude and sophisticated permanent housing? (crude are rough and unfinished; sophisticated are made from modern materials). RESPONSE: Not sure—crude are built to stay longer and sophisticated is not that long.

7. Name some types of crude permanent housing. (igloo, adobe, log cabin). RESPONSE: Log cabin, adobe hut, igloo.

8. What are some materials from which sophisticated permanent housing is made? (wood, iron, steel). RESPONSE: I think one of the houses are igloos made out of snow—or I think wood. [Anything else?] Steel.

9. What determines where sophisticated, permanent houses are built? (location of materials). RESPONSE: Well, if they were wood, they would be by a forest.

10. *If you had the choice between living in an igloo, a log cabin, or an adobe hut, which would you choose and why? (discuss climate and comfort). RESPONSE: Igloo, or log cabin . . . Well, I would choose an igloo because it keeps you warm. Maybe a log cabin; it was built like a house—and that's what we mostly live in, like in cabins in the woods. [So which would you choose?] Log cabin 'cause it's built like a house.

11. *Of all the types of housing mentioned in the passage—temporary and permanent, crude permanent, and sophisticated permanent—which type do you live in? (permanent sophisticated). RESPONSE: I think sophisticated. [Is it permanent or temporary?] Permanent.

12. *Do climate and environment still govern what materials we use to build houses today? (discuss climate, environment, today's construction). RESPONSE: Not sure. [Do you think people can build any kind of house no matter what the climate is?] Well, not exactly—don't know how to explain it.

Louisa's Responses

1. environment
   RESPONSE: The things around you.

2. determines
   RESPONSE: They . . . . say it, they predict.
   TEACHER: Can you use the word *determine* in a sentence?
   RESPONSE: He determined that the number was gonna be five.

3. available
   RESPONSE: That it's . . . I can't explain it.
   TEACHER: Then use it in a sentence.
   RESPONSE: This pen is available for anybody that wants to use it.

4. temporary
   RESPONSE: It's not built to stay long.

5. permanent
   RESPONSE: That it stays there . . . the house stays up longer.

6. sophisticated
   RESPONSE: I don't know the meaning of that word from the other thing, but I think I know another meaning.
   TEACHER: OK. Tell me the meaning you know.
   RESPONSE: Well, I don't know how to explain it.
   TEACHER: Could you put it in a sentence?
   RESPONSE: This is a sophisticated truck.
   TEACHER: What does that mean about the truck?

   (continued)

Figure 7.13 Louisa's Responses to Questions About the Passage on Housing

*These questions require the student to go beyond the information presented in the reading passage.

RESPONSE: That it's in a kind of motion of something. A kind of way.

7. insulator
RESPONSE: Some sort of machine to make things hot. (Could not clarify when reviewing context, "The snow acts as an insulator.")

8. adobe
RESPONSE: Don't know.

(Reinspected context and figured out that it was "some stuff to build with.")

9. igloo
RESPONSE: A snow house for eskimo . . . like made of snow blocks.

10. nomad
RESPONSE: Don't know.
(Reinspected the context and corrected to "Someone who moves around a lot.")

Figure 7.13   Continued

This probing of Louisa's vocabulary knowledge indicated that she is able to read with good understanding when the vocabulary is familiar or well defined in context. However, when the selection or questions used to discuss the selection are unfamiliar and not explicitly defined in the text, she had more difficulty. Her teacher decided that specific vocabulary should be addressed in prereading and that Louisa should receive systematic instruction in inferring word meanings from context.

Further Exploration

When students' comprehension seems affected by vocabulary knowledge, you can further explore aspects of their vocabulary knowledge by probing with both standardized and informal assessment tools. You might choose to do this after having given a screening device, such as a group test, and selecting the bottom-stanine students to probe further. With standardized tests, if the standardized scores are going to be calculated, you must use the administration guidelines for giving the test. However, you can return the test to the student at a later time, after the scores have been registered, to use it for probing. What is important is to keep the two administrations and the data gained from them separate and to make sure that the standardized data are gathered before any probing takes place.

Probing Power or Speed.   If you administer a standardized test with vocabulary subtests, you can probe deeper into a student's understanding by doing some of the following probing after the test has been administered using the standardized procedures. As with all standardized tests, you need to look at a student's answer sheet. Does a raw score of 50 out of 100 represent 50 correct out of 100 answered? Or did a student get all of the first 50 correct but only finish half the test? This can tell you something about a student's working style and ability to access vocabulary quickly. Many students have been classified as having vocabulary problems when their real "problem" is slow and careful work. To probe on this hunch, return the test to the student along with the answer sheet and a colored pencil. Then rescore after the student has had ample time for completion. For this type of student, test-taking skills development might be more beneficial than special work on vocabulary.

Decoding Problem or Vocabulary Problem.   Sometimes students miss items on standardized vocabulary tests because they cannot decode the words. Administering missed test items orally, with the students reading aloud to you, will help you figure out if this is the real source of a low vocabulary score. If they are unable to decode a word correctly, you pronounce it and see if they can then choose a correct synonym.

Lack of Prior Knowledge Versus Lack of Vocabulary Knowledge.   Once the student can decode or hears the word and still can't provide a correct meaning or association, try to find out if the incorrect response is due to lack of prior knowledge of specific vocabulary. For example, a student who misses *igloo* can be asked what she knows about the Arctic. This can be done by asking the student to free-associate by telling you all she knows. If her associations are limited, this can be an indicator of lack of prior knowledge. A student with limited conceptual knowledge can't be expected to know specific vocabulary.

Sometimes, however, you will find a student who has the concepts but not the specific vocabulary. For example, after telling about the Arctic and the Inuit, the student was talking about their houses:

> You know, they're those round ones made out of snow blocks. You see them on Eskimo pies.

For this student, some direct specific vocabulary instruction might be in order.

Lack of Use of Context.   Many times, in a testing situation, students will not answer questions about vocabulary items that are explicitly explained in the text. Check to see if they can use the context by asking them to locate the word in the text, read the sentences before and after it, and then try the question a second time. For words that are implicitly defined in the context, try a questioning probe such as was done with Louisa above.

Language or Concepts: Potentially English Proficient Students.   With students for whom English is not their first language, you may wish to probe whether or not the vocabulary is the problem or the concepts are not well established. Using the Peabody Picture Vocabulary Test-Revised (Dunn & Dunn, 1981), where students can respond in their native languages, will help you get a sense of their level of oral vocabulary. If you are not a fluent speaker of their language, ask an adult speaker or foreign language teacher to help you translate for scoring. That person can also tell you when the picture or item is a cultural unknown so you can correct the scoring.

Pulling It All Together

Once individual assessment and probing are completed, you can plan mini-lessons or corrective instruction based on your findings. An example of a vocabulary diagnosis profile sheet is shown in Figure 7.14.

Name:_____   **Date:**_____

Grade:_____

Initial Observation:

Louisa seems at sea in social studies class, yet she is bright and capable in discussions after lectures. I need to look at her vocabulary knowledge.

Profile

Measure	Results	Observation/Probe
Standardized test	*verbal:* 1st percentile *math:* 5th percentile	Test sheet shows she finished; not a speed problem.
Decoding	95% of words decoded correctly	Used standardized test for reread and also IRI.
Concepts	On IRI, had problem with *sophisticated, crude* —missed questions related to terminology and vocabulary	Probed with IRI on second day. Had no knowledge of terms. Could go back and use context for explicit one, not for implicit one.
Oral vocabulary	PPVT-R: 5th percentile	Has good general oral vocabulary.

Plan:

Louisa has a good, everyday general vocabulary but lacks literary and textbook vocabulary. She also has a problem inferring meaning from the text, perhaps because there are too many words she doesn't know. Also, she is involved in learning English and often has a superficial knowledge of words even when she seems to have a deeper knowledge.

Goals

1. Make sure that prereading work establishes some of the critical vocabulary and concepts.
2. Make sure that postreading work clarifies sophisticated connections.
3. Do mini-lessons on inferring meaning from context.

Figure 7.14   Vocabulary Diagnostic Profile Sheet

Looking Back and Looking Ahead

In this chapter, we have presented several different ways of thinking about assessment. The type of assessment you use depends on your goal. If you want information that will directly inform your instruction, you can choose from many instructional activities that contain an assessment option, do structured or informal observation, have students do their own self-evaluations, or construct your own test. For large-scale assessment or for specific diagnostic needs, a standardized measure or probed informal reading inventory can be used. And for all of these, thoughtful record keeping is an added dimension. We hope, at this point, you are "looking ahead" to your own interpretation and use of some of the ideas we have presented in this book. Use the appendices, which appear later in the book, to find book, game, dictionary, and media resources for your classroom.

For Further Learning

Barr, R., Blachowicz, C. L. Z, Katz C., & Kaufman, B. (2001). *Reading diagnosis for teachers: An instructional approach*. White Plains: Longman. (Includes useful chapter on individual assessment of vocabulary)

Cooter, R. B. (1990). *The teacher's guide to reading tests*. Scottsdale, AZ: Gorsuch Publishers. (A concise guide to commercial and standardized assessment tools)

Johnson, D. D. (2000). *Vocabulary in the Elementary and Middle School*. Boston: Allyn & Bacon.

CHAPTER 8

VOCABULARY INSTRUCTION FOR LEARNERS WITH SPECIAL NEEDS

☑ Prepare Yourself

Prepare yourself by evaluating your own knowledge. Rate your ability to answer some of the key questions for this chapter. Check the boxes that best describe your prereading knowledge.

Key concept questions	Well informed	Aware	Need ideas
1. *What are some **instructional considerations** for **students with special needs** in relation to vocabulary?*	❏	❏	❏
2. *How do I make connections in general vocabulary instruction for **words that are related by topic or theme**?*	❏	❏	❏
3. *How can I use **imagery** to help make connections between words and their meanings?*	❏	❏	❏
4. *How do I make connections in vocabulary instruction for **students whose native language is not English**?*	❏	❏	❏

☑️ Strategy Overview Guide

This chapter presents background, ideas, and strategies to help you develop instruction in vocabulary that may be appropriate for some learners with special needs. Using the theme of making connections, we once again discuss making connections between words based on topic, but this time in the context of general vocabulary development. We elaborate on the use of synonyms to make connections between words, and we emphasize how connecting words with their antonyms can be a powerful concept for word learning. The difficulty of teaching students the connotations of words is addressed. Making connections between images and definitions can help students remember word meanings, so the keyword method is outlined. Finally we examine making connections when English is a second language. The following chart can help you choose suitable instructional strategies for your classroom.

Instructional strategy	Goal—use when you want to . . .	Comments
Word fluency (p. 170)	Help students use their own knowledge to categorize words.	Fun and harder than the students think initially. Good for ESL students.
Synonym webs (p.173)	Draw contrasts between synonyms for the same word.	Best as a class activity.
Synonym feature analysis (p. 173)	Focus on characteristics that distinguish one synonym of a word from another.	Can be added to over time.
Alphabetic antonyms (p. 177)	Have students learn meanings for a variety of unrelated words.	Best done in groups. A puzzler!
Analogy lines (p. 178)	Teach students the different forms of analogy.	A real eye-opener for some students.
Keywords (p. 178)	Link difficult words with their definition.	Can result in superficial learning.
Songs (p. 185)	Teach English as a second language.	Fun and motivating.
ESL buddies (p. 186)	Teach ESL students in the regular classroom.	A form of peer tutoring.

In earlier chapters, we introduced strategies for vocabulary learning and instruction that can be used with and by *all* children. Since each of us has unique human experiences, the way any of us learns a particular word will be idiosyncratic. However, some general principles for vocabulary learning have guided our discussion so far.

These principles, such as the need to connect new learning to prior knowledge and the importance of developing an active learner (see Chapter 1), hold true for all students, but some students may require particular attention because of some special needs. In this chapter, we introduce some strategies and techniques that are especially appropriate for such learners, although they can also be used with the general student population.

Any textbook on learners with special needs has lists of classifications used in our schools—LD, BD, EMH, TMH, ADD, visually challenged, auditorily challenged, and others. We have not made any attempt to address the needs of these particular groups separately. We have included a section in this chapter on students who are learning English as a second language because we consider differentiated vocabulary instruction to be a special need in their case. For all these groups, careful and systematic planning and instruction are the keys to successful vocabulary learning. For ESL students, there is the special case of making connections between two labels for a concept—one label in the native language and one label in English.

So far in this book, we have not discussed developing a student's vocabulary in situations that are not linked to some other form of instruction such as reading, writing, or oral language development. With some students, however, it may be appropriate to make vocabulary the focus of instruction simply to develop their knowledge of word meanings. We are not maintaining that the meanings of all the words that students need to know in school can be taught (see Chapter 1), but we do believe that students can benefit from being taught vocabulary without any other instructional purpose. Playing with language and being interested in words per se have benefits in many areas of the curriculum and beyond school.

As we learn vocabulary, the process of categorization is a way of ordering and organizing concepts. We have argued that part of vocabulary learning is making associations. For learners with special needs, we feel that this process needs to be strengthened through careful use of categorization and classification (O'Rourke, 1974). Such an approach should be systematic in terms of selecting the words to be learned and in grouping words for instruction according to some criteria. Under such a system, for example, young children would not learn the words *bed, potato, table, chair, carrot, cabbage, couch,* and *beans* on the same day, but would focus on vegetables for one day and furniture on another, building knowledge about a category along with the new words. By categorizing words using some criterion, students are able to more easily see and learn the connections between them. Some experts advocate the use of lists of core words that students in each grade level or those belonging to a particular population should learn, but we believe that these lists can be misused, and teachers are better able to select words for their particular students that will meet specific needs. So, while making these connections between words is important for *all* students, making them explicitly and systematically can be particularly important for those who have special needs. The focus of the chapter is, therefore, on making connections.

For learners with special needs, we offer the following guidelines for instruction:

1. Vocabulary should be addressed as a separate subject for instruction, not just in relation to other areas of the curriculum.

2.   Careful attention should be paid to the selection of appropriate words for systematic instruction and reinforcement.

3.   Meanings should be made explicit and comprehensible through demonstration, discussion, usage, and further discussion.

4.   Multiple modalities and avenues of expression should be used in instruction and learning.

5.   Attention should be paid to creating categories, such as semantic, thematic, or morphemic, for example, and not teaching isolated words.

In the following sections, we suggest strategies that use categories for instruction—those based on making connections through topic relatedness, through word relatedness, and with imagery. These strategies are not supposed to be used in isolation, but may be utilized together with some of those from previous chapters to develop a careful and systematic program. The principles of vocabulary instruction suggested in Chapter 1 also apply. In the final section, we briefly address making connections between English and another language.

MAKING CONNECTIONS THROUGH TOPIC RELATEDNESS

In previous chapters, we have emphasized the importance of presenting vocabulary in a meaningful context and in relation to words about the same or similar themes. These suggestions are usually related to instruction in reading, oral language, or the content areas. In this section, we present two techniques for teaching words that are related by topic, but that can also be used when the focus of instruction is to develop general vocabulary.

Word Fluency

Readence and Searfoss (1980) outline a technique that encourages students to use categorization to learn vocabulary. The task initially seems very simple—to name as many words as possible in 1 minute. In the beginning, the task can be demonstrated with one student before the class works in pairs. The teacher needs a watch or a clock with a second hand and pencil and paper. With the chosen student, the following directions can be given:

> I want to see how many words you can name in one minute. Any words will do, like *story, book,* or *friend.* When I say "ready" you begin and say the words as rapidly as you can and I will count them. Using sentences or counting numbers is not allowed. You must use separate words. Go as rapidly as you can. (Readence & Searfoss, 1980, p. 43)

The teacher can tally the words as the student says them. If students hesitate for 10 seconds or more, she can clue them to look around the room or to think about an activity the class did recently. Sophie, a fourth-grade student, managed the list in column 1 in Table 8.1 when she tried this the first time. Once the students have had a

Table 8.1 Sophie's Word Lists

Before Categorization	Thinking in Categories
tree	*Computer Stuff*
fish	CD Rom
computer	printer
picture	box
bee	*Birds*
eye	albatross
you	robin
see	crow
touch	*Tools*
feel	wrench
flour	knife
table	hammer
chair	monkey wrench
bear	screwdriver
flowers	nails
window	nut
cars	bolt
books	*Buildings*
door	tar
	roof
	bricks
	signs
	chair
	radiator
	playground
	Transport
	car
	bus
	truck

chance to work in pairs to see how many words they can name, the teacher asks for them to time her. The teacher models naming words in *categories*, which is much easier and faster than choosing random words. When Sophie had practiced thinking in categories, she was able to generate the longer list in column 2 in Table 8.1.

Students can practice this every day and graph their increased ability to name words. They might use these rules for scoring:

1. No repetitions, no number words, no sentences

2. One point for each word

3. One point for each category of four words or more

Once students are familiar with the activity, the teacher can ask them to name words on a particular topic or theme—animals, science, or families, for example.

Word fluency could also be used with a unit of study to reinforce vocabulary that has been taught in another way. Students in groups can also take turns to say a word on a particular topic that has been studied, for example, the Revolutionary War. If they do not say a word in 10 seconds, they lose a "life" out of three "lives." The student who remains alive longest is the winner.

List–Group–Label

Readence and Searfoss (1980) also outline a technique called list-group-label, which they attribute to Hilda Taba. The name of the technique summarizes its procedure, which asks students to list words on a particular topic, group them, and then specify the criterion they have used for grouping with a label. For example, the teacher could ask students to think of words to do with *danger*. The list might include:

enemy	alarm	fire	red
shout	snake	scare	cry
siren	fright	shoot	wolf
poison	warn	escape	run
bug	safe	peril	shelter
hazard	die		

Students might select *enemy, snake, wolf, poison,* and *bug* as being things that are dangerous. Others might select *shout, cry, shoot, run, alarm,* and *scare* as things that they do if there is danger. The teacher can collect different categories of words (allowing words to be in more than one category) and display them. If certain words do not fit in any category, a miscellaneous category can be created, or students can brainstorm words that might go with them to create a new category. Readence and Searfoss recommend keeping the list to about 25 words, depending on ability and grade level.

These two categorization exercises allow students to practice and develop their vocabularies without having to be concerned with definitions or supplying meanings. The categorizing in itself supplies sufficient structure for students to begin to learn meanings with which they are unfamiliar or to refine their understanding of meanings partially known.

MAKING CONNECTIONS THROUGH WORD RELATEDNESS

This section addresses teaching word meanings through focusing on the semantic relatedness of words. The idea seems almost tautological—when you relate a word to a meaning, then you must be talking about semantic relationships. What we mean, however, is that a teacher chooses a group of words for instruction based on its semantic relatedness rather than on some other criterion (such as theme or orthographic similarity). Three specific criteria will be examined—synonymy and antonymy. A third, morphology (using units of meaning within words), is addressed in the next chapter. In addition, we look at analogies as a way of demonstrating the semantic relation between particular words.

Synonyms

In Chapter 6, we talked about using synonyms in a word map to help students understand when they "knew" a word (see pp. 118–119). We argued that synonyms are especially useful in helping define adjectives and adverbs, such as *big* and *tall* or *badly* and *poorly*. However, as can be seen from these examples, all synonyms have a *slightly* different meaning than the target word has. While a *big* tree is usually a *tall* tree, we would not normally think of a *big* mushroom as being *tall*. If words did not differ slightly in meaning, why would there be a need for two words? Understanding these shades of meaning is something that can be problematic for students. Two instructional techniques that are extensions of ideas we presented earlier can help—synonym webs and synonym feature analysis.

Synonym Webs.   A **synonym web** is similar to a semantic map, but it refines the idea of a semantic map, which includes *all* types of related concepts, to an examination of relationships that are *only* synonymic. This type of web is particularly useful with words that have multiple meanings (Paul & O'Rourke, 1988).

Figure 8.1 shows a synonym web for the word *loose*. To complete such a web, follow the steps shown in Teaching Idea File 8.1.

While this activity makes clear the synonymic connections, it does not distinguish between the denotations and connotations of words (see the following sections). Students can, however, talk about this as they construct the web.

An alternative synonym web can be developed with usage attached to each synonym (see Figure 8.2). The advantage of this web is that it reminds students of appropriate uses of the word. The disadvantage is that it does not show the immediate connections between the synonyms. We have tried a combination of the two types of web, but found that it becomes cumbersome and confusing to many students.

As with many webbing activities, the discussion that goes along with the webbing may have the strongest impact on students' learning. The usage web may be more helpful, therefore, for less advanced students who need the usage to remind them of class or group discussions about appropriate contexts for using the word.

Connotations: Synonym Feature Analysis.   Since even synonyms have slightly different meanings, it is important for students to learn the difference between the denotations and the connotations of words. The **denotation** of a word is its general or literal meaning. For example, while *clothing* and *raiment* may have the same denotation, the connotation is very different. Thus *clothing* is "what people wear," but the word has connotations that would normally include the mundane or utilitarian, such as outdoor clothing. The **connotation** of a word is what may be suggested by or associated with the use of the word. The connotation for *raiment* is something splendid, such as clothing worn by princes and princesses on formal occasions, even though the denotation is still what people wear. Students often use words inappropriately when they understand the general meaning of a word, but not its connotation. So a student might write, "He put on his raiment to go out in the rain." In Chapter 4, we presented semantic feature analysis as one way of helping students recognize the distinguishing characteristics of words that belong to the same category

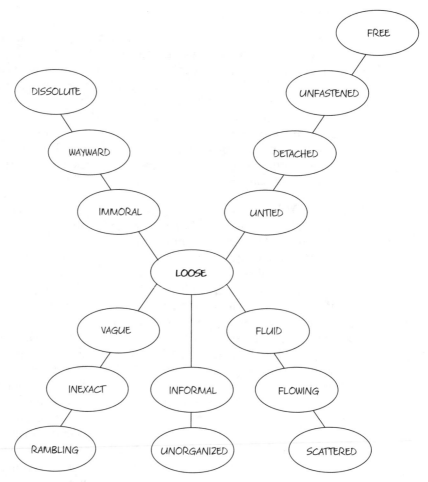

Figure 8.1   A Synonym Web for *Loose*

Teaching Idea File 8.1

Constructing a Synonym Web

1. Students brainstorm various synonyms and use a thesaurus to identify others.
2. The teacher then works with the students to determine which of the words "go together." This requires the students to categorize the words in some way and to demonstrate an understanding of how the meanings are related.
3. The words are connected on a web to show their relationship.
4. The students copy the web into their vocabulary notebook.

From Blachowicz & Fisher, *Teaching Vocabulary in All Classrooms*, p. 164.

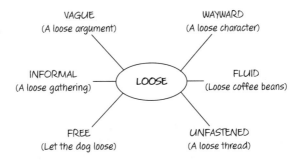

Figure 8.2   A Synonym Web with Usage

Table 8.2   Feature Analysis for *Gather* and Synonyms

	Done with People	Done to Things	Formal	Deliberate	Work	etc.
gather	+	+	?	+	?	
collect	+	+	?	+	?	
harvest	–	+	?	+	+	
accumulate	–	+	–	–	–	
assemble	+	+	+	+	?	
congregate	+	–	–	+	?	

(for example, people who deal with money; types of houses). This technique can also be used to clarify the connotations of synonyms.

Baldwin, Ford, and Readence (1981) suggest a method of using feature analysis that utilizes a thesaurus. They suggest that, before developing the feature analysis, teachers draw students' attention to connotative differences between synonyms by presenting words in a sentence frame. The teacher writes a sentence frame for a word (for example, *gathered*), and the students use a thesaurus to substitute possible synonyms in the frame. For example,

> The friends *gathered* in front of the ice cream stand.

> The friends *collected* in front of the ice cream stand.

> The friends *harvested* in front of the ice cream stand.

> The friends *accumulated* in front of the ice cream stand.

> The friends *assembled* in front of the ice cream stand.

> The friends *congregated* in front of the ice cream stand.

The teacher and the students then discuss the differences they notice between the meanings of the sentences, and they decide which sentences are acceptable and which are not. Sometimes sentences result that students find amusing, as in the third sentence above. Once students understand the denotative meaning of the word, the teacher and students together can create a feature matrix (Table 8.2).

If the teacher then provides an *appropriate* sentence context for each synonym, attention can be drawn to distinctive features. For example, the teacher might provide the sentence, "Congress *assembles* in Washington after each election." The students can note that Congress does not *accumulate* in Washington because people do not *accumulate*. Also when Congress *assembles*, it is a more formal *gathering* than when people *congregate*. As students complete the matrix, they can add distinguishing features that help them remember when to use one synonym or another. There may be differences of opinion about the distinguishing characteristics, but this allows for good discussion where students have to justify their thinking. Finally, it may be appropriate to "explore the matrix" (Baldwin, Ford, & Readence, 1981). The teacher can ask questions that explore the use of each synonym. For example, "If you wanted to describe how people *gathered* for a wedding, which would be the best word? If you were *gathering* signatures for a petition, which would be the best word to describe what you were doing?" Baldwin, Ford and Readence maintain that this system of presenting words in context, determining distinguishing features, and then reinforcing them in new contexts is a more effective and naturalistic way of instructing students in connotations than traditional methods, which tend to present words in isolation.

Teaching connotative meanings is extremely difficult. Even effective users of the English language may have difficulty verbalizing why they use one synonym rather than another in certain contexts. For learners with special needs, particularly ESL students, exercises that make connotative differences between words as clear as possible can help develop confidence in language use.

Antonyms

Although many words do not have antonyms (for example, *tree*), the use of polarity in defining words sets clear parameters in meaning. If you know that something is an opposite, then you understand along which dimensions, or by which features, the two words differ. Thus, knowing *big* is the antonym of *small*, you know that size is the characteristic in which they are opposites. If you know that *gather* is the antonym of *disperse*, you know that the dimension on which they differ is aggregation.

Powell (1986) argues that the use of antonyms can be one of the most powerful tools in vocabulary instruction. He notes that semanticists identify three main types of word opposition: contradictories (complementaries), contraries, and reciprocal (converse) terms. These relations are clarified in Table 8.3.

Contradictories are mutually exclusive (*single/married, part/whole*). **Contraries** allow for gradations (*big/small, transparent/opaque*). In **reciprocal** terms, one word reverses or undoes the meaning of the other (*buy/sell, gather/disperse*). However, for instructional purposes, Powell (1986) suggests drawing a distinction between polar antonyms and scalar antonyms. **Polar antonyms** are categorical and allow no intermediate terms (*husband/wife, buy/sell*). In other words, the assertion of one denies the possibility of the other. Both contradictories and reciprocals would fall into this category. **Scalar terms,** in contrast, allow gradations between extremes (*gigantic, big, large, small, tiny*). One of the instructional techniques possible with scalar terms is a semantic gradient (Chapter 5, pp. 95–96). Antonyms are also used on a word map (pp. 118–119) and in other defining exercises (Chapter 6).

Table 8.3 Types of Antonymy

Polar Antonyms		Scalar Antonyms
Contradictories	**Reciprocals**	**Contraries**
single/married	buy/sell	big/small

Teaching Idea File 8.2

Constructing an Alphabet-Antonyms Table

(Based on Powell, 1986)

1. The teacher selects words beginning with the same letter.
2. She prepares a two-column table, with the antonyms of the target words listed in the first column.
3. Students complete the table, in groups or individually, knowing only that the words in the second column begin with the same letter.
4. After a 5-minute period, students may use a thesaurus, a synonym dictionary, or other resource.
5. Students share their tables and display a completed table for reference.

From Blachowicz & Fisher, *Teaching Vocabulary in All Classrooms*, p. 167.

Table 8.4 Alphabet-Antonyms Table

Antonyms	Target Words
succeed	
allow	
remember	
whole	
back	

Powell (1986) suggests an alphabetic-generative activity that requires students to use their vocabulary knowledge and a dictionary, thesaurus, or synonym/antonym dictionary (see Teaching Idea File 8.2).

An example might be if a teacher selects *fail, forbid, forget, fraction,* and *front* as target words. She then presents the antonyms to the students, without the target words—in this example *succeed, allow, remember, whole,* and *back* as in Table 8.4. The students have to guess the target words, knowing that they all begin with the letter *f*. For younger students, the activity can be done with the whole class or in groups. For older students, the teacher can use a word list where she wants students to learn the meanings of the words she gives them, rather than the words beginning with the same letter. See Table 8.5, for example.

Students enjoy puzzles such as this and can easily learn to construct them for each other using a synonym/antonym dictionary or a thesaurus.

Table 8.5 Alphabet-Antonyms Table for Older Students

Antonyms	Target Words
broad	narrow
pleasant	nasty
wisdom	nonsense
obsolete	new
dispensable	necessary

Analogies

Hofler (1981) suggested a way of using scalar terms to teach analogies to students. He used a word line, which is similar to a semantic gradient, like the word lines shown in Figure 8.3. The teacher can demonstrate how to develop an antonym analogy, a synonym analogy, and a degree analogy in relation to the words on a particular line. Then students can use a thesaurus or dictionary to construct their own word lines and analogies and try them out on each other. With many scalar terms, there may be some discussion about which term goes where on the word line, for example whether *murky* or *gloomy* is closer to *dark* on the word line in the figure. This discussion, as with those about synonyms in the activities described earlier, can help students clarify their understandings of terms.

MAKING CONNECTIONS WITH IMAGERY

It is important to recognize that although vocabulary learning has to be verbal in nature, other modalities can be used to help reinforce and supplement learning. One of the strongest techniques for linking word meanings and images is the keyword method, which has received much attention in the literature for ESL instruction and developmental education (Mastropieri, 1988; McCarville, 1993).

The Keyword Method

The keyword method of vocabulary instruction has a long history of effectiveness for teaching the definitions of words (Pressley, Levin, & Delaney, 1983). In the **keyword method,** imagery is used to connect words with their definitions, which has proved effective with various special populations (Mastropieri, 1988). The method is a mnemonic device that uses both auditory and visual cues to enhance the learning of information about word meanings. One recommended procedure for teaching the method to students is using the steps of recoding, relating, and retrieving (Mastropieri, 1988).

Recoding.   **Recoding** involves selecting part of the target word that looks like or sounds like a word with which the student is familiar. For example, for the word *apex*, a student might select the word *ape*. For the word *corpuscle*, a student might select *corpse*. In other words, students recode the original word into a word that they can easily picture.

Figure 8.3 Word Lines: Analogies

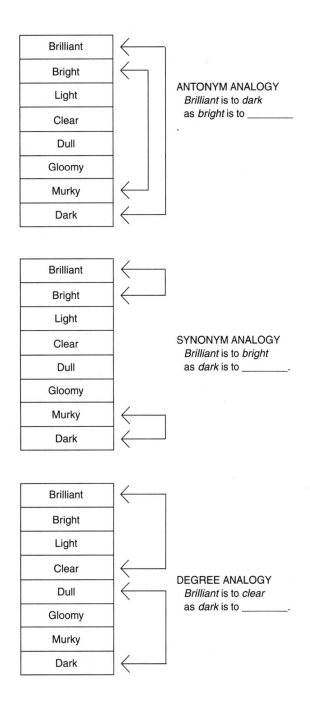

Brilliant
Bright
Light
Clear
Dull
Gloomy
Murky
Dark

ANTONYM ANALOGY
Brilliant is to *dark*
as *bright* is to _____
.

Brilliant
Bright
Light
Clear
Dull
Gloomy
Murky
Dark

SYNONYM ANALOGY
Brilliant is to *bright*
as *dark* is to _____.

Brilliant
Bright
Light
Clear
Dull
Gloomy
Murky
Dark

DEGREE ANALOGY
Brilliant is to *clear*
as *dark* is to _____.

Table 8.6   Keywords for Scientific Word Parts

Word Part	Keyword	Interactive Illustration
ornith	oar	bird carrying an oar
thero	thermos	wild animal drinking from a thermos
paleo	pail	old people carrying pails
sauro	saw	a lizard sawing
bronto	bronco	a bronco bucking in thunder

Note. From "Using the Keyword Method" by M. A. Mastropieri, *Teaching Exceptional Children, 20* (Winter), 1988, 4–8. Copyright 1988 by The Council for Exceptional Children. Reprinted with permission.

Relating.   The next step for students is **relating** the recoded word to the definition of the original word using imagery. For example, since the definition of *apex* is a highest point, a student might relate the recoded word *ape* to the definition by imagining an ape at a very high point (King Kong on the Empire State Building?). The definition of *corpuscle* is a blood cell, so a student might imagine a corpse traveling around the arteries of a body reaching out with "dead" arms to pick up oxygen or attacking disease-carrying germs in the form of monsters.

Retrieving.   The last step is **retrieving,** or recalling, the meaning of the target word. When a learner sees the word, the first step is to think of the keyword for that word (*ape* or *corpse*). Next, the picture or image related to that word has to be recalled—the ape on a high place, the corpse in the bloodstream. Finally the image must be linked to the definition.

To teach the keyword method, the teacher must model the process using familiar words. Mastropieri (1988) includes an account of teaching the morphemes shown in Table 8.6 to middle school LD students, who then applied the meanings to figuring out the dinosaur terms *ornithopoda, theropoda, paleopoda,* and *brontosaurus.*

Since the keyword method uses a mnemonic device, it does not result in an extended understanding of a word's meaning. However, it does provide a beginning from which students can develop a more elaborated understanding through subsequent exposures to the word.

MAKING CONNECTIONS WHEN ENGLISH IS A SECOND LANGUAGE

Nationally, in 1993–94, 46% of schools contained LEP students, with 17.8% having bilingual programs and 42.7% having ESL programs (National Center for Educational Statistics, 1997). Most educators are not surprised by these numbers, especially classroom teachers who are aware of more and more students in their classes whose native language is not English. Despite the growth in the number of ESL programs and across the country, students who do receive ESL support spend only a fraction of their time in school in support classrooms. When they are in regular classrooms, the vast majority of LEP students have teachers who have had no ESL training (Clair, 1995). This limited availability of informed ESL instruction means that all teachers need to become more knowledgeable about the issues in ESL instruction. One major part of that instruction is teaching English vocabulary. This section focuses on teaching word meanings to nonnative speakers of English in regular literacy classrooms. Bilingual education classrooms, where the teacher is bilingual in English and another language, have different dynamics than ESL classrooms, where students may speak multiple languages and the teacher cannot speak them all.

It might appear logical that a primary focus of language instruction in multilingual classrooms is teaching word meanings, but the history of ESL instruction shows that the issue can be more complex. Carter and McCarthy (1988) and Maiguashca (1993) provide historical views of the role of vocabulary instruction in second-language learning. They note the movement from controlled vocabulary lists in the late 1930s and 1940s, through structural approaches that emphasized the importance of teaching grammar, to a focus on a communicative approach, to a more recent emphasis on teaching vocabulary. Although all these approaches still have advocates, several books on teaching vocabulary to second-language learners (Carter & McCarthy, 1988; Huckin, Haynes, & Coady, 1993; Nation, 1990; Taylor, 1990) and a series of annotated bibliographies (Meara, 1983, 1987, 1993) demonstrate this concern with vocabulary as a focus for non-native English speakers. Some of these texts and references are more concerned with learners of English as a foreign language (EFL), but in addition what many of these texts presuppose is that the students are being taught in settings where all the students are nonnative English speakers and where vocabulary is the primary focus of instruction. However, the needs of classroom teachers who are teaching literacy to both native English speakers and ESL students are not often addressed. We will focus here on principles of ESL instruction in regular classrooms, and some techniques for vocabulary instruction that meet those principles.

Several researchers (Garcia, 1994; Gersten, 1996; Truscott & Watts-Taffe, 1997) have developed guidelines for literacy instruction for second-language learners. As Garcia (1994) notes, "Second language learners of English will have different instructional needs depending on their ages, educational experiences, language backgrounds, cultures and communities" (first page). However, some general guidelines can be developed in relation to most students. Rather than iterate these in a block, we will present them one at a time with specific implications for vocabulary instruction. The order in which they are presented is not meant to be hierarchical, and does not imply that one guideline is more important than any other.

Activate and Use Prior Knowledge

This is so much a part of our regular literacy instruction, that this recommendation does not appear to be very helpful. Yet with ESL students, drawing on their existing understanding of words may be vital. Students may know a concept and a word for it in their native language, and all we have to do is provide an English equivalent. If, however, they do not have the concept, richer vocabulary instruction may be necessary. Two prereading vocabulary activities that we have mentioned before lend themselves well to the activation and utilization of prior knowledge.

Table 8.7 Knowledge rating for *Peck, Slither and Slide*

	Can Define It	Know About It	Never Heard It
build			
wade			
woodpecker			
walrus			
reach			
slither			
leopard			
peck			

In/out is an exclusion brainstorming exercise that asks students to decide, usually as a group, which words presented by the teacher will appear **in** a text or **out** of a text or passage that they will read. It works well at any level, but in this example a first-grade teacher with some ESL students is going to read the book *Lunch* by Denise Fleming out loud to her students. The book tells the tale of a mouse who eats a variety of vegetables and fruits for his lunch. Each two-page spread gives a clue to the next menu item by presenting a picture of part of the vegetable or fruit and a color. The teacher is concerned that in order to participate in the activity the students need to know the names of the items and the colors associated with them. She asks them to decide which of the following words will appear—*apple, carrot, frog, turnip, peas, bicycle, berries, grapes, computer, corn, watermelon, seeds*. After showing and reading each word to them, she stops and asks, "Will this be *in* the story?" When the students respond, she says, "Why?" This step is important because it requires some prediction of text content and thus activates prior knowledge. With this book, and with her expectations, when students correctly identify a fruit or a vegetable, the teacher also asks, "What color are peas?" This ensures that all students can participate in using the picture and word clues to predict what menu item will be appearing next.

A second activity, a knowledge rating (Blachowicz, 1986), also asks students to examine teacher-selected words prior to reading a text. This exercise draws on students' prior knowledge and encourages them to monitor their own knowledge. It is particularly appropriate for second-language learners because it addresses partial knowledge of words. The teacher selects some easy and some hard words that will appear in the passage, and asks students to decide whether they know the meaning of the word (perhaps a definition), know something about the word, or have never heard it. Having students complete a table like that in Table 8.7 for *Peck, Slither and*

Slide by Suse MacDonald (1997) allows students to work individually or in pairs. This book is a wonderfully illustrated vocabulary lesson on words used to describe the motion of various animals.

Incorporate Tasks That Use Language Purposefully

This guideline focuses on the importance of the functional use of language for learning to occur. Many school tasks, such as completing a phonics worksheet, may not seem purposeful to students. We know that language learning occurs best when language is used to communicate for authentic reasons. Having students participate in literature discussion groups, engaging them in collaborative learning, and involving them in a process approach to writing are examples of classroom occasions when language can be used purposefully. Perez (1994, 1996) has conducted research on instructional conversations, which she defines as "true conversations in which both the teacher and students are engaged as partners in the pursuit of some new understanding" (1996, p. 174). One of her examples demonstrates how students can explore the meanings of new words as they try to solve problems. The second/third-grade teacher has created a situation in which students are making bubbles, and in which they must find how bubbles vary in size and color according to the type of solutions used to make them. In her directions she says, "The vocabulary I want to hear is *experiment, measure, solution, observe,* and *results*" (Perez, 1996, p. 176). The transcripts of the conversations reveal that the students *do* explore the meanings of these words, as when Esperanza says, "Na-ah! We can—can't just guess. We 'pose to be doing an esperment" (Perez, 1996, p. 176). Instructional conversations clearly work best when they are about concrete experiences that children are interested in, and where students work in small groups so that the teacher and fluent English speakers can provide linguistic modeling and scaffolding. Perez warns that it is important to allow time for students to learn the vocabulary of a topic—they may need to listen for two or three sessions before they are willing to contribute. This is an excellent reminder to us that learning words and their meanings takes time, especially when concepts are new.

Scaffold the Use of English

Certainly instructional conversations are situations in which teachers and students can model and scaffold the use of English. However, it would be an unusual classroom where these types of conversations occur all the time. Besides organizing students into linguistically heterogeneous groups, what other literacy activities scaffold the use of English? The one that appears most commonly in classrooms, but is valuable nonetheless, is the teacher reading aloud to students, especially if followed by choral reading. For example, the teacher might read a big book and then have students join in on repeated lines. The syntax and vocabulary will become internalized as students read and reread the same text. Partner reading, while not providing the same level of support, also allows scaffolding to occur. Finally, although it is not always appropriate, providing an oral meaning of words can be a form of scaffolding.

Just as when a two-year-old asks the meaning of a word (such as *ebony*), we don't rush to the dictionary but provide a contextually appropriate meaning (such as "the black keys on a piano are made of ebony"), so with students in our classrooms. Often we give students more information than they need about a word, or more information than they can process. A use of the word in a sentence that provides sufficient information for understanding, and also a second example of the use of the word, may be more meaningful than some formal definition.

Focus on Comprehension

We all learn words gradually, and it is important to allow ESL students to demonstrate some understanding through approximations. Allowing and respecting these partial meanings is one component of effective vocabulary instruction for all learners, but is especially important for students struggling to make themselves understood in a new language. An activity like the knowledge rating outlined above is helpful in this respect. But in addition to accepting partial knowledge of words, focusing our reading instruction on meaning or comprehension of extended text allows students to compensate for the lack of understanding of some words by demonstrating a general understanding of the main points of the text. One prediction activity that focuses students on vocabulary, but also demonstrates that approximation is appropriate, is a story impression. In this activity the teacher presents words and phrases from a story that is about to be read, and students try to construct the story line themselves before reading the original story. For example, before reading *Harry and the Terrible Whatzit* by Dick Gackenbach (1977), a teacher might present the following words and phrases:

> Harry, Mom
> dark cellar
> Terrible Whatzit
> strike, broom
> smaller and smaller
> pouf and vanish
> Mom, safe
> scream next door

Students generally have no problem working out that Harry saves his Mom from the Terrible Whatzit in the dark cellar by hitting it with a broom. The vanishing and the scream from next door often produce different predictions. When the students read the text, they find that the gist of their stories matches the original, with some interesting variations. They are thrilled that they "got it right," and at the same time have learned about approximations being OK and have used their prior experiences and vocabulary in their learning. When developing a story impression, it is often best to use words that describe the setting, characters, problem, actions, and resolution, and to keep the list of words fairly short. This allows the construction of stories with an outline similar to the original, but different enough that interesting variations can occur.

Incorporate Various Media

The use of pictures and charts allows ESL students to better understand difficult words and texts. Labeling items around the room may be appropriate with some grade levels and new ESL students. Using audiotapes and videotapes allows students who have difficulty with reading to process the information in more than one format. Computers are a wonderful tool for teachers of ESL students. We recently watched a third-grade student, who had arrived from Korea 6 weeks prior to our visit, spend 15 to 20 minutes with a computer program that highlighted and "read" text to her, asked her to read along, and then asked her to read by herself. She diligently did so, even though the text was similar to "Run, Spot, run." The combination of the visual pictures (of Spot running), the audio, and highlighted text motivated this little girl in a way that only one medium could not have done. By the time she became bored with the program, she had certainly learned the meaning of the word *run* (as well as several other words), and also how to read and say it. In a world that increasingly emphasizes graphic information, it is encumbent upon us to utilize graphic sources in our literacy and language teaching.

Have Students Use Multiple Modalities

We often have students respond to text in writing, such as answering questions or keeping a literature log, but less often allow them to respond through pictures and acting. When students perform charades, where they choose a word that they think is important from the passage they have read, and act out the word for other students to guess, meanings may be more easily demonstrated by ESL students than through writing. Similarly, having them choose a word to illustrate may be appropriate on occasions. Asking peers not just to guess the word, but to discuss *why* they think that word was chosen from the passage, adds an extra dimension to the learning. It encourages students to be more thoughtful in their choice of words, and it focuses students back on what the passage was about, as well as on the word itself.

Using songs as part of a foreign language curriculum is hardly a new idea, but in an age where popular singers are known worldwide, it would be strange to ignore such an obvious source of vocabulary learning. In addition to building on students' natural interest in popular culture, music addresses the right brain in contrast to most vocabulary instruction, which has to rely largely on left-brain approaches. Guglielmino (1986) argues that songs bridge the hemispheres, strengthening the retention of language through the complementary functioning of the right brain as it learns the melody.

Although every song is an opportunity for students to expand their vocabulary, Guglielmino (1986) suggests these guidelines for selecting songs:

1. The tune should be easy to learn and easy to sing. Students will not relax if they are trying to reach a high note.
2. The words and structures should closely represent standard spoken English. Learning about "Herring boxes without topses" from "Clementine" may be more confusing than helpful!

3.   The content of the song should be related to the lesson.

4.   Students should be able to view the words to the song at some point in the lesson.

5.   Activities should be designed around the song—for example, an antonym or synonym search.

6.   For those students who are just beginning to learn English, the teacher should try to select songs with repetitive lyrics or with a chorus.

Teaching students songs without connecting the vocabulary to meaning is like teaching students phonics and not allowing them to read real books. Melody can be a great tool for learning, but the full enjoyment of singing songs is in their interpretation.

Provide Opportunities for Literacy Work in Students' Native Languages

This is hard to do when the teacher does not understand the language, but it is important to honor the various languages that may be represented in the classroom and to celebrate the diversity. One way is for students to learn the words for regularly used concepts, not just in English, but in some other languages. Words of praise and encouragement are popular—it's wonderful to be able to say "Great job" in several languages. Another activity that works well at the end of a unit of study is a categories game (see page 216). To celebrate the linguistic diversity in a class, the teacher could allow words in languages other than English.

ESL Buddies

Many schools are experimenting with buddies for all types of instruction. Eighth-grade students read to kindergartners or write down their stories. Fifth-grade students show second graders how to use computers. More and more teachers are recognizing how peer tutoring helps not just the tutee, but also the tutor. As teachers we know that we *really* get to know a subject when we have to teach it! Having ESL buddies in schools can help both those students who are proficient in English and those who are not. The nature of the buddy system will be as varied as the curriculum and the children in the school. When two students collaborate on a research project, the ESL student may learn as much vocabulary as during a more structured vocabulary lesson. The tutor may learn new perspectives from the tutee and develop a better understanding of the nature of our multicultural society.

Buehler and Meltesen (1983) suggest that the teacher present four rules for native English-speaking students to use when instructing their buddies:

- Speak in short, simple sentences.

- Speak naturally, but slowly. Leave pauses after each phrase and after each sentence.

- Use gestures and act out meanings of words. Don't hesitate to draw pictures and use props, if that would help.

- Don't try to teach too much. Check to see that she [the student] understands two or three items thoroughly before going on to teach more. (p. 120)

They go on to outline some strategies that buddies can use for writing, spelling, ESL drill, phonics, and vocabulary. For buddy work with vocabulary, the suggested focus is on the use of picture cards with words on the back, usually in categories such as food, animals, and clothes.

Freeman and Freeman (1993) describe a school in which the buddies are required to speak Spanish rather than English. The teacher tells students that "English is all around. You are the experts for the younger kids who need primary language instruction" (p. 558). The argument here is that knowledge of the processes of literacy, and the content of the curriculum, will transfer faster when children are experts in their primary language prior to learning the English equivalent.

It is important that linguistically diverse classrooms are places where risk taking is allowed so that students can learn English without fear of failure. As teachers, we need to make our communication explicit, to structure classroom routines so that they are easily understandable and predictable, and to clearly state expectations for success and participation. Rules and criteria for success that may be apparent to native English speakers may be less so to ESL students. In classroom environments where procedures and expectations are clear, students will be more comfortable and become better learners. After all, vocabulary and language learning will occur whatever we do, but it is our task as teachers to make the learning easy and rapid and as much fun as possible.

Looking Back and Looking Ahead

For students with special needs, systematic and careful instruction may be a necessity for developing vocabulary knowledge. In this chapter, we have outlined how to make some connections between word meanings by using topics and themes, synonymy, antonymy, and imagery. We have also addressed principles of instruction for ESL students. None of these methods is sufficient in itself, but must be combined with other techniques that begin with the student and with the student's knowledge so that meaningful learning can occur. One of the methods that can be important for all learners, but especially for nonnative English speakers, is using morphology, which is addressed in the next chapter.

For Further Learning

Freeman, D. E., & Freeman, Y. S. (1993). Strategies for promoting the primary languages of all students. *The Reading Teacher, 46,* 552–558. (Describes ways of having students help each other with language learning)

Hatch, E., & Brown, C. (Eds.). (1995). *Vocabulary, semantics, and language education.* Cambridge University Press. (Primarily a theoretical book with some practical suggestions)

Pressley, M., Levin, J. R., & Delaney, H. D. (1983). The mnemonic keyword method. *Review of Educational Research, 52,* 6–91. (An extensive review of the keyword method)

http://mind.ucsc.edu/vip.

Vocabulary Improvement Project (VIP). The Vocabulary Improvement Project (VIP) is a national research program funded by the U.S. Department of Education. The project's main goal is to develop intervention strategies aimed at helping children who are learning English develop vocabulary.

http://idea.uoregon.edu/~ncite/documents/techrep/tech14.html.

NCITE Reading Research Synthesis. NCITE Research Synthesis: Reading and Diverse Learners NCITE staff reviewed reading research on the design of instructional materials for diverse learners in six general areas—vocabulary literacy, phonological amateurs, and metacognitive strategies acquisition, word recognition, text organization, emergent.

http://www.web-books.com/Language.

Interactive Audio-Picture English Lessons. This site offers interactive ESL with pronunciation and pictures.

http://www.englishclub.net.

EnglishCLUB.net This site features grammar and vocabulary activities, word games, pen pal listings, and question-and-answer service. Includes free classroom handouts for ESL teachers.

http://www.englishday.com.

Learn English—Have Fun. This site offers online English crosswords, ESL word games, jokes, tests, and word search puzzles. New games and crosswords added regularly.

http://www.aitech.ac.jp/~itesls.

Interesting Things for ESL Student. This site has a free web-based textbook and fun study activities. There is a daily page for English, proverbs, slang, anagrams, quizzes, and more.

CHAPTER 9

VOCABULARY AND SPELLING INSTRUCTION USING STRUCTURAL ANALYSIS

☑ **Prepare Yourself**

Prepare yourself by evaluating your own knowledge. Rate your ability to answer some of the key questions for this chapter. Check the boxes that best describe your prereading knowledge.

Key concept questions	Well informed	Aware	Need ideas
1. What are **morphemes**, and how are they connected to **vocabulary instruction**?	❏	❏	❏
2. Which **affixes** are important for students to know, and how should I teach them?	❏	❏	❏
3. How do I make **connections** between **vocabulary and spelling instruction**, and why is it important?	❏	❏	❏
4. What is **etymology**, and where can I find **sources** for word origins?	❏	❏	❏

Strategic Overview Guide

This chapter introduces the connection between spelling and meaning instruction. It describes ways in which students who are in the later grades (third grade and above) can learn the importance of deriving meaning from word parts or morphemes. It outlines how morphemes can impact on the spelling of a word, and the ways in which students can learn about this derivational constancy.

Instructional strategy	Goal—use when you want to . . .	Comments
Generating compound words (p. 191)	*Begin structural analysis instruction.*	*Collect interesting combinations and meaning changes.*
Incidental morphemic analysis (p. 192)	*Develop understanding of morphemes and how they impact meaning.*	*Use words from texts that students are reading.*
Teaching prefixes through a context and definition procedure (p. 193)	*Focus on affixes and how they change meaning.*	*It is useful to begin with words which are familiar to students.*
Constructing "affixionaries" (p. 193)	*Develop students' understanding of prefixes and suffixes.*	*Fun at all grade levels.*
Teaching word families (p. 195)	*Teach about root words.*	*Involves analogical reasoning.*
Words sorts (p. 198)	*Teach spelling patterns that involve a change in pronunciation through the addition of affixes.*	*An inductive task for small groups and individuals.*
Teaching root words with manipulatives (p. 200)	*Reinforce root words and affixes.*	*Very motivational.*

We have all at one time or another used our knowledge of word parts and Latin or Greek roots to help decipher the meaning of an unfamiliar word. Often we do this by analogy with other words and an effective use of the context in which the word is spoken or written. For example, we might work out the meaning of *bicuspid* in relation to the bi- in *bicycle* or *biplane* and our knowledge of the word *cusp* and recognize from the fact that a dentist is talking to us that it is a tooth with two points. Some of us will have learned the meaning of most of these roots through analogy, but many of us were taught them in school. It is also important to teach students particular meanings of affixes and root words so that inferences about meaning can become transparent, and the process of determining meaning through structural analysis is internalized.

English spelling is impacted by the semantic or meaning system. Although the *a* in *relative* is pronounced as a schwa (a vowel that is pronounced as *uh*), students can understand the reason for the spelling when they see the word family *relate, relation, relative*. The system of vowel alternation, and other similar patterns, only makes sense if you understand that it is based in meaning. The teaching of word families that are related in this way often occurs in spelling instruction. In this way spelling and vocabulary instruction are linked.

Second-language learners can also benefit from structural analysis. We know that loan translation is a common process in second-language learning, and knowledge of common morphemes in both languages can help in making such learning a positive experience. Those of us who have tried learning another language know that cognates can be both helpful and deceptive. It is really helpful that *excellent* in English and *excelente* in Spanish have comparable meanings. However, false cognates can cause problems—such as *excusado*, which means *toilet*. Theorists and educators differ on the usefulness of teaching cognates, but whatever they believe, we know that learners will still engage in loan translation. Consequently morpheme instruction may play a positive role with second-language learners.

In this chapter we explore the way in which we can make morphological connections for students to explicate meanings. We then explore how spelling and vocabulary instruction may be linked through morphology, and indicate common spelling patterns that should be taught. Finally, we provide a brief introduction to etymology.

MORPHOLOGICAL CONNECTIONS

As part of vocabulary instruction, the structural analysis of words can draw students' attention to the morphemes that compose a word; and from an analysis of the meanings of the individual morphemes, students are helped to understand the meaning of the whole word. A **morpheme** is the smallest unit of meaning in a language. For example, *cats* has two morphemes: *cat* and the plural *s*.

A word may have several morphemes, but there is a general distinction between free morphemes, which can stand alone (for example, *cut*), and bound morphemes, which need to be attached to another morpheme (for example, *-ing* in *cutting,* or *un-* in *uncut*). Free morphemes are commonly called **root words,** whereas bound morphemes are **affixes** (prefixes and suffixes). Two free morphemes can bind together to form compound words, such as *airplane*. There is no agreement about the best way to structure lessons for teaching morphemic analysis, so in this section, we describe instruction that relates to compound words, incidental morphemic analysis, affixes, and root words.

Compound Words

Young children can have strange ideas about how compound words get their meanings. Gleason (1969, reported in Lapp & Flood, 1986) found that one small boy thought that an *airplane* was so called because it was a *plain* thing that went in the *air*. Another child believed it was the quickness with which it was consumed before school that made the meal *breakfast*. What both of these children understood, however, was that you could try to work out a word's meaning from its parts. A good place to begin instruction about structural analysis, therefore, is to have students generate as many compound words as they can. Once you have the list, ask students to divide the words into the following categories:

1.   Words where the meaning is a combination of the two parts (for example, *sidewalk, birthday*).

2.   Words where the meaning is related to, but not completely represented by, the meaning of the two morphemes (for example, *cowboy, shipyard*).

Notice that there may be some words where idiomatic or figurative use has changed the meaning (for example, *moonstruck*), but these are uncommon. Students can then discuss how words in the second category may have developed different meanings. Students may also draw pictures to show a possible meaning as compared with the real meaning. This activity can introduce how word meanings may change over time and can prepare students for the idea that spellings, as well as meanings, change (see Templeton, 1983, and below).

Incidental Morphemic Analysis

Manzo and Manzo (1990) argue that morphemic analysis is best taught incidentally. They recommend watching for words in reading assignments that may be unfamiliar to students but that have familiar word parts. The procedure suggested is:

1.   Present the word with helpful morphemic elements underlined. For example, *seis mo graph.*

2.   Ask students to use the underlined words to determine the meaning if they can and to explain their reasoning. If they correctly predict the word meaning, write it under the word and go on to steps 3 and 4.

3.   Give extra "level-one clues" to the students by writing easier words using the same morphemes underneath (see Table 9.1). Ask for predicted meanings.

4.   Give extra "level-two clues," which are the morpheme meanings, and ask for predictions until the students determine the correct meaning.

Table 9.1   Incidental Morphemic Analysis

	Seis	**mo**	**Graph**
Level-One Clues	Seizure		telegraph
			graphic
Level-Two Clues	to shake		written
Definition	An instrument that records earthquakes.		

Note. Reprinted with the permission of Simon & Schuster, Inc. from the Merrill/Prentice Hall text *Content Area Reading: A Heuristic Approach* by Anthony Manzo and Ula Manzo. Copyright © 1990 by Prentice Hall, Inc.

You can see that although this is incidental instruction, the method includes using familiar words to help students make analogies with the new word. For some students, it may be appropriate to teach affixes more formally.

Affixes

Knowledge of the meanings of common affixes may help students generate the meanings of new words that they encounter. Fortunately, words with common affixes (such as *return*) are a part of most children's speaking vocabulary. This means that instruction can begin from what students know and proceed to the unknown.

Graves and Hammond (1980) argue that there are three reasons for teaching prefixes: First, there are relatively few prefixes, and many are used in a large number of words. Second, most prefixes have relatively constant meanings that are easily definable. And third, prefixes tend to have consistent spellings. Harris and Sipay (1990) report the most commonly used prefixes, noting that according to some calculations 4 prefixes (*un-, re-, in-,* and *dis-*) account for about half of the common prefixed words in English, and that 20 prefixes account for nearly all prefixed words. Breen (1960) argues that 11 suffixes and their variants account for the most common meanings. These suffixes do not include inflectional endings, such as *-ed* or *-ing*. (A list of the most common affixes and their meanings is shown in Table 9.2.)

For teaching prefixes, Graves and Hammond (1980) used a context and definition procedure that transferred to new words that seventh-grade students had not encountered before during instruction (see Teaching Idea File 9.1). They found that this method of instruction was more effective than teaching the students just the words, without separating the prefix.

Irwin and Baker (1989) recommend teaching one prefix at a time and constructing original words with the students. They suggest:

1. Explain the prefix, for example, *mono-*.

2. Have students construct a word family list (for example, *monotony, monocycle, monocle, monologue*).

3. Develop original words and definitions with the students (for example, "one-headed" would be *monoheaded*).

4. Have students create their own new words and illustrate them. Create an *Our Own Words* dictionary.

Irwin and Baker emphasize that this is an activity to demonstrate how prefixes work and that it should be applied to meaningful reading tasks.

A similar dictionary-type activity has been suggested by Lindsay (1984). Students construct their own "affixionaries" in which affixes are listed alphabetically, with one page for each affix. The entry on each page might have the definition at the top, followed by words using the affix and sentences that have examples of the words. Table 9.3 shows what this might look like for the *con-* words used previously. Students may choose to list the prefixes and the suffixes separately to avoid confusion.

Table 9.2 Common Affixes and Their Meanings

Affix	Meaning	Examples
Prefixes		
ab	away from	absent
ad, ap, at	to, toward, near	advance, appeal, attract
bi	two	bicycle, binoculars
com, con, col, co	with, together	combine, conference, collide, cooperate
de	from, reverse	defect, decompose
dis	not, opposite from	disappear, disconnect
em, en	in, into	embed, enroll
ex	out, former, beyond	explode, ex-husband, exceed
in, im	in, into, not	inside, immortal, incorrect
mono	one	monorail
ob, op	against	obstruct, oppose
post	after	postpone
pre	before	prefix, prewar
pro	in favor of, ahead of	pro-taxes, progress
re	back, again	return, replay
sub	under	submarine, subsoil
super	over, greater than normal	supervise, superstar
trans	across	translate
tri	three	triangle
un	not, the opposite of	unequal, unpopular
Suffixes		
al	referring to	optical
ble	likely to be	divisible, probable
ence, ance, ancy	act of, state of	difference, acceptance, truancy
er, or	someone who does	teacher, professor
ful	full of, tending to	powerful, forgetful
ian	someone who is an expert in	musician, tactician
ic, ical	like, referring to	symbolic, geographical
ist	someone who does or believes in	pianist, scientist, abolitionist
less	without	painless, hopeless
ly	in the manner of	kindly, safely
ment	result of, act of	discouragement, punishment
ness	state of being	happiness
ous, ious	like, full of	nervous, tedious
tion, sion	act of	locomotion, permission
ty, ity	quality of	tasty, rapidity
ward	in the direction of	backward

Teaching Idea File 9.1

Teaching Prefixes

(Based on Graves & Hammond, 1980)

1. Present the prefix in isolation and also attached to four words (for example, *con-, construct, converge, conference, connect*).
2. Define the prefix. For example, *con-* means "to put together."
3. Use the whole words in sentences. For example,

    Builders *construct* houses.

    The train and the bus *converged* at incredible speeds.

    The *conference* on dieting attracted 2,000 people.

    He *connected* the TV to the VCR with a cable.
4. Define the whole words. For example,

    To *construct* means to put or fit together.

    To *converge* means to come together at a point.

    A *conference* is a kind of meeting, where people come together to talk formally about a topic.

    To *connect* things is to join them together.
5. After completing steps 1 through 4 for several prefixes, with these familiar words, have students practice matching different prefixes to their meanings, and root words to prefixes.
6. Have students identify the meanings of new words with familiar prefixes.

Table 9.3   A Page from an Affixionary

The Prefix *con-* means *"together"*

Construct	Builders construct houses.
Converge	The train and the bus converged at incredible speeds.
Conference	The conference on dieting attracted 2,000 people.
Connect	He connected the TV to the VCR with a cable.

For bilingual Spanish/English classrooms, teachers may be able to use some affixes and root words that are common to both English and Spanish. One such list is given in Table 9.4.

Root Words

Breen (1960) analyzed one list of words commonly used by elementary school children and found that only 82 Latin roots and 6 Greek roots occur 10 or more times in children's vocabulary. Templeton (1983) suggests that instruction should begin with the Greek roots first, since they are easier to locate within words, although typically instruction begins with Latin roots. For example, it is easier to work with the

Table 9.4 Prefijos, Sufijos, y Raices (Prefixes, Suffixes, and Roots)

Prefijos	Significado	Ejemplos
anti-	contra [opposed]	antiséptico [antiseptic]
co- [co- or con-]	junto con [with]	cooperar [cooperate]
re-	de neuvo [repetition]	reajustar [readjust]
sub-	debajo [under]	subterráno [subterraneous]
Sufijos		
-able, -ible	digno de o se puede [worthy to or able to]	demostrable [demonstrable]
-ción, sión, -xión	acción o efecto [action or effect]	invención [invention]
-iento	parecido o tendencia [resemblance; tendency to]	crecimiento [increase or increment]
-oso	lleno de [full of]	luminoso [luminous, shining]
Raices		
bio	vida [of living things, life]	anfibio, biologia [amphibious, biology]
geo	tierra [earth]	geografia, geologia [geography, geology]
cracia	gobierno [government]	democracia [democracy]
hidro	agua, liquido [water, liquid]	hidrosfera [hydrosphere]

Note. From *Learning in Two Worlds: An Integrated Spanish/English Biliteracy Approach* by Bertha Perez and Maria E. Torres-Guzman. Copyright © 1992 by Longman Publishers. Reprinted by permission.

Table 9.5 The Most Common Latin Roots in the Vocabulary of Children

Root	Meanings	Examples
fac, fact (facere)	to make or do	facile, factory
fer (ferre)	to bear, carry	transfer, ferry
mis, mit (mittere)	to send	admissible, transmit
mov, mot (movere, motus)	to move	movement, motion
par (parare)	to get ready	prepare, repair
port (portare)	to carry	export, portable
pos, pon (posito, ponere)	to place, put	position, opponent
spect, spic (specere)	to look	inspect, conspicuous
stat, sta (stare)	to stand	station, stanza
tend, tens (tendere, tensus)	to stretch	extend, tension
ven, vent (venire)	to come	convention, event
vid, vis (videre, visus)	to see	provide, vision

Note. Adapted from L. C. Breen, *The Reading Teacher*, November. 1960, in *How to Increase Reading Ability* by Harris & Sipay, 1990, Longman.

Greek *tele-*, as in *telephone* and *telegraph*, than it is with the Latin *regere*, which takes the forms *reg* (as in *regular*), *rect* (as in *direct*), and *rul* (as in *ruler*). A list of the most useful Latin root words appears in Table 9.5.

Templeton (1983) suggests that, after the most common Greek roots, the Latin roots that have the most stable form and meanings should be the focus of root word instruction—namely, *spect* (to look), *press* (to press), *port* (to carry), *form* (to shape), *pose* (to put or place), *tract* (to draw or pull), *spir* (to breathe), and *dict* (to say or speak). A good procedure is to work by analogy in a manner similar to that outlined for affixes. The teacher could begin with a word the students know (such as *porter*) and develop with the students a list of words that have the same root (*export, transport,* and *teleport,* for example). The methodology is similar for all word families, whether teaching affixes or root words.

The advantage of teaching words in families is that students learn new words by analogy with familiar words, which is what you want them to do when they come across an unfamiliar word. However, the research on the advantage of teaching root words is sparse, and there seems to be no agreement about the grade levels at which particular morphemes are best taught.

SPELLING AND MORPHEMIC ANALYSIS

In the early grades, spelling instruction focuses on teaching students the orthographic structure of words for which they know the meanings. This makes sense. After all, they will only use words in their personal writing with which they are familiar. However, by the middle grades (5, 6, and 7) students are encountering many more words in their reading which are unfamiliar in meaning, especially in the content areas. They may be required to use these words in essays, reports, etc. In order to become good spellers, they need to understand the relation of meaning to spelling and the reason why words such as *divine* and *divinity* look alike although they are pronounced differently.

Templeton and Morris (1999) observe that children's knowledge of English orthography (rules of spelling) develops in fairly predictable stages, from understanding the alphabetic principle to recognizing patterns across words, and, finally, to grasping how meaning impacts spelling. This final stage is sometimes referred to as the "derivational constancy" stage (Bear, Invernezzi, Templeton, & Johnson, 1996). Although there is some disagreement about the exact stages in developmental spelling, and whether every change in spelling-error patterns is a developmental stage (Gentry, 2000), nobody disputes that some errors are related to a misunderstanding of how meaning, or morphemes, impacts on English spelling.

Several authors (for example, Bear et al., 1996; Ganske, 2000) have pointed out how morphemic analysis helps with spelling. Once again, although there are no generally agreed upon recommendations for instruction, it is common to begin with showing how silent consonants make sense when studied in relation to morphemes (such as *sign/signal* and *condemn/condemnation*). A possible four-stage sequence of instruction includes:

1. Silent/sounded consonants in related words

2. Vowel and consonant alternations (for example, *sane/sanity* and *(admire/admiration)*

3. Absorbed or assimilated prefixes (for example, the *ad-* in attached)

4. Roots and combining forms

We will examine each of these in more detail, but before doing so we will describe a word-sorting activity. Since the words appropriate for students in the derivational constancy stage are best learned by comparison of the orthographic structure, a good way of presenting them is through a word-sorting or grouping activity.

Word Sorts

Word sorts are classification tasks designed to help students develop word knowledge. Words are written on small index cards (or half-cards) and given to a student or a group of students with the direction to read the words aloud and sort them into columns. Reading the words aloud is necessary to check for correct pronunciation. A closed sort might begin with four exemplars at the top of each column. For example, if you were sorting consonant alternations, you might have the exemplars *explode, explosion, extend,* and *extension.* The students would be expected to sort the other words into the appropriate categories. For an open sort, there would be no exemplars, and the students would be expected to establish the categories without teacher help. There are two basic tenets for word sorting in this manner. First, a student's understanding develops inductively—there is little or no direct instruction. You are aiming for students to internalize patterns and understand rules, which is better accomplished if they see them for themselves. Second, the teacher's role is to model. Modeling provides the scaffolding where necessary for successful completion of the task.

Operating Principles

1. Always work from the known to the unknown. Use exemplars that are familiar words to the students.

2. Usually work with up to four columns. When you have more than four columns, the number of words may be confusing, and the physical manipulation of the cards begins to interfere with learning.

3. Usually have a maximum of six words in each column. This allows students to work easily on desktops.

4. Don't explain an error—model the correct response. Since you want to use the power of inductive learning, it is better to take the card that has been placed in the wrong column and put it in the correct place while saying "No—watch me—listen while I read." If you are having students work without you, model the appropriate response before leaving them to work alone.

5. When all the words have been placed in appropriate columns, have students explain their reasoning for each column.

6. Look for speed and automaticity. Initially students may take some time to see the rationale behind each category. You may need to have them sort two or three times before it becomes automatic.

Since word sorts work through comparison and contrast, you may wish to sort both within and across the following categories. For instance, you could sort vowel alternation in contrast to consonant alternation, or sort different vowel alternation patterns against each other.

Silent/Sounded Consonants

There are several words with silent consonants in English where the consonant is sounded in another member of the word family. For example, *sign, signal*. When working with these words, it may sometimes be necessary to introduce an unfamiliar word to make the spelling transparent. For instance, a student who misspells *debt* as *det* may be introduced to the word *debit*. The latter word then becomes a mnemonic for remembering the correct spelling. For silent *n*, some useful words to sort are *autumn, autumnal; column, columnist; hymn, hymnal; condemn, condemnation; solemn, solemnity*. For silent *g*, words might include *sign, signal; design, designate; malign, malignant; resign, resignation; assign, assignation*. For other silent consonants, some word choices are *crumb, crumble; doubt, dubious; fast, fasten; moist, moisten; muscle, muscular; soft, soften*.

Consonant and Vowel Alternations

There are various forms of vowel and consonant alternations. One of the commonest is /t/ to /sh/ at the end of a word, as in *construct, construction*. A few examples in each category are listed here, although the list of categories is not comprehensive.

   /t/ to /sh/: inspect, inspection; predict, prediction; subtract, subtraction; digest, digestion; prevent, prevention; attract, attraction
   /s/ to /sh/: compress, compression; express, expression; impress, impression; obsess, obsession; recess, recession; process, procession
   /k/ to /sh/: clinic, clinician; electric, electrician; magic, magician; optic, optician; politic, politician; tactic, tactician
   /t/ to /sh/ *with e-drop*: anticipate, anticipation; create, creation; educate, education; hesitate, hesitation; locate, location; promote, promotion
   /s/ to /z/ *with e-drop*: confuse, confusion; fuse, fusion; immerse, immersion; revise, revision; supervise, supervision; televise, television
   /d/ to /sh/ or /zh/: comprehend, comprehension; conclude, conclusion; decide, decision; divide, division; invade, invasion; suspend, suspension
   Long vowel to short vowel: cave, cavity; volcano, volcanic; serene, serenity; wise, wisdom; telescope, telescopic; introduce, introduction
   Long vowel to schwa: famous, infamous; prepare, preparation; define, definition; compose, composition; divide, dividend; relate, relative
   Short vowel to schwa: personality, personal; excel, excellent; critic, criticize; economics, economy; mobility, mobile; fatality, fatal

Absorbed or Assimilated Prefixes

This spelling instruction would assume that students are familiar with most of the prefixes, and have engaged in activities like those outlined above in the section on affixes. An assimilated prefix is a prefix that loses some of its letters when it joins with a root word beginning in a consonant, commonly a root word of Latin origin. The letters are "absorbed" by the root word, which doubles its initial consonant. The most commonly absorbed prefixes are *ad-, com-, in-, ob-*, and *sub-*.

ad (to): addict, accept, accident, affect, allow, annul, appear, approach, assent, assist, attendance

com (with, together): collapse, correspond, correct, collide, collect, corrupt, commission

in: illegal, immature, immigrate, immoral, irrational, immerse, irresistible

ob (to): oppose, offend, occupy, offer, opponent, opposite, occasion

sub (under): suffix, support, suppose, surrender, surround, suffice, supply, suggest

Roots and Combining Forms

We have already talked about root words and some ways of teaching them. It is important to remember in relation to spelling instruction that it helps if students learn not only how the root words combine, but also what the various roots mean.

One way to teach how to combine various roots and affixes is through manipulables. You may choose to use word-sort cards or to create cards with words and affixes that can be put together. An alternative is to purchase commercial materials such as Reading Rods (ETA/Cuisenare, 2000) which are plastic cubes on which the roots and affixes are written, and which can be attached to each other to show appropriate combinations. The kits also provide lessons to accompany the rods. A sample lesson is shown in Figure 9.1.

ETYMOLOGY

Some students become absorbed and excited about the study of word origins. They find it interesting that a *sandwich* is named after the Earl of Sandwich, who placed meat between two pieces of bread when he had little time to eat during fighting in the Crimean War. Studying and exploring the origins of words can contribute to students' vocabulary knowledge and facilitate their comprehension of texts. We will mention two common sources of word origins in addition to Latin and Greek roots–words from mythology and word related to specific people or events.

Words from Mythology

Many middle school students study mythology. The most common sources for such words in English are Greek and Roman myths. Just a few are:

Titans: This race of giants in Greek mythology ruled the world before they battled the gods and lost. Our word from them is *titanic*.

Hypnos: The word *hypnosis* comes from this Greek god of sleep.

Psyche: In the Greek myth she was loved by Cupid and was made immortal. Consequently, *psyche* was used to refer to the human soul or spirit and gave rise to our words *psychiatry, psychic, psychological,* etc.

A good source for such words is *Words from the Myths* (Asimov, 1960).

Purpose
Students will be introduced to the idea that Latin and Greek roots and affixes have particular meanings using the root *graph* and the prefix *tele*.

Materials
Latin/Greek root word cube *graph/press/meter/metr;* prefix cube *tele/tri/anti/pro.* Extra letter cubes. Other prefix and root cubes as needed.

Group
Small group.

Procedure
1. Ask students to build the word *telephone*. Share with them that the prefix *tele* means "over a distance." Explain that the root *phon* has a meaning "about sound" (as in *phonics*). Ask them how this helps them understand the meaning of *telephone*. Now ask them to use the root cubes to generate more *tele* words (for example, *telegram, telescope, television, televise, telephoto, telegraph*). Ask them how the meaning "over a distance" helps them understand the meaning of each word.
2. Ask the students to build the word *telegraph*. Tell them that the root graph means "about writing". Ask them how this helps them understand the meaning of the word. Have them make other words that include *graph* (for example, *paragraph, photograph, monograph, autograph, geography*). Ask them how the meaning "about writing" helps them understand the meaning of the word. Use the opportunity to introduce the meanings of new roots.
3. Ask the students to use all the roots and prefixes that they have used so far to make new words (that is, *gram, scop, vis, photo, phon, para, mono, auto, geo*). As they build and share the words, ask them to try to work out what these roots mean.

Evaluation
Ask the students to choose three *tele* words and three *graph* words, and to write the definitions explaining how the root meaning is related to the definition.

Extension
Have students use *tele* and *graph* in combination with other roots and affixes to build "crazy words" for which they must write a definition. They can choose the best word of the ones they make, illustrate it, and display it.

Adapted from ETA/Cuisenaire (2000) *Reading rods: Prefixes, suffixes and root words: Teacher's Resource Guide* (pp. 26–27). Vernon Hills, IL: ETA/Cuisenaire

Figure 9.1   Sample Possible Reading Rods Lesson

Words from People and Events

When words are used to name things after people, they are called *eponyms* (*epi* + *onoma*, meaning *after* + *name*). Some of our favorites:

> *Bloomers,* after Amelis Bloomer, an late 19th Century feminist
> *Magnolias,* after the French botanist, Pierre Magnol
> *Malapropism,* after Mrs. Malaprop in Sheridan's play
> *Virginia,* after the virgin queen, Elizabeth I

A good source of such words is *NTC's Dictionary of Word Origins* (Room, 1990).

Looking Back and Looking Ahead

We have explored the uses of morphology in teaching both vocabulary and spelling. For some students such teaching can lead to a fascination with words—how they are constructed and how they originated. For others, it may develop their understanding without an increased motivation to learn. However, we believe word learning can be fun, and in the next chapter we describe some games that most students will enjoy.

For Further Learning

Gentry, R. J. (2000). A retrospective on invented spelling and a look forward. *The Reading Teacher, 54,* 318–332. (Reviews various theories and the implications for practice)

Nation, I. S. P. (1990). *Teaching and learning vocabulary.* Boston: Heinle & Heinle. (A good section on morphology)

Templeton, S., & Morris, D. (1999). Questions teachers ask about spelling. *Reading Research Quarterly, 34,* 102–112. (Very strong theoretical and practical review of what is known about spelling instruction)

www.worldwidewords.org

The home page of this site is subtitled "Investigating international English from a British viewpoint," and it is written by Michael Quinion. Much of this site may be above the heads of elementary and middle school students, but teachers may find some fun information here, to either share with their students or have their students search for on the site.

www.wordexplorations.com

This site describes itself as an advanced English vocabulary site that will expand visitors' vocabularies by focusing on Latin and Greek elements used in English. There are two features that might be useful for teachers. First, by clicking on "Oxymora," visitors will reach a page listing a multitude of oxymora (plural of *oxymoron*), including famous quotations that seem to be oxymoronic. Second, there is a list of redundant phrases and quotes ("Pleonastic Redundancies"), which might be fun for students to explore. Both oxymora and redundancies allow students to expand their vocabulary and sharpen their logic skills.

CHAPTER 10

WORDPLAY IN THE
CLASSROOM

☑ **Prepare Yourself**

Prepare yourself by evaluating your own knowledge. Rate your ability to answer some of the key questions for this chapter. Check the boxes that best describe your prereading knowledge.

Key concept questions	Well informed	Aware	Need ideas
1. *Why do wordplay in the classroom?*	❏	❏	❏
2. *How can I use books about words in my classroom?*	❏	❏	❏
3. *How can I use riddles, jokes, and puns in my classroom?*	❏	❏	❏
4. *How can I use word games in my classroom?*	❏	❏	❏
5. *How can I use art for wordplay in my classroom?*	❏	❏	❏
6. *How can I use drama for word learning in my classroom?*	❏	❏	❏
7. *How can I use puzzles for word learning in my classroom?*	❏	❏	❏
8. *How can I use computers for word learning in my classroom?*	❏	❏	❏

Strategy Overview Guide

This chapter presents background, ideas, and strategies to help you include wordplay as an important part of word learning in your classroom. The following chart can help you choose suitable assessment for your classroom.

Instructional strategy	Goal—use when you want to . . .	Comments
Using books about words (p. 205)	*Use interpretation to look at the variety of word genres.*	*Helps build variety in classroom library as well.*
Riddles, jokes, and puns (p. 209)	*Emphasize connotation, denotation, and multiple meanings.*	*Often taken home to share.*
Word games, cards, board games, memory, bingo, pencil-and-paper games, and guessing games (p. 210)	*Provide motivating ways to practice new words.*	*Develops independence.*
Art, word animals, word personifications, bulletin boards, and cartoons (p. 218)	*Provide for multiple intelligences in learning.*	*Great for ESL.*
Drama, synonym string, situations, and charades (p. 221)	*Provide for multiple intelligences in learning.*	*Gives lots of chances for usage.*
Puzzles, word circles, crosswords, codes, and jumbles (p. 222)	*Make practice pleasurable.*	*Can build a lifelong hobby.*
Computers (p. 223)	*Motivate.*	*Builds comfort with technology as well.*

WHY DO WORDPLAY IN THE CLASSROOM?

All teachers know the motivational value of play. Things we enjoy and view as sources of pleasure stay with us throughout our lives. Research bears out this belief in many ways as well; studies relating motivation to learning are too numerous to list. For example, in one highly controlled study of vocabulary learning in the middle grades (Beck, Perfetti, & McKeown, 1982), a curious phenomenon surfaced. Out of all the classrooms involved in the research project, students in one classroom learned more incidental vocabulary, words no one was attempting to teach. When trying to locate the source of this learning, researchers were unable to come up with any instruction or materials that could account for the difference.

Then one researcher noted a poster of interesting words in the classroom. When the teacher was asked about it, she noted that it was the **word wall,** a place where students could write new words they encountered in reading, in conversation, on TV, in their daily experiences. If they could write the word, talk about where they heard or saw it, and use it, they received points in a class contest. Very little expense, instructional time, or effort was involved, but the students became "tuned in" to learning new words in a way that positively affected their learning. They actively watched and listened for new words and shared them with their peers. They were motivated word learners.

Part of creating this "positive environment for word learning" involves having activities, materials, and resources that allow students to play with words. One necessary requirement is that teachers are models of word learning. We can all remember the year we learned lots of new words in school, when we had a teacher who was an avid punster, crossword puzzle aficionado, or otherwise involved in wordplay. This chapter presents ideas for stimulating word learning in your classroom—ideas involving word books, word games, art, drama, puzzles, and computers.

USING BOOKS ABOUT WORDS

Word Books for Interpretation

Word awareness can be stimulated by having students read and share books about words and books in which wordplay and plays on words are an important part of the book's humor (see Appendix B). For example, the *Amelia Bedelia* books by Peggy Parish are full of fun and humor derived from the fact that Amelia Bedelia takes figurative language literally. In *Amelia Bedelia* (Parish, 1963), Mrs. Rogers, Amelia's employer, asks her to "draw the drapes" so the carpets won't fade from the sun. Amelia's response is shown in Figure 10.1.

On a simpler level, books by Fred Gwynne, such as *The King Who Rained* (1970), provide simple, single-phrase examples of confusing **homophones** (words like *rained-reigned,* which sound alike but have different meanings and spellings) and words with more than one meaning.

To encourage interpretation and to share the fun, have students share these funny misconceptions in reader's workshop, act them out dramatically, or show two interpretations in art to explain the mix-ups. Since we all have stories like these in our backgrounds, students might like to make a collection of their own misconceptions, with illustrations. The students in one fourth-grade class collected their own book of examples, which included:

"Amelia Bedelia, the sun will fade the furniture.
I asked you to draw the drapes," said Mrs. Rogers.
"I did! I did! See," said Amelia Bedelia.
She held up her picture.

Figure 10.1　Amelia Bedelia Draws the Drapes

Figure 10.2 Interpretation of Possible Multiple Meaning

Jake
I remember being really confused in first grade when we were going to read a story about a cowboy. I thought of a half boy and half cow like some of those characters in my books. (See Figure 10.2.)

Jesse
When my grandmother asked me, "Are you blue?" I looked at her like she was crazy. Of course I wasn't blue! I was skin colored.

Interviewing parents and adults can provide more examples and more laughs.

Along with books for younger students, many chapter books for older students also engage interest and curiosity. *The Phantom Tollbooth* (Juster, 1962) offers many sophisticated plays on words grounded in music, mathematics, science, mythology, and linguistics. For example, when meeting monsters that get in his way, Milo, the main character, meets "the Terrible Trivium, demon of petty tasks and worthless jobs, ogre of wasted effort, and monster of habit" (p. 213). A monster familiar to every "over-meeting-ed" teacher!

In addition to using books that exemplify wordplay, include books on words and wordplay in your classroom library. Riddle, joke, and pun books abound for all ages, and there are many enjoyable books that deal with etymologies and interesting word forms that students will read independently (see Appendix B).

Including books on words in your classroom collection, reading excellent examples to the class, and having students use the ideas in art, drama, and their own writing provide models for wordplay and help to develop word awareness. You can also use these sources as references to investigate different types of word genres and interesting categories of words, the most familiar of which are synonyms and antonyms.

Investigating Word Genres

Books on words can also be used as resources for developing curiosity about different types of words. Most school curricula deal with common word categories or genres, such as synonyms, antonyms, similes, and metaphors. But what about acronyms, portmanteau words, imported words, slang, collective words, and other creative categories of words? Include these in your investigation of words.

Portmanteau Words.   When you pack a suitcase, or portmanteau, sometimes you scrunch things together to make room. For example, you might put your socks in your shoes. **Portmanteau words** are "packed" words formed by merging portions of one word with another. For example, *smog* is a common portmanteau word based on a combination of *smoke* and *fog*. English has a rich history of new words created in this way, a tendency readily picked up by Madison Avenue, journalists, and comic book writers. Advertising has given us the *motel* (*motor* + *hotel*), cartoons provided *zap* (*zip* + *slap*), science the *beefalo* (*beef* + *buffalo*), and political journalism such words as *insinuendo* (*insinuation* + *innuendo*) (McKenna, 1978).

Other Word Genres.   Students enjoy compiling sets of these creative genres, making bulletin boards, crosswords, word search puzzles, and other games with these interesting types of words. Espy (1975) has authored many books on words and suggests investigating some of the following:

Acronym: A word formed from the initial letters of other words (e.g., *scuba* = self-contained underwater breathing apparatus)

Anagram: A word or phrase formed by scrambling the letters of a word (e.g., *dear/read*)

Borrowed words: Words used in English from other countries and continents (e.g., *cafe, lariat, pretzel*)

Collective words: Words that label a group, typically of animals (e.g., a *gaggle* of geese, a *pride* of lions)

Lipogram: A word or phrase lacking a certain letter or letters (e.g., Pete wed Helen when he met her. (All vowels are missing except *e*.)

Malapropism:* Use of an incorrect word for a similar-sounding one (e.g., He reached a new platitude (plateau) of achievement.)

Mixed metaphor: A confusing or incongruous mixing of two parts of other well-known metaphors (e.g., A stitch in time waits for no man.)

Onomatopoeia: A word whose sound relates to its meaning (e.g., *buzz, gulp*)

Oxymoron: A phrase composed of words that seem contradictory (e.g., plastic silverware)

Palindrome: Words or phrases that read the same forward or backward (e.g., mom, dad, Able was I ere I saw Elba)

Spoonerism: * An unintentional transposition of sounds (e.g., Please pass the salt and shecker papers.)

You might have your students research the origins of the words marked with an asterisk (*), which refer to people or characters.

USING RIDDLES, JOKES, AND PUNS

Students become interested in riddles and jokes in the early grades, and pun-o-mania hits in the middle grades. Riddle and joke books abound and quickly circulate in most classrooms. Creating riddles, jokes, and puns is one way to stimulate exploration of words and to build interest and flexibility in word learning.

Word Riddles

Mike Thaler, a prolific author and conference speaker, has collected many ideas for riddle and joke making (Thaler, 1988). One way to make **word riddles,** questions with pun-like responses, involves choosing a subject and generating a list of related terms. For example, if your subject is "pig," your list might contain the words:

ham	pork
pen	grunt
hog	oink

and so forth. You take the first letter off one of the words and make a list of words that begin with the remaining letters. (See Teaching Idea File 10.1.) If you choose *ham,* you would make a list that begins with *am* such as:

ambulance	amnesia
amphibian	America

Then you put back the missing letter:

Hambulance	Hamnesia
Hamphibian	Hamerica

and make up riddles for the words.

Riddle: How do you take a pig to a hospital?
Answer: In a hambulance!

Riddle: What do you call it when a pig loses its memory?
Answer: Hamnesia!

Creating Word Riddles

1. Pick a subject (e.g., pig).
2. Generate a list of related words (e.g., *ham, pen, hog*).
3. Pick a word (e.g., *ham*), drop the first letter(s) to get a shortened version (e.g., *am*), and find a list of words that begin the way the shortened version begins (e.g., *ambulance, amnesia*).
4. Put back the missing letter (*h*) (*hambulance*).
5. Make up a riddle for which this word is the answer. (What do you use to take a pig to the hospital? A hambulance!)

Adapted from Mike Thaler (1988, April–May). Reading, writing and riddling. *Learning*, pp. 58–59.

From Blachowicz & Fisher, *Teaching Vocabulary in All Classrooms*, p. 186.

Name Riddles

Thaler also suggests name riddles. Look for names with the related word part. For example, remaining in the "pig mode,"

> *Riddle:* What pig discovered the theory of relativity?
> *Answer:* Albert Swinestein!

Tom Swifties

Tom Swifties are created by writing a quotation followed by a descriptive adjective or verb that has some relationship to the quotation. They get their name from the verbal manipulations of a fictional character named Tom Swift, who appeared in several books written for boys by Edward Stratemeyer from 1910 to 1935.

> "Let's hurry," said Tom swiftly.

> "Your sewing is extremely sloppy," she needled.

> "Catch that stray dog!" he barked at the bystanders.

Students enjoy creating and explaining Tom Swifties.

USING WORD GAMES

Word awareness can be encouraged by using both homemade and commercial games (see Appendix D) that focus on words and wordplay. To select games to make, use, and adapt, consider the guidelines shown in Teaching Idea File 10.2.

Many class-constructed games follow one of four models: matching card games (like rummy or fish), race-and-chase board games (like Parcheesi), memory board games (such as concentration), or bingo.

Teaching Idea File 10.2

Guidelines for Selecting and Using Word Games

1. Games should be simple to use without teacher intervention.
2. Vocabulary level should be appropriate.
3. Play should call on students to use the words in some meaningful way.
4. Games should utilize outside resources (e.g., a dictionary or class notebook) for self-checking.
5. Games should limit the number of players so that all players are involved.

From Blachowicz & Fisher, *Teaching Vocabulary in All Classrooms*, p. 187.

Figure 10.3   Card Pair for Card Games

Card Games

Card games work on the pairing principle. A pair is made when a student matches a word with one of the following: a synonym, a definition, an antonym, a cloze sentence in which it makes sense, a picture symbolizing its meaning, an English translation, or some other match appropriate to your class. Prepare a deck of at least 40 word cards with pair cards, such as the one shown in Figure 10.3, which was constructed by students from words across their curriculum for the week. Their deck made pairs of words and synonyms or definitions. Cards are shuffled and seven are dealt to each player. Each player can choose a card and discard one card in turn. Pairs may be placed on the table. The first player to pair all cards wins.

Fish.   For "fish," all the cards are dealt and players pick one card from the player on their left in turn. Pairs may be placed on the table. The first player to pair all cards wins.

Old Teacher   (A variation of old maid). An extra card is prepared with a drawing of the teacher—or some generic teacher. This is played like fish. The person who is left with this card is the "old teacher."

In all card games, students must read their pairs and can be challenged by another student if the group does not agree with the pair. The dictionary settles disputes. A challenger who is correct may take an extra turn. If the challenger is incorrect, the player gets an extra turn.

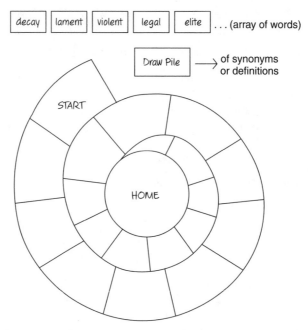

Figure 10.4   Race-and-Chase Board

Race-and-Chase Board Games

Race-and-chase games require a posterboard game board and moving pieces. Many teachers like to construct "generic" race-and-chase boards that can be used with many sets of cards. If the card space fits the cards from the card games, cards prepared for one purpose can be used for many others. A 2"×3" index card cut in halves or thirds is an excellent size for word cards. Movers can be commercially purchased at teacher stores or taken from old garage sale games. In addition, dice or spinners are useful.

One of the easiest race-and-chase formats is synonym match. The stack of word cards is placed in the center of the board and the synonym cards are arranged, face up, next to the board (see Figure 10.4).

Each student rolls a die and picks up a word card. If the student can correctly locate the synonym match, she can move the number of spaces on the die. The group, and outside reference, again supplies the check. Harder versions involve using the words in original sentences.

Memory Games

Like commercial memory games, word memory involves finding matches and remembering cards. Play this game with a maximum of 25 cards—12 word cards, 12 match cards, and 1 wild card. All of the cards are shuffled and placed face down in a 5"×5" grid (see Figure 10.5).

A Match!

Figure 10.5 Memory Grid

For each turn, a student turns over and reads two cards. If the cards are a match, the student takes the cards. If they are not a match, they are turned back over and left in the same place. Play continues in turn until only a single card remains. Students may use the wild card only if they can supply a suitable match orally. This can be checked at the end of the game by looking at the remaining card. The student with the most cards wins.

Bingo

This popular game can be played by any size group. Students each have sets of word cards from which they construct a 5″ × 5″ grid. They lay out their cards in any manner they choose, placing a "free" card in the space of their choice (see Figure 10.6).

The caller chooses definitions from the definition pile and reads them out. Students can place markers on the words that match. The first student to mark an entire row, column, or diagonal wins. Students check by reading the words and definitions. The cards are reshuffled, new cards are composed, and the winner becomes the caller for the next game.

Pencil-and-Paper Games

Categories.   One of the most popular pencil-and-paper games is categories. Students draw a suitable size grid (2″ × 2″ for younger students, 5″ × 5″ for older, or some size in between) and label each vertical row with a category (or the teacher may provide a category). Then one student flips through a book and chooses a word whose number of letters matches the number of columns. For example, students in a ninth-grade study hall working on the Civil War constructed the grid shown in Figure 10.7.

Players are given a designated time limit to fill in as many squares as they can (a kitchen timer is useful). At the end of the time limit, points are totaled. Players get 5 points for every category square they fill in, but that no other player has filled; 2 points for every category square filled in that others have filled in, but with other words; and 1 point for every category square filled in where someone else has the same term. Inappropriate entries may be challenged and carry no point totals if they are not suitable. Categories can be related to content and thematic units, but using a few "fun" or "silly" categories in each grid adds spice and laughter.

Word Challenge.   Word challenge is another category game in which the categories are preset to think about particular characteristics of words (Abromitis, 1992). For example, common categories might include synonym/similar, antonym/different, example, and related word (see Figure 10.8). This is played the same way as categories.

Guessing Games

Hink Pink.   Hink pink asks students to come up with a pair of rhyming words to match a defining phrase. Each word in the pair has the same number of syllables. The person who creates the phrase clues the guesser with the term *hink pink* (two 1-syllable words), *hinky pinky* (two 2-syllable words), *hinkety pinkety* (two 3-syllable words), and so forth. For example,

Student Cards

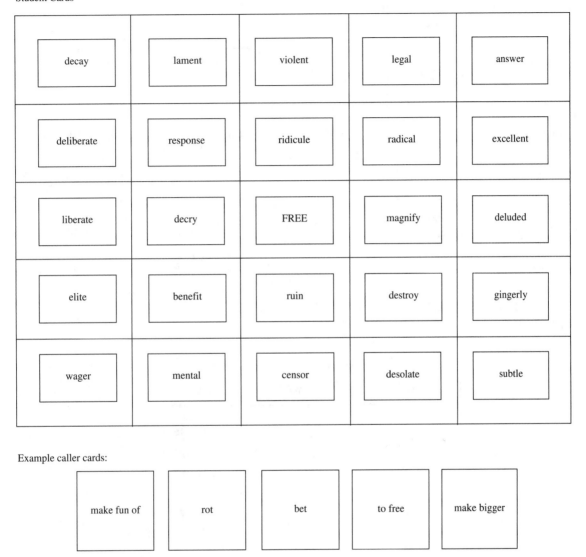

Example caller cards:

Figure 10.6 Bingo Cards

Clue: Hink pink—an angry father
(*Answer:* mad dad)

Clue: Hinkety pinkety—an evil clergyman
(*Answer:* sinister minister)

Hink pinks are lots of fun, and, often, students can come up with more than one answer for a clue. Any meaningful answer is acceptable.

	R	U	L	E	S
Specific Confederacy Words	rebel		Lee		
Specific Union Words		union	Lincoln		Sherman
Military Words					sniper
Other Civil War Vocabulary	Recon-struction			emancipa-tion	scallywag
Authors Who Wrote on Civil War	Russell		Longley		

Figure 10.7   Categories Grid

Word	Synonym/Similar	Antonym/Different	Example	Related Word
deride	speak badly about	praise	You deride teams you don't like.	criticize
subtle	understated	loud	Gray is a subtle color.	restrained

Figure 10.8   Word Challenge Grid

20 Questions.   20 questions is an excellent verbal game that can be adapted to help students think about words they are learning. The student who is "it" selects a word card from a prepared stack. Other students can ask questions in turn, using only ones that require a yes-or-no answer. The "asking" team gets 20 questions. A turn ends with a "no." If one correctly guesses the word, that player becomes "it" for the next round. If the player does not guess the word, "it" gets another turn. For example, in one class, the questions went like this:

S1: Is it a noun—a person, place, or thing? (1)
IT: Yes.
S1: Is it something in this classroom? (2)
IT: Yes.
S1: Is it something we use for science? (3)
IT: No.
S2: Is it something we might have in our desk? (4)
IT: No.
S3: Is it a word from social studies? (5)
IT: Yes.
S3: Did we have it in this week's lesson? (6)
IT: No.
S1: Does it have to do with the Civil War? (7)
IT: No.
S2: Does it have to do with our interviews? (8)
IT: Yes.
S2: Is it *outline?* (9)
IT: No.
S3: Is it something we have to hand in? (10)
IT: Yes.
S3: Is it our *learning log?*
IT: Yes. (Student 3 becomes "it".)

Word of the Day.   Many teachers do the venerable "word of the day" in a guessing-game format. Each day a set of clues is prepared and put on the board. An envelope is taped below for guesses that are discussed at the end of the day (see Figure 10.9).

As a variation, a teacher can choose a word that she uses throughout the day. For example, in the morning, she might say, "Oh, I had such a bad headache this morning I had to medicate myself. I took two aspirin." Later in the day, discussing the death of Lincoln and its aftermath, she will say, "I wonder what Dr. Mudd used to medicate John Wilkes Booth? I don't think they had aspirin then."

At the end of the day, she asks students if they could identify the word of the day and what it meant. Students become keen listeners for new words when this approach is used.

Adapting Commercial Games

Besides teacher-made games, many commercial games (see Appendix D) can be adapted for class use. For general word learning, Scrabble, Probe, and Boggle can be excellent. Teachers can also add dictionary use as a component of play. Facts in Five and Scattergories are variations of the category game and can build general word learning. Outburst and Outburst Junior help develop networks by association. All are worthwhile for general vocabulary development.

Word of the Day

1. When the doctor gives you a pill, s/he _____s you.
2. This is something Dr. Mudd did to John Wilkes Booth before he fixed his leg.
3. This is on the same page of the dictionary as the word <u>medicine.</u>

ANSWERS

Figure 10.9   Word of the Day

USING ART FOR WORDPLAY

Students love to play with words using art and drawing. Not only does art offer a multisensory way to provide keys to word learning, but it can also provide a playful way for students with nonverbal talents to relate to word learning.

Combination Animals

For example, for high school students studying word parts, a drawing activity is a natural way to show learning. If students are studying Latin combining forms, such as:

pento	=	five
ped	=	feet
tri	=	three
cornis	=	horned

they can create and label their own original animals. See, for instance, Figure 10.10, which shows the pentopedi (five-footed) tricornoptis (three-horned) animal that one high school student drew.

Word Personifications

Students may want to use word personification drawings to evoke a word's meaning. See Figure 10.11, for example. The student has used shaky letters as a personal

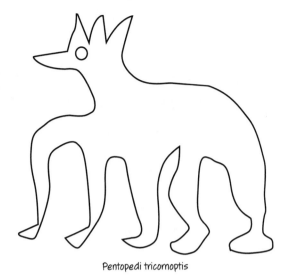

Pentopedi tricornoptis

Figure 10.10 Combination Animal for Studying Word Parts

Figure 10.11 Word Personification

reference to the meaning of the word. Using this method, students not only have to think about words and their characteristics, but also have to create personal images for new words.

Bulletin Boards

Students who enjoy art can also create monthly bulletin boards showing new vocabulary words in a graphic way. For example, when studying acronyms (words created from the first initials of other words), students created the bulletin board shown in Figure 10.12 with a self-check for the viewers.

Cartoons

Because many cartoons are based on wordplay, they can be used and created to have fun with words (Goldstein, 1986). For example, students can create collections of word cartoons (such as the one in Figure 10.13) in a class book. They can create cartoons for some of the word misconceptions we discussed earlier in this chapter or can use cartoons as models. For instance, from the Funky Winkerbean cartoon, students created their own versions.

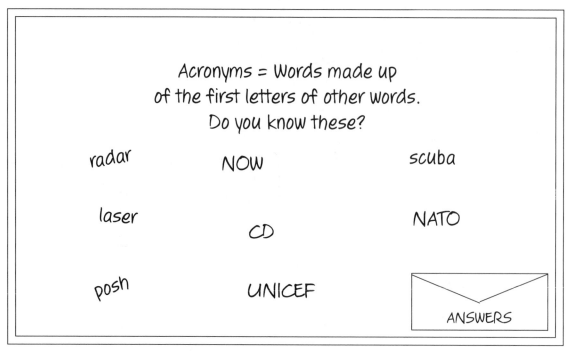

Figure 10.12   Acronym Bulletin Board

Figure 10.13   Example of a Cartoon Using Wordplay

Note. From "Funky Winkerbean" by Tom Batiuk. Copyright © by and permission of North America Syndicate.

Word: amble

Meaning: to walk slowly, to stroll

Situation: You are walking home from school with a friend you really like. You know that you have chores to do at home, so you take your time and stop at the convenience store. You buy a snack and slowly walk home talking and joking.

Question: When was the last time you ambled? Describe what the circumstances were.

Figure 10.14 Word Cards for Situations Game

USING DRAMA

Synonym String

Use drama to build a set of related words, the synonym string. Divide the class into teams and present each team with a starter word, such as *walk*. Each group needs to come up with as many synonyms for the word as it can and illustrate each dramatically. For example, the students might *stroll, saunter, sashay, amble,* and so forth. This is a good game for use with a thesaurus. The teacher can also present a list of words if this seems more appropriate. This game can also lead to a discussion of connotation and denotation and shades of meaning.

Situations

Students can use dramatization of words to create meaningful situations or contexts that clarify word meaning (Duffelmeyer, 1980). Prepare a set of word cards each with a word, its meaning, an example of a situation in which the word is used, and a question (see Figure 10.14). Then form groups of students and give one card to each group. The actors have time to discuss the word and plan a skit (limit to 5 minutes or so). They can use the situation on the card or plan their own.

When presenting their skit, one member of the group writes the word on the board and pronounces it. The skit is acted out and a cast member asks the audience the

Teaching Idea File 10.3

Signals for Charades

1. Choose your word.
2. Hold up the number of fingers that matches the number of syllables.
3. Indicate the syllable you are acting out by putting that number of fingers on your arm.
4. Hold your ear before acting to indicate "sounds like."
5. Make a big circle with your hands to indicate you are acting out the whole concept rather than the individual syllables.

From Blachowicz & Fisher, *Teaching Vocabulary in All Classrooms*, p. 199.

question and meaning of the word. At this point, the teacher can provide feedback, and all class members enter the word in a vocabulary file along with the meaning and some personal context.

A commercial set of materials, Word Theater, is designed for a similar process with words selected for grades 4–6.

Charades

Charades can be played with a phrase as well as single words. Words or phrases are placed on word cards and placed in a stack. The class is divided into teams. One member of a team draws a card and attempts to act out each word or syllables of the word using a series of signals. A timekeeper from the other team keeps track of the time; and the team with the lowest time score after a full round wins. (See Teaching Idea File 10.3 for a description of signals students can use while playing charades.)

USING PUZZLES

The number of word puzzle magazines and books that line the shelves of any newsstand or bookstore serves as proof of the popularity of word puzzles. Involvement in creating and doing puzzles can build a lifelong interest in words for students.

Word Circles

Word circles are simple forms of crossword puzzles. They involve only a few words and are easy for students to create for one another. Figure 10.15 illustrates a word circle.

Crosswords

Crossword puzzles are probably the most popular types of word puzzle. They are so familiar that we won't go into detail about them here. One thing for teachers to note is that, though crosswords are familiar to most of us, the process is not familiar to

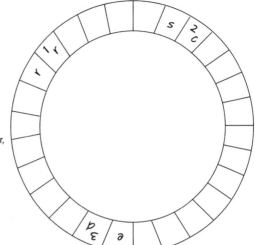

1. a line segment from center to outside of circle

2. the measurement around a circle

3. the line segment from one side of circle to the other, passing through the center

Figure 10.15   Word Circle

most children. Take the time to work through a puzzle with your students until they get the general idea of how the puzzles are completed. Keep blank grids in your classroom for creating puzzles since this is also a wonderful way to stimulate thinking about words and definitions.

Codes

Students love secret codes. Decoding a word, phrase, or sentence demands a substantial use of context and inference. Many books of coded and encrypted messages can be purchased in bookstores and supermarkets and at newsstands.

Jumbles

Jumbles call for readers to unscramble words and letters to match a clue, sometimes in cartoon form. Most newspapers run a daily jumble that can provide good classroom material—as well as an incentive to browse the paper each day. This can be a good starter in middle school or high school advisory or homeroom periods. Figure 10.16 shows a typical jumble.

USING COMPUTERS

Many commercial programs are available for wordplay. For example, there are create-a-crossword programs, semantic mapping programs, dictionaries and thesauruses, word clustering programs, computer forms of commercial word games, as well as instructional programs that are less playful. Students can also use the

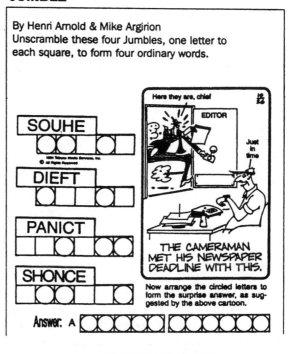

Figure 10.16 Typical Letter and Word Jumble

computer to create text or Hypercard personal word banks that can be easily alphabetized, coded, and clustered. See Appendix C for a list of computer resources for word learning.

Looking Back and Looking Ahead

In this chapter, we have presented ideas for making word learning playful in your classroom. Not only are these strategies motivational, but they also provide wonderful practice in contextual situations. Using new words in conversation, drama, art, games, and writing gives ownership to the learner. The appendices that follow present numerous resources for your classroom: dictionaries and other references, books for word learning, and computer resources and games.

For Further Learning

Espy, W. R. (1975). *An almanac of words at play.* New York: Clarkson N. Potter. (A book by the "dean" of wordplay)

Goldstein, B. S. (1986, April). Looking at cartoons and comics in a new way. *Journal of Reading, 29,* 657–661. (Excellent ideas for using comics)

Thaler, M. (1988). Reading, writing and riddling. *Learning* (April–May), pp. 58–59. (A very "punny" set of ideas for teachers)

www.mindfun.com/wordscramble.htm

This game is an online version of the classic game of Boggle (without the trade-marked name). It is easy to figure out how to play, and the computer scores answers automatically. A new scramble of letters appears each time, so this can be played over and over. One potential problem with this website: After visitors have played a few times, they are asked to register to win free prizes for their scores. There is a warning that registrants must be over 18, but this may not stop children from giving away personal information.

APPENDIX A

SCHOOL DICTIONARIES

Preschool Dictionaries/Wordbooks

American Heritage Picture Dictionary—Houghton Mifflin
Good Morning Words—Scott Foresman
Macmillan/McGraw–Hill Picture Word Book
My Pictionary—Scott Foresman

Early Elementary School Dictionaries

Lincoln Reading Dictionary for Children—Harcourt Brace Jovanovich
Macmillan First Dictionary
My First Dictionary—Scott Foresman
My First Picture Dictionary—Scott Foresman
Very First Dictionary—Macmillan
Words for New Readers—Scott Foresman

Upper Elementary/Junior High School Dictionaries

American Heritage Children's Dictionary—Houghton Mifflin
Childcraft Dictionary—World Book
Gage Canadian Dictionary
Longman Dictionary of American English
Macmillan School Dictionary
Scott Foresman Intermediate Dictionary
Scribner Intermediate Dictionary
Webster's New World Children's Dictionary
World Book Student Dictionary

High School Dictionaries

Longman Dictionary of Contemporary English
Macmillan Dictionary for Students
Scott Foresman Advanced Dictionary
Scribner Dictionary
Thorndike-Barnhart Student Dictionary
World Book Dictionary

APPENDIX B

BOOKS FOR EXPANDING VOCABULARY AND WORDPLAY

Adams, R. (1994). *The cowboy dictionary: The chin jaw words and whing-ding ways of the American west.* New York: Pedigree Books. (6th grade and up)

Asher, S. (1989). *Wild words and how to tame them.* New York: Walker. (5th grade and up)

Asimov, I. (1986). *Words from the myths.* Boston: Houghton Mifflin. (6th grade and up)

Awdry, C. (1992). *Thomas's big book of words.* New York: Random House. (preschool to 1st grade)

Bowler, P. (1994). *The superior person's second book of weird and wondrous words.* New York: Laurel. (6th grade and up)

Campbell, G. (1992). Words: *A potpourri of fascinating origins.* Santa Barbara, CA: Capra Press. (6th grade and up)

Carle, E. (1985). *My very first book of words.* New York: Crowell. (preschool to 1st grade)

Cutler, C. (1994). *O brave new words: Native American loanwords in current English.* Norman, OK: University of Oklahoma Press. (4th grade and up)

Dickson, P. (1992). *The Dickson's word treasury: A connoisseur's collection of old and new, weird and wonderful, useful and outlandish words.* New York: Niley. (9th grade and up)

Dusseau, J. (1993). *Bugaboos, chimeras & Achilles' heels: 10,001 difficult words and how to use them.* Englewood Cliffs, NJ: Prentice Hall. (9th grade and up)

Flexner, S. (1993). *Wise words and wives' tales: The origins, meanings and time-honored wisdom of proverbs and folk sayings, olde and new.* New York: Avon Books. (9th grade and up)

Freeman, M. (1993). *Hue and cry and humble pie: The stories behind the words.* New York: Plume. (6th grade and up)

Funk, C. (1993). *2107 curious word origins, sayings and expressions from white elephants to a song & dance.* New York: Galahad. (6th grade and up)

Gill, N. (1985). *Vocabulary boosters.* Belmont, CA: David S. Lake. (3rd to 6th grade)

Graham-Barber, L. (1991). *Mushy: The complete book of Valentine words.* New York: Bradbury. (2nd grade and up)

Graham-Barber, L. (1993). *Gobble! The complete book of Thanksgiving words.* New York: Avon. (2nd grade and up)

Graham-Barber, L. (1993). *Ho ho ho! The complete book of Christmas words.* New York: Bradbury. (2nd grade and up)

Grambs, D. (1994). *The endangered English dictionary: Bodacious words your dictionary forgot.* New York: W.W. Norton. (6th grade and up)

Gregorich, B. (1990). *Positional words and opposite words.* Grand Haven, MI: School Zone Publishing Co. (kindergarten and 1st grade)

Healey, T. (1993). *My wonderful word box.* New York: Readers Digest Kids. (preschool to 3rd grade)

Hendrickson, R. (1994). *Grand slams, hat tricks, and alley-oops: A sport's fans book of words.* New York: Prentice Hall. (4th grade and up)

Hill, E. (1985). *More opposites.* Los Angeles: Price, Sten, Sloan. (preschool and kindergarten)

Hill, E. (1988). *Spot's big book of words.* New York: Putnam. (preschool to 1st grade)

Hoban, T. (1987). *Over, under and through.* New York: Macmillan. (preschool to 3rd grade)

Jeans, P. (1993). *Ship to shore: A dictionary of everyday words and phrases derived from the sea.* Santa Barbara, CA: ABC-C40. (6th grade and up)

Linfield, J. (1993). *Word traps: A dictionary of the 7,000 most confusing sound-alike and look-alike words.* New York: Collier. (6th grade and up)

Maestro, B. (1990). *Delivery van: Words for town and country.* New York: Clarion. (preschool to 3rd grade)

Maestro, B. (1990). *Taxi: A book of city words.* New York: Clarion. (preschool to 3rd grade)

Maestro, B. (1992). *All aboard overnight: A book of compound words.* New York: Clarion. (1st to 4th grade)

Martin, B. (1993). *Words.* New York: Simon & Schuster. (kindergarten to 2nd grade)

Michaels, A. (1993). *Suffix obsession.* Jefferson, NC: McFarland. (9th grade and up)

Mills, J. (1993). *Womanwords: A dictionary of words about women.* New York: Henry Holt. (9th grade and up)

Moncure, J. (1984). *Word bird makes words with duck.* Elgin, IL: Children's Press. (kindergarten to 2nd grade)

Moncure, J. (1993). *Butterfly express.* Elgin, IL: Children's Press. (1st to 3rd grade)

Potter, B. (1993). *Learn with Benjamin Bunny: A book of words.* New York: Derrydale Books. (preschool to kindergarten)

Rovin, J. (1994). *What's the difference? A compendium of commonly confused and misused words.* New York: Ballantine Books. (6th grade and up)

Sarnoff, J. (1981). *Words: A book about the origins of everyday words and phrases.* New York: Scribner. (4th to 8th grade)

Scarry, R. (1976). *Early words.* New York: Random House. (preschool to 1st grade)

Scarry, R. (1992). *Richard Scarry's best little word book ever.* Racine, WI: Western Publishing Co. (preschool and kindergarten)

Schur, N. (1994). *2000 most challenging and obscure words.* New York: Galahad. (9th grade and up)

Schwartz, L. (1978). *The usage sleuth.* Santa Barbara, CA: Learning Works. (4th to 6th grade)

Smitherman-Donaldson, G. (1994) Black talk: Words and phrases from the hood to the amen corner. Boston: Houghton Mifflin. (6th grade and up)

Supraner, R. (1977). *I can read about homonyms.* Mahwah, NJ: Troll Association. (2nd to 5th grade)

Supraner, R. (1977). *I can read about synonyms & antonyms.* Mahwah, NJ: Troll Association. (2nd to 5th grade)

Terban, M. (1989). *Superdupers: Really funny real words.* New York: Clarion. (4th to 8th grade)

Williams, D. (1995). *NTC's dictionary of easily confused words: With complete examples of correct usage.* Lincolnwood, IL: NTC. (6th grade and up)

APPENDIX C

COMPUTER PROGRAMS WITH A VOCABULARY FOCUS (INCLUDING PUBLISHERS' RECOMMENDED LEVELS)

101 Misused Words and How to Use Them Correctly. Learning Seed. (4th grade and up)
American Heritage III Dictionary. Softkey. (3rd grade and up)
Analogies I & II. Intellectual. (9th grade and up)
Analogies Tutorial. Hartley. 5th and 6th. (also HS versions)
Antonyms. Intellectual. (9th grade and up)
Antonyms/Synonyms. Hartley. (4th to 6th grade)
Billiards 'n' Antonyms. Heartsoft. (3rd to 8th grade)
Billiards 'n' Homonyms. Heartsoft. (3rd to 8th grade)
Billiards 'n' Synonyms. Heartsoft. (3rd to 8th grade)
Bubblegum Machine. Heartsoft. (2nd grade and up)
Cat 'n Mouse. MindPlay. (kindergarten to 6th grade)
Compound Words and Contractions. Hartley. (1st to 3rd grade)
Crosswords Deluxe. Sierra. (6th grade to adult)
Dictionary Skills. Intellectual. (4th to 8th grade)
Dropin. Research Design. (Teachers)
English Vocabulary I. American Ed. (1st to 3rd grade)
English Vocabulary II. American Ed. (4th to 6th grade)
Fay's Word Rally. Didatech. (kindergarten to 3rd grade)
Figurative Language. Hartley. (7th to 9th grade)
From ABC to XYZ. Hartley. (1st to 6th grade)
Game Show. Advanced Ideas. (1st grade and up)
GOAL Reading Vocabulary. Davidson. (Adult)
Homonyms. Hartley. (2nd to 5th grade)
Homonyms, Antonyms and Synonyms. Gamco. (3rd grade and up)
Improving Your Vocabulary Skills. Intellectual. (3rd grade and up)

Lucky 7 Vocabulary Games, Elementary Level. Intellectual. (3rd to 6th grade. Also intermediate and advanced levels)

Mission Control Word Games. Gamco. (3rd to 9th grade)

Mutanoid Word Challenge. Legacy. (3rd grade to adult)

Oliver's Crosswords. Micrograms. (3rd to 6th grade)

Practical Vocabulary. Intellectual. (9th to 12th grade)

Reading Blaster: Invasion of the Word Snatchers. Davidson. (1st to 4th grade)

Roots and Affixes. Hartley. (4th to 6th grade)

Scrabble Deluxe. Virgin Games. (5th grade and up)

Snoopy's Skywriter Scrambler. American School Publisher. (3rd to 6th grade)

Spell Dodger. Arcadia. (1st to 8th grade)

Spinner's Choice. Heartsoft. (3rd to 8th grade)

Survival Wordplay. J Weston Welch. (6th to 10th grade)

TEAM Reading and Vocabulary. Davidson. (at risk)

Vocab. Research Design. (6th grade and up)

Vocab Lab. Substance Abuse. (4th grade to adult)

Vocabulary Detective. Southwest EdPsych. (3rd to 12th grade)

Vocabulary Development. Weekly Reader. (3rd to 6th grade)

Vocabulary Machine. Southwest EdPsych. (1st to 12th grade)

Vocabulary Quest in the Land of the Unicorn. Unicorn. (4th to 9th grade)

Vocabulary Tutor Series. MindPlay. (4th to 12th grade)

Wizard of Words. Advanced Ideas. (1st grade and up)

Word Attack 3. Davidson. (5th grade to adult)

Word Capture. Heartsoft. (2nd grade and up)

Word City. Magic Quest. (3rd to 9th grade)

Word Master Vocabulary Builder. Unicorn. (3rd to 8th grade)

WordSearch Deluxe. Nordic Software. (1st grade and up)

Wordstore. Research Design. (Teachers)

APPENDIX D

VOCABULARY/WORD GAMES

Blurt! The Webster's Game of Word Racing—Players take turns reading a definition aloud, while others blurt out guesses in a race for the right word. Ages 10–adult; includes a junior version for ages 7–9. ISBN 0-9628275-4-1. Made by the Riverside Publishing Company, 1992.

Boggle Junior—Players associate words with pictures and find letters on cubes that match the letters in the words. Ages 3–6. Made by Parker Bros., 1988.

Boggle Master—3-Minute Word Game—Players link letters up, down, sideways, and diagonally to form words within the time limit. Ages 8 and up. Made by Parker Bros., 1993.

Claymania—Players draw cards with words that depict the object into which the clay must be molded within the 45-second time limit. Ages 12 and up. Made by Classic Games, 1993.

Gestures—The Game of Split-Second Charades—Players act out four words at a time within a given time limit. Ages 12 and up. Made by Milton Bradley Co., 1990.

Go to the Head of the Class—Deluxe Edition—Players answer quiz questions that are divided into three knowledge levels and that cover every subject. Ages 8–adult. Made by Milton Bradley Co., 1986.

Hangman—The Original Word Guessing Game—Players guess letters of their opponent's word, trying not to make incorrect guesses, each of which would expose another part of the hangman. Ages 8–adult. Made by Milton Bradley, 1988.

Outburst Junior—Players on a team have 60 seconds to yell out answers that fit familiar categories within a given time limit. Ages 7–14. ISBN 0-307-04253-7. Made by Western Publishing Co. under license from Hersch and Col., 1989.

Overturn—Players find words from randomly placed letters that must be in a continuous line in order to form the word. Ages 8–adult. Made by Pressman Toy Corp., 1993.

Pictionary Junior—The Classic Game of Quick Draw for Kids—Players sketch clues for teammates who have to quickly guess the word from the card that was drawn. Ages 8–14. Made by Golden and Design, 1993.

Scattergories Junior—Players draw cards that have six categories on them. They must roll the die to determine which letter their answers must begin with to fill each of the six categories. Ages 8–11. Made by Milton Bradley, 1989.

Scrabble Crossword Game—Players connect letter titles up and down and across the board to make words of various point values. Ages 8–adult. Made by Milton Bradley, 1989.

Tribond Kids—Players answer questions by using association and grouping methods to obtain the correct answer. Ages 7–11. Made by Big Fun A Go Go, Inc., 1993.

REFERENCES

Abromitis, B. (1992). *New directions in vocabulary.* Rolling Meadows: Blue Ribbon Press.

Allen, J. (1999). *Words, words, words: Teaching vocabulary in grades 4–12.* York, ME: Stenhouse.

Alverman, D. E., & Hynd, C. R. (1989). Study strategies for correcting misconceptions in physics: An intervention. In S. McCormick & J. Zutell (Eds.), *Cognitive and social perspectives for literacy research and instruction.* Thirty-eighth Yearbook of the National Reading Conference.

Anders, P., Bos, C., & Filip, D. (1984). The effect of semantic feature analysis on the reading comprehension of learning-disabled students. In J. A. Niles & L. A. Harris (Eds.), *Changing perspectives on research in reading/language processing and instruction.* Rochester, NY: National Reading Conference.

Anderson, R. C., Wilson, P., & Fielding, L. (1988). Growth in reading and how children spend their time outside of school. *Reading Research Quarterly, 23,* 285–303.

Asimov, I. (1989). *Words from the myths.* Boston, MA: New American Library.

Atwell, N. (1987). *In the middle.* Portsmouth, NH: Heinemann.

Baldwin, R. S., & Schatz, E. I. (1985). Context clues are ineffective with low frequency words in naturally occurring prose. In J. A. Niles & R. V. Lalik (Eds.), *Issues in literacy: A research perspective.* Thirty-fourth Yearbook of the National Reading Conference (pp. 132–135). Rochester, NY: National Reading Conference.

Baldwin, R. S., Ford, J. C., & Readence, J. E. (1981). Teaching word connotations: An alternative strategy. *Reading World, 21*(2), 103–108.

Balmuth, M. (1984). Early English dictionaries in historical perspective. *New Horizons, 25,* 124–133.

Bannon, E., Fisher, P. J. L., Pozzi, L., & Wessel, D. (1990). Effective definitions for word learning. *Journal of Reading, 34,* 301–302.

Barr, R., Blachowicz, C. L. Z., Katz, C., & Kaufman, B. (2001). *Reading diagnosis for teachers: An instructional approach.* White Plains, NY: Longman.

Barr, R. C., & Johnson, B. (1990). *Teaching reading in elementary classrooms.* White Plains, NY: Longman.

Barron, R. F. (1969). The use of vocabulary as an advance organizer. In H. L. Herber & R. F. Barron (Eds.), *Research in reading in the content areas: First year report.* Syracuse, NY: Syracuse University Press.

Bean, T. W., Singer, H., & Cowen, S. (1985). Acquisition of a topic schema in high school biology through an analogical study guide. In J. A. Niles and R. V. Lalik (Eds.), *Issues in literacy: A research perspective.* Thirty-fourth Yearbook of the National Reading Conference.

Bear, D. R., Invernezzi, M., Templeton, S., & Johnston, F. (1996). *Words their way: Word study for phonics, vocabulary and spelling instruction.* Columbus, OH: Merrill/Prentice Hall.

Beck, I., Perfetti, C., & McKeown, M. (1982). The effects of long-term vocabulary instruction on lexical access and reading comprehension. *Journal of Educational Psychology, 74,* 506–521.

Beck, I. L., & McKeown, M. G. (1983). Learning words well—A program to enhance vocabulary and comprehension. *The Reading Teacher, 36,* 622–625.

Beck, I. L., McKeown, M. G., McCaslin, E. S., & Burkes, A. M. (1979). *Instructional dimensions that may affect reading comprehension: Examples from two commercial programs* (LRDS Publication, 1979/20). Pittsburgh: University of Pittsburgh, Learning Research and Development Center.

Becker, W. C. (1977). Teaching reading and language to the disadvantaged—What we have learned from field research. *Harvard Educational Review, 47,* 518–543.

Beyersdorfer, J. M., & Schauer, D. K. (1989). Semantic analysis to writing: Connecting words, books, and writing. *Journal of Reading, 32,* 500–508.

Blachowicz, C. L. Z. (1986). Making connections: Alternatives to the vocabulary notebook. *Journal of Reading, 29,* 643–649.

Blachowicz, C. L. Z.(1993). C2QU: Modeling context use in the classroom. *Reading Teacher, 47,* 268–269.

Blachowicz, C. L. Z. (1994). Problem-solving strategies for academic success. In G. P. Wallach & K. G. Butler (Eds.), *Language learning disabilities in school-age children and adolescents: Some principles and applications* (pp. 304–322). Englewood Cliffs, NJ: Merrill/ Prentice Hall.

Blachowicz, C. L. Z., & Fisher, P. J. L. (1989). Defining is an unnatural act: A study of written definitions. In S. McCormick & J. Zutell (Eds.), *Cognitive and social perspectives for literacy research and instruction* (pp. 181–188). Thirty-eighth Yearbook of the National Reading Conference.

Blachowicz, C. L. Z., & Fisher, P. J. L. (2000). Vocabulary instruction. In R. Barr, M. L. Kamil, P. B. Mosenthal, & P. D. Pearson (Eds.) *Handbook of reading research* (Vol. III). White Plains, NY: Longman.

Blachowicz, C. L. Z., Fisher, P. J. L., Costa, M., & Pozzi, M. (1993). *Researching vocabulary learning in middle school cooperative reading groups: A teacher-researcher collaboration.* Paper presented at the Tenth Great Lakes Regional Reading Conference, Chicago.

Blachowicz, C. L. Z., Fisher, P. J. L., Wohlreich, J., & Guastafeste, P. (1990). *Children using dictionaries: A think-aloud study.* Paper presented at the American Educational Research Association Annual Convention, Boston.

Blachowicz, C. L. Z., & Leipzig, F. (1989). Reading detectives and writing architects: A collaborative "adventure" in action research. *Illinois Schools Journal, 69,* 3–19.

Blachowicz, C. L. Z., & Zabroske, B. (1990). Context instruction: A metacognitive approach for at-risk readers. *Journal of Reading, 33,* 504–508.

Breen, L. C. (1960). Vocabulary development by teaching prefixes, suffixes and root derivatives. *Reading Teacher, 14,* 93–97.

Brigance, A. H. (1983). *Brigance diagnostic comprehension inventory of basic skills.* New York: Curriculum Associates.

Bromley, K. D. (1984). Teaching idioms. *Reading Teacher, 38,* 272–276.

Buehler, E. C., & Meltesen, D. (1983). ESL buddies. *Instructor, 93*(2), 120–124.

Buikema, J. L., & Graves, M. F. (1993). Teaching students to use context clues to infer word meanings. *Journal of Reading, 36* (6), 450–457.

Campion, M. F., & Elley, W. B. (1971). *An academic vocabulary list.* Wellington, New Zealand: New Zealand Center for Educational Research.

Carey, S. (1978). Child as word learner. In M. Halle, J. Bresnam, & G. Miller (Eds.), *Linguistic theory and psychological reality.* Cambridge, MA: MIT Press.

Carr, E. M. (1985). The vocabulary overview guide: A metacognitive strategy to improve vocabulary comprehension and retention. *Journal of Reading, 28,* 684–689.

Carr, E. M., & Mazur-Stewart, M. (1988). The vocabulary overview guide: A metacognitive strategy to improve vocabulary comprehension and retention. *Journal of Reading, 28,* 648–669.

Carris, J. D. (2001). *SAT word flash.* Princeton, NJ: Petersons.

Carter, R., & McCarthy, M. (1988). *Vocabulary and language teaching.* White Plains, NY: Longman.

Clair, N. (1995). Mainstream classroom teachers and ESL students. *TESOL Quarterly, 29,* 189–196.

College Entrance Examination Board. (1993). *Introducing the New SAT: The College Boards' Official Guide.* Princeton, NJ: College Board Publishers.

Conrad, P. (1989). *Prairie songs.* New York: Harper & Row.

Cooter, R. B. (1990). *The teacher's guide to reading tests*. Scottsdale, AZ: Gorsuch Publishers.

Courtland, M. C. (1992). Teacher change in the implementation of new approaches to literacy instruction. *Journal of Reading, 35*, 542–548.

Dale, E. (1965). Vocabulary measurement: Techniques and major findings. *Elementary English, 42*, 895–901.

Dale, E., & O'Rourke, J. P. (1976). *The living word vocabulary*. Chicago: Field Enterprises.

Dale, E., Razik, T., & Petty, W. (1973). *Bibliography of vocabulary studies*. Columbus, OH: Ohio State University.

Davey, B. (1983). Think-aloud-modeling the cognitive processes of reading comprehension. *Journal of Reading, 27*, 44–47.

Davis, F. B. (1943). Fundamental factors of comprehension in reading. *Psychometrika, 9*, 185–197.

Davis, F. B. (1968). Research in comprehension in reading. *Reading Research Quarterly, 3*, 499–544.

Degrees of reading power. (1995). Brewster, NY: Touchstone Applied Science Associates.

Downing, J., & Leong, C. K. (1982). *Psychology of reading*. New York: Macmillan.

Duffelmeyer, F. A. (1980). The influence of experience-based vocabulary instruction on learning word meanings. *Journal of Reading, 24*, 35–40.

Duin, A. H., & Graves, M. F. (1987). Intensive vocabulary instruction as a prewriting technique. *Reading Research Quarterly, 22*, 311–330.

Dunkling, L. (1988). *A dictionary of days*. New York: Facts on File Publications.

Dunn, L. M., & Dunn, L. M. (1997). *Peabody Picture Vocabulary Test—Third Ed.* Circle Pines, MN: American Guidance Service.

Durkin, D. D. (1978–79). What classroom observations reveal about reading comprehension instruction. *Reading Research Quarterly, 14*, 481–533.

Durrell, D. D., & Catterson, J. H. (1980). *Durrell analysis of reading difficulty*. New York: The Psychological Corporation.

Eeds, M., & Cockrum, W. A. (1985). Teaching word meanings by expanding schemata vs. dictionary work vs. reading in context. *Journal of Reading, 28*, 492–497.

Eller, G., Pappas, C. C., & Brown, E. (1988). The lexical development of kindergartners: Learning from written context. *Journal of Reading Behavior, 20*, 5–24.

Elley, W. B. (1988). Vocabulary acquisition from listening to stories. *Reading Research Quarterly, 24*, 174–187.

Espy, W. R. (1975). *An almanac of words at play*. New York: Clarkson N. Potter.

ETA/Cuisenaire (2000). *Reaching Rods: Prefixes suffixes and root words: Teacher's resource guide*. Vernon Hills, IL: ETA/Cuisenaire.

Fisher, D. (2000). *Miss Alaineus: A Vocabulary Disaster*. San Diego: Harcourt Brace.

Fisher, P. J. L., Blachowicz, C. L. Z., Pozzi, L., & Costa, M. (1992). *Vocabulary teaching and learning in middle school literature study groups*. Paper presented at the National Reading Conference, San Antonio, TX.

Fisher, P. J. L., Blachowicz, C. L. Z., & Smith, J. C. (1991). Vocabulary learning in literature discussion groups. In J. Zutell & S. McCormick (Eds.), *Learner factors/teacher factors: Issues in literacy research and instruction* (pp. 201–209). Fortieth Yearbook of the National Reading Conference. Chicago: National Reading Conference.

Fisher, P. J. L., Kent, D. M., & Blachowicz, C. L. Z. (1990). *Examining dictionary instruction in basal readers*. Paper presented at the American Educational Research Association Annual Convention, Boston, MA.

Fleming, D. (1996). *Lunch*. NY: Henry Holt.

Frayer, D. A., Frederick, W. C., & Klausmeier, H. J. (1969). *A schema for testing the level of concept mastery* (Working paper No. 16). Madison: University of Wisconsin.

Freebody, P., & Anderson, R. C. (1983a). Effects of differing proportions and locations of difficult vocabulary on text comprehension. *Journal of Reading Behavior, 15*, 19–39.

Freebody, P., & Anderson, R. C. (1983b). Effects of vocabulary difficulty, text cohesion, and schema availability on reading comprehension. *Reading Research Quarterly, 18*, 277–294.

Freeman, D. E., & Freeman, Y. S. (1993). Strategies for promoting the primary languages of all students. *Reading Teacher, 46*, 552–558.

Funk, C. E. (1993). *2107 Curious Word Origins*. Lavergne, TN: Ingram Book Co.

Gackenbach, D. (1977). *Harry and the terrible whatzit*. New York: Clarion Books.

Ganske, K. (2000). *Word journeys: Assessment-guided phonics, spelling and vocabulary instruction*. New York: Guildford Press.

Garcia, G. E. (1994). Supporting second language literacy: Enhancing the English literacy development of students who are learning English as a second language. *Illinois Reading Council Journal, 22*(1), special pullout section.

Gentry, R. J. (2000). A retrospective on invented spelling and a look forward. *The Reading Teacher, 54*, 318–332.

George, J. C. (1972). *Julie of the wolves.* New York: Harper & Row.

Gersten, R. (1996). Literacy instruction for language-minority students: The transition years. *The Elementary School Journal, 96*, 227–244.

Gillet, J. W., & Temple, C. (1986). *Understanding reading problems: Assessment and instruction.* Boston: Little, Brown.

Gipe, J. P. (1979–80). Investigating techniques for teaching word meanings. *Reading Research Quarterly, 14*, 624–645.

Goldstein, B. S. (1986). Looking at cartoons and comics in a new way. *Journal of Reading, 29*, 657–661.

Graves, M., & Hammond, H. K. (1980). A validated procedure for teaching prefixes and its effect on students' ability to assign meanings to novel words. In M. Kamil & A. Moe (Eds.), *Perspectives on reading research and instruction* (pp. 184–188). Washington, DC: National Reading Conference.

Graves, M. F. (1984). Selecting vocabulary to teach in the intermediate and secondary grades. In J. Flood (Ed.), *Promoting reading comprehension* (pp. 245–260). Newark, DE: International Reading Association.

Graves, M. F. (1986). Vocabulary learning and instruction. In E. Z. Rothkopf (Ed.), *Review of research in education* (Vol. 13 pp. 49–89). Washington, DC: American Educational Research Association.

Graves, M. F., & Slater, W. H. (1987). *The development of reading vocabularies in rural disadvantaged students, inner-city disadvantaged, and middle class suburban students.* Paper presented at the Annual Meeting of the American Educational Research Association, Washington, DC.

Guglielmino, L. M. (1986). The affective edge: Using songs and music in ESL instruction. *Adult Literacy and Basic Education, 10*, 19–26.

Gwynne, F. (1970). *The king who rained.* New York: Simon & Schuster.

Haas, M. E. (1988). *An analysis of the social science and history concepts in elementary social studies textbooks Grades 1–4* (ERIC Document No. ED 305310). Paper presented at the Annual Meeting of the National Council for the Social Studies.

Haggard, M. R. (1982). The vocabulary self-selection strategy: An active approach to word learning. *Journal of Reading, 26*, 203–207.

Haggard, M. R. (1985). An interactive strategies approach to content reading. *Journal of Reading, 29*, 204–210.

Harris, A. J., & Sipay, E. R. (1990). *How to increase reading ability.* New York: Longman.

Heimlich, J. E., & Pittelman, S. D. (1986). *Semantic mapping: Classroom applications.* Newark, DE: International Reading Association.

Herber, H. (1978). *Teaching reading in the content areas.* Englewood Cliffs, NJ: Prentice Hall.

Herman, P. A., Anderson, R. C., Pearson, P. D., & Nagy, W. E. (1987). Incidental acquisition of word meaning from expositions with varied text features. *Reading Research Quarterly, 22*, 263–284.

Herman, P. A., & Dole, J. (1988). Theory and practice in vocabulary learning and instruction. *Elementary School Journal, 89*, 43–54.

Hofler, D. B. (1981). Word lines: An approach to vocabulary development. *The Reading Teacher, 35*, 216–218.

Huckin, T., Haynes, M., & Coady, J. (Eds.). (1993). *Second language reading and vocabulary learning.* Norwood, NJ: Ablex.

Irwin, J. W., & Baker, I. (1989). *Promoting active reading comprehension strategies.* Englewood Cliffs, NJ: Prentice Hall.

Jenkins, J. R., Matlock, B., & Slocum, T. A. (1989). Approaches to vocabulary instruction: The teaching of individual word meanings and practice in deriving word meaning from context. *Reading Research Quarterly, 24*, 215–235.

Jenkins, J. R., Stein, M. L., & Wysocki, K. (1984). Learning vocabulary through reading. *American Educational Research Journal, 21*, 767–787.

Jiminez, R. J. (1997). The strategic reading abilities and potential of five low-literacy Latina/o readers in middle school. *Reading Research Quarterly, 32*, 224–243.

Johnson, D. D. (2000). *Vocabulary in the elementary and middle school.* Boston: Allyn & Bacon.

Johnson, D. D., & Pearson, P. D. (1984). *Teaching reading vocabulary* (2nd ed.). New York: Holt, Rinehart & Winston.

Johnson, D. D., Toms-Bronowski, S., & Pittelman, S. D. (1982). *An investigation of the effectiveness of semantic mapping and semantic feature analysis with intermediate grade level students* (Program Rep. No. 83–3). Madison: Wisconsin Center for Education Research, University of Wisconsin.

Johnson, D. W., Johnson, R. T., & Holubec, E. J. (1986). *Circles of learning: Cooperation in the classroom.* Edina, MN: Interaction Book Company.

Jukes, M. (1983). *No one is going to Nashville.* New York: Harper & Row.

Juster, N. (1962). *The phantom tollbooth.* New York: Bullseye Books/Alfred Knopf.

Kameenui, E. J., Carnine, D. W., & Freschi, R. (1982). Effects of text construction and instructional procedures for teaching word meanings on comprehension and recall. *Reading Research Quarterly, 17,* 367–388.

Karlsen, B., & Gardner, E. F. (1984). *Stanford Diagnostic Reading Tests.* New York: Harcourt Brace Jovanovich.

Karp, R. S., & Corcoran, F. (1991). *Dictionaries for adults and children.* Chicago: American Library Association.

Kister, K. F. (1992). *Kister's best dictionaries for adults & young people: A comparative guide.* Phoenix, AZ: Oryx Press.

Koeze, S. (1990). The dictionary game. *Reading Teacher, 43,* 613.

Krashen, S. (1989). We acquire vocabulary and spelling by reading: Additional evidence for the input hypothesis. *The Modern Language Journal, 73,* 440–464.

Langer, J. A. (1989). *The process of understanding literature* (Report Series 2.1). Albany: State University of New York, Center for the Learning and Teaching of Literature.

Lapp, D., & Flood, J. (1986). *Teaching students to read.* New York: Macmillan.

Lapp, D., Flood, J., & Farnan, N. (1989). *Content area reading and learning.* Englewood Cliffs, NJ: Merrill/Prentice Hall.

Lewis, C. S. (1950). *The lion, the witch and the wardrobe.* New York: Collier Books.

Lindsay, T. (1984). The affixionary: Personalizing prefixes and suffixes. *Reading Teacher, 38,* 247–248.

Lobel, A. (1981). *On market street.* New York: Scholastic.

MacDonald, S. (1997). *Peck, slither and slide.* New York: Scholastic.

MacGinitie, W. H., & MacGinitie, R. K. (1989). *Gates-MacGinitie Reading Tests* (3rd ed.). Chicago: The Riverside Publishing Co.

Maiguashca, R. U. (1993). Teaching and learning vocabulary in a second language: Past, present and future directions. *The Canadian Modern Language Review, 50,* 83–99.

Manzo, A., & Manzo, U. (1990). *Content area reading: A heuristic approach.* Columbus, OH: Merrill/Prentice Hall.

Maria, K., & MacGinitie, W. (1987). Learning from texts that refute the reader's prior knowledge. *Reading Research and Instruction, 26,* 222–238.

Marshall, J. D. (1989). *Patterns of discourse in classroom discussions of literature* (Report Series 2.9). Albany: State University of New York, Center for the Learning and Teaching of Literature.

Marshall, N. (1989). Overcoming problems with incorrect prior knowledge: An instructional study. In S. McCormick & J. Zutell (Eds.), *Cognitive and social perspectives for literacy research and instruction.* Thirty-eighth Yearbook of the National Reading Conference.

Marzano, R. J., & Marzano, J. S. (1988). *A cluster approach to elementary vocabulary instruction.* Newark, DE: International Reading Association.

Mastropieri, M. A. (1988). Using the keyboard [*sic*] method. *Teaching Exceptional Children, 20* (Winter), 4–8.

Mayer, M. (1973). *What do you do with a kangaroo?* New York: Scholastic.

McCarville, K. B. (1993). Keyword mnemonic and vocabulary acquisition for developmental college students. *Journal of Developmental Education, 16*(3), 2–4, 6.

McGinley, W. J., & Denner, P. R. (1987). Story impressions: A prereading/writing activity. *Journal of Reading, 31*(3), 248–253.

McKenna, M. (1978, March). Portmanteau words in reading instruction. *Language Arts, 55,* 315–317.

McKeown, M. (1990). *Making dictionary definitions more effective.* Paper presented at the American Educational Research Association Annual Convention, Boston, MA.

McKeown, M. G. (1985). The acquisition of word meaning from context by children of high and low ability. *Reading Research Quarterly, 20,* 482–496.

McKeown, M. G., & Beck, I. L. (1989). *The assessment and characterization of young learners' knowledge of a topic in history.* Paper presented at the National Reading Conference, San Antonio, TX.

Meara, P. (1983). *Vocabulary in a second language.* London: Center for Information on Language Teaching.

Meara, P. (1987). *Vocabulary in a second language* Vol. II. London: Center for Information on Language Teaching.

Meara, P. (1993). *Vocabulary in a second language,* Vol III. (Special Issue) *Reading in a Foreign Language, 9.*

Merriam, E. (1987). *The Halloween ABC.* New York: Macmillan.

Mezynski, K. (1983). Issues concerning the acquisition of knowledge. Effects of vocabulary training on reading comprehension. *Review of Educational Research, 53,* 263–279.

Miller, G. A., & Gildea, P. M. (1987). How children learn words. *Scientific American, 257,* 94–99.

Nagy, W. E., (1988). *Teaching vocabulary to improve reading comprehension.* Newark, DE: International Reading Association.

Nagy, W. E., & Anderson, R. C. (1984). How many words are there in printed school English? *Reading Research Quarterly, 19,* 303–330.

Nagy, W. E., & Herman, P. A. (1987). Depth and breadth of vocabulary knowledge: Implications for acquisition and instruction. In M. G. McKeown & M. E. Curtis (Eds.), *The nature of vocabulary acquisition.* Hillsdale, NJ: Erlbaum.

Nagy, W. E., Herman, P. A., & Anderson, R. C. (1985). Learning words from context. *Reading Research Quarterly, 20,* 233–253.

Nation, I. S. P. (1990). *Teaching and learning vocabulary.* Boston: Heinle & Heinle.

Nicol, J. E., & Graves, M. F. (1990). *Building vocabulary through prefix instruction.* Unpublished manuscript, University of Minnesota.

Noyes, G. E. (1943). The first English dictionary, Cawdrey's Table Alphabeticall. *Modern Language Notes, 58,* 600–605.

Nussbaum, J. (1979). Children's conceptions of the earth as a cosmic body: A cross-age study. *Science Education, 63,* 83–93.

Nussbaum, J., & Novick, S. (1982). Alternative frameworks, conceptual conflict and accommodation: Toward a principled teaching strategy. *Instructional Science, 11*(3), 183–200.

Ogle, D. (1986). K-W-L: A teaching model that develops active reading of expository text. *Reading Teacher, 39,* 564–570.

O'Rourke, J. P. (1974). *Toward a science of vocabulary development.* The Hague, The Netherlands: Mouton.

Otterman, I. M. (1955). The value of teaching prefixes and word-roots. *Journal of Educational Research, 48,* 611–616.

Palincsar, A. S., & Brown, A. L. (1984). Reciprocal teaching of comprehension-fostering and monitoring activities. *Cognition and Instruction, 1*(2), 117–175.

Pany, D., & Jenkins, J. R. (1978). Learning word meanings: A comparison of instructional procedures and effects on measures of reading comprehension with learning disabled students. *Learning Disability Quarterly, 1,* 21–32.

Parish, P. (1963). *Amelia Bedelia.* New York: Harper & Row.

Patberg, J. P., Graves, M. F., & Stibbe, M. A. (1984). Effects of active teaching and practice in facilitating students' use of context cues. *Changing perspectives on research in reading/language processing and instruction.* Thirty-third Yearbook of the National Reading Conference (pp. 146–151). Rochester, NY: National Reading Conference.

Paul, P. V., & O'Rourke, J. P. (1988). Multimeaning words and reading comprehension: Implications for special education students. *Remedial and Special Education, 9*(3), 42–52.

Paulsen, G. (1985). *Dogsong.* New York: Bradbury Press.

Pearson, P. D., & Johnson, D. D. (1984). *Teaching reading comprehension.* New York: Holt, Rinehart, & Winston.

Perez, B. (1994). Spanish literacy development: A descriptive study of four bilingual whole-language classrooms. *JRB: A Journal of Literacy, 26,* 75–94.

Perez, B. (1996). Instructional conversations as opportunities for English language acquisition for culturally and linguistically diverse students. *Language Arts, 73,* 173–181.

Perez, B., & Torres-Guzman, M. E. (1992). *Reasoning in two worlds: An integrated Spanish/English biliteracy approach.* New York: Longman.

Perkins, D. N., & Simmons, R. (1988). Patterns of mis-understanding: An integrative model for science, math, and programming. *Review of Educational Research, 58,* 303–326.

Petrosky, A. R. (1980). The inferences we make: Children and literature. *Language Arts, 57,* 149–156.

Pittelman, S. D., Heimlich, J. E., Berglund, R. L., & French, M. P. (1991). *Semantic feature analysis: Classroom applications.* Newark, DE: International Reading Association.

Powell, W. R. (1986). Teaching vocabulary through opposition. *Journal of Reading, 29,* 617–621.

Pressley, M., Levin, J. R., & Delaney, H. D. (1983). The mnemonic keyword method. *Review of Educational Research, 52,* 6–91.

Readence, J. E., Baldwin, R. S., & Head, M. H. (1986). Direct instruction in processing metaphors. *Journal of Reading Behavior, 18,* 325–339.

Readence, J. E., & Searfoss, L. W. (1980). Teaching strategies for vocabulary development. *English Journal, 69,* 43–46.

Rhodes, L. K. (1993). *Literacy assessment: A handbook of instruments.* Portsmouth, NH: Heinemann.

Riccio, O. M. (1980). *The intimate art of writing poetry.* Englewood Cliffs, NJ: Prentice-Hall.

Robinson, A. (1993). *Word smart: Building an educated vocabulary.* New York: Villard Books.

Room, A. (1990). NTC's dictionary of word origins. Skokie, IL: National Textbook Co.

Rothstein, V., & Goldberg, R. Z. (1993). *Thinking through stories.* Weare, NH: Options, Inc.

Sauer, J. L. (1943). *Fog Magic.* New York: Viking Press.

Scharer, P. L. (1992). Teachers in transition: An exploration of changes in teachers and classrooms during implementation of literature-based reading instruction. *Research in the Teaching of English, 26,* 408–445.

Schatz, E. I., & Baldwin, R. S. (1986). Context clues are unreliable predictors of word meanings. *Reading Research Quarterly, 21,* 439–453.

Schiller, A., & Jenkins, W. A. (1977). *In other words: A junior thesaurus.* Glenview, IL: Scott Foresman.

Scholfield, P. (1982). Using the English dictionary for comprehension. *TESOL Quarterly, 16,* 185–194.

Schwartz, R. M., & Raphael, T. E. (1985). Concept of definition: A key to improving students' vocabulary. *Reading Teacher, 39,* 198–205.

Scott, J., & Nagy, W. E. (1990). *Definitions: Understanding students' misunderstandings.* Paper presented at the American Educational Research Association Annual Convention, Boston.

Scruggs, T. E., Mastropieri, M. A., & Levin, J. R. (1985). Vocabulary acquisition of retarded students under direct mnemonic instruction. *American Journal of Mental Deficiency, 89,* 5451–5456.

Searls, E. F., & Klesius, J. P. (1984). 99 multiple meaning words for primary students and ways to teach them. *Reading Psychology, 5,* 55–63.

Sentell, C., & Blachowicz, C. L. Z. (1989). Hear ye! Hear ye! Court is in session. *Reading Teacher, 42,* 347–348.

Silverstein, S. (1974). *Where the sidewalk ends.* New York: Harper & Row.

Silverstein, S. (1974). *A light in the attic.* New York: Harper & Row.

Smith, J. B. (1983). "Pique": A group dictionary assignment. *Exercise-Exchange, 29*(1), 35.

Snow, C. E. (1991). *Unfulfilled expectations: Home and school influences on literacy.* Cambridge, MA: Harvard University Press.

Sobol, D. J. (1967). *Encyclopedia Brown gets his man.* New York: Scholastic.

Stahl, S. (1983). Differential knowledge and reading comprehension. *Journal of Reading Behavior, 15,* 33–50.

Stahl, S., & Fairbanks, M. (1986). The effects of vocabulary instruction. A model-based meta-analysis. *Review of Educational Research, 56,* 72–110.

Stahl, S., & Vancil, S. (1986). Discussion is what makes semantic maps work in vocabulary instruction. *Reading Teacher, 40,* 62–69.

Stahl, S. A. (1985). To teach a word well: A framework for vocabulary instruction. *Reading World, 24*(3), 16–27.

Stanford Diagnostic Reading Test (1995). San Antonio: Harcourt Educational Measurement.

Stauffer, R. G. (1969). *Directing reading maturity as a cognitive process.* New York: Harper & Row.

Sternberg, R. (1987). Most vocabulary is learned from context. In M. G. McKeown & M. E. Curtis (Eds.), *The nature of vocabulary acquisition.* Hillsdale, NJ: Erlbaum.

Taylor, L. (1990). *Teaching and learning vocabulary.* New York: Prentice Hall.

Templeton, S. (1983). Using the spelling/meaning connection to develop word knowledge in older students. *Journal of Reading, 27,* 8–14.

Templeton, S., & Morris, D. (1999). Questions teachers ask about spelling. *Reading Research Quarterly, 34,* 102–112.

Thaler, M. (1988, April–May). Reading, writing, and riddling. *Learning,* 58–59.

Tierney, R. J., Readence, J. E., & Dishner, E. K. (1985). *Reading strategies and practices: A compendium* (2nd ed.). Newton, MA: Allyn & Bacon.

Truscott, D. M., & Watts-Taffe, S. M. (1997). *Literacy instruction for second language learners: A study of best practice.* Paper presented at the National Reading Conference, Scottsdale, AZ.

Upton, A. (1973). *Design for thinking: A first book on semantics.* Palo Alto, CA: Pacific Press.

Valencia, S. W., & Pearson, P. D. (1986). Reading assessment: Time for a change. *Reading Teacher, 40,* 726–732.

Viorst, J. (1972). *Alexander and the Terrible, Horrible, No Good, Very Bad Day.* New York, Atheneum.

Vosniadou, S., & Ortony, A. (1983). Testing the metaphoric competence of the young child: Paraphrase versus enactment. *Human Development, 29,* 226–230.

Welker, W. A. (1987). Going from typical to technical meaning. *Journal of Reading, 31,* 275–276.

White, T. G., Graves, M. F., & Slater, W. H. (1989). Growth of reading vocabulary in diverse elementary schools. *Journal of Educational Psychology, 42,* 343–354.

White, T. G., Sowell, J., & Yanagihara, A. (1989). Teaching elementary students to use word-part clues. *The Reading Teacher, 42,* 302–308.

Whittlesea, B. W. (1987). Preservation of specific experiences in the representation of general knowledge. *Journal of Experimental Psychology: Learning, Memory, & Cognition, 13*(1) 3–17.

Winthrop, E. (1985). *The castle in the attic.* New York: Holiday House.

Wood, A., & Wood, D. (1985). *King Bidgood's in the bathtub.* New York: Harcourt, Brace, Jovanovich.

Woodcock, R. W., Mather, N., & Barnes, E. (1987). *Woodcock Reading Mastery Tests—Revised.* Circle Pines, MN: American Guidance Service.

Word Theater. (1980). New York: Barnell Loft.

Wysocki, K., & Jenkins, J. R. (1987). Deriving word meanings through morphological generalization. *Reading Research Quarterly, 22,* 66–81.

Yolen, J. (1991). *Greyling.* New York: Philomel.

Zarrillo, J. (1989). Teachers' interpretation of literature-based reading. *Reading Teacher, 43,* 22–28.

NAME INDEX

SUBJECT INDEX